Caribbean Divers' Guide

First published by Immel Publishing Ltd 1991
Edited and written by Peter Vine
Illustrated and designed by Jane Stark, Connemara Graphics
Copy edited by Michael Bennie
Typesetting: Shirley Kilpatrick, Icon Publications Ltd
Photographic contributors: W. Gregory Brown, John Murray,
F. Busonero, Joan C. Bourge, Chris Huxley, Pat McCoole, David George,
Paul L. Janosi
Cover photographs, left to right: W. Gregory Brown (2), David George,
John Murray (2), Paul Janosi

British Library Cataloguing in Publication Data
Caribbean Divers' Guide
    1. Caribbean region. Recreations. Underwater diving.
    1. Vine, Peter *1945* –
    797.2309729

ISBN 0-907151-60-4

Immel Publishing Ltd,
Ely House, 37 Dover Street, London W1X 3RB.
Tel: 071 491 1799; Fax: 071 493 5524

Other Marine Books by Peter Vine and Immel Publishing Ltd:-

The Red Sea
Red Sea Invertebrates
Red Sea Explorers
Red Sea Safety

Also published by Immel Publishing:-

Red Sea Reef Fishes by Dr J. E. Randall
Diver's Guide to Red Sea Reef Fishes by Dr J. E. Randall
Sharks of Arabia by Dr J. E. Randall
Sea Life of Britain and Ireland edited by Dr E. Wood
Guide to Inshore Marine Life by David Erwin and Bernard Picton
Marine field course guide. 1. Rocky Shores. Dr Steve Hawkins

MESSAGE FROM THE PUBLISHERS

ACKNOWLEDGEMENTS

This guidebook is the product of the efforts of a large number of divers throughout the Greater Caribbean region. A project such as this one is directly dependent on the close co-operation of many people with special-ised local knowledge and experience. It has been my pleasant duty to collate their contributions and to create from their efforts a country-by-country account of Caribbean diving and the facilities available for visiting divers. It is my great pleasure to list below the people who have thus assisted in the production of this book.

Iain Grummitt (Anguilla); Gloria Newby, Mark Bowers (Antigua and Barbuda); Martin Molina, Walter Chai (Aruba); Sarah J. Davis, Allan Jardine, Al Catalfumo, Eddy Statia (Bonaire); Alan Baskin, Russel Harrigan, Bert and Gayla Kilbride, Jim Scheiner (British Virgin Islands); Wayne Hasson, John Murray, Bob Carter, Stuart Freeman (Caymans); Pat McCoole (Cuba); Kiki (Curaçao); Derek Perryman (Dominica); Mercedes Perdello (Dominican Republic); Mosden Cumberbatch and Anne Marie Marecheau (Grenada); Theo and Hannie Smit-van Valen, Karen McCarthy and Anne Marie Francis (Jamaica); Jacques Guannel (Martinique); L. Ayala (Mexico); Chris Mason (Montserrat); Karen Vega and Harry Schmidt (Puerto Rico); Susan Walker, Joan and Louise Bourque, and Wilson McQueen (Saba); Judy Brown (St. Eustatius); Auston Macleod (St. Kitts and Nevis); Joyce and Chris Huxley, Nick Troobitscoff (St Lucia); LeRoy French (St. Maarten); Bill Tewes and Karen Mills (St. Vincent); James Young (Tobago); Julie Archibald (US Virgin Islands). I should like to offer my sincere thanks to all the above people, together with all the underwater photographers whose work is separately credited. I also wish to apologise to those people who have played a part in the production of the book whose names may have been inadvertently omitted from the list.

Whilst every care has been taken in the preparation of information in this guide, the editorial responsibility for errors which may have occurred is mine and mine alone. It is sincerely hoped that even greater co-operation will take place on future editions, so that the book can serve the needs of visiting divers for years to come.

Contents

3 : COUNTRYFILES

1 : INTRODUCTION

Much has been written about diving in the Caribbean and it is pertinent to ask whether another book on the subject is either necessary or desirable. On reviewing the available sources of information, however, one very soon discovers that virtually all the published material falls into a particular category in terms of its limited geographical coverage, its scientific pitch, or its depth of real insight with regard to diving conditions. The purpose of this book is to (a) assist divers who are visiting the Caribbean to locate suitable areas for their particular purposes; (b) help them find the right kind of accommodation; (c) advise them on arranging their diving with competent local diving companies; (d) introduce them to local divesites; (e) provide a very brief synopsis of marinelife; (f) advise them on special conservation regulations; (g) highlight items of special interest; and, finally, (h) ensure that they are pre-warned about local facilities for hyperbaric treatment of diving accidents. The book has been written, collated and edited by divers who have first-hand knowledge of the areas concerned together with a deep appreciation of the actual needs of divers at all grades of experience.

Throughout the entire Caribbean there has been an awakening of appreciation of the enormous economic potential of healthy marine environments as key attractions for tourists. Increasingly, visitors who come to the islands to learn to dive and gain internationally recognised qualifications return to explore the reefs and other marine habitats of these fascinating tropical waters. As the number of visitors has increased, diving facilities have also grown and new hotels have been built. All this has brought increased pressure on the reefs themselves and governments throughout the Caribbean have been actively engaged in finding legal and practical ways of protecting their priceless marine heritage. In this move to conserve the richness and beauty of the marine environment, diving companies themselves have made the running, since it is they who have most to gain or lose from the state of their coastal waters.

Almost all diving in the Caribbean is carried out in the company of professional dive-guides who ensure that visitors appreciate the fragility of sealife. Whether one is accompanied or not however, if one discovers an area of great beauty or richness underwater one can be certain that it has either enjoyed the careful protection of the authorities and diving concerns, or else is a virtually virgin diving site! The lesson here is that *regular* diving at any marine site is bound to have a deleterious effect *unless* great care is taken to preserve marinelife. Readers of this book are urged to take positive action to avoid damaging Caribbean reefs and their associated marinelife. Such action includes the selection of flippers which are not too long and unwieldy; careful adjustment of lead-weights so that one is not stumbling over the seabed; correct use of buoyancy compensators for the same reason; avoidance of handling or resting on reef areas where delicate forms live; and needless to say, absolutely no collection of marinelife of any form.

The sport of spearfishing and the hobbies of shell- or coral-collecting ought by now to be things of the past. Today, underwater photography can provide greater challenges and better souvenirs of our time underwater. Many of the Caribbean diving centres have special courses in underwater photography and also rent equipment and offer on-site processing of colour films. Even underwater video has become commonplace and offers divers unique opportunities to create impressive records of their experiences. The warm, clear waters of the Caribbean are the perfect place to develop one's skills in both diving and underwater photography. Hopefully this guidebook will help visitors to gain the most from their visits. Since the publishers intend to provide a regular updating of the guide, readers are encouraged to send comments, information or suggested additions to the editor (Peter Vine) care of Immel Publishing, Ely House, 37 Dover Street, London W1X 3RB (fax 071-493 5524).

2.0 : MARINELIFE

2.1 : INVERTEBRATES

2.1(i): HARD CORALS

From the viewpoint of a diver who has cut his or her teeth on Indo-Pacific coral-reefs, the Caribbean offers enhanced possibilities for one to master the identification of coral species since the numbers are less daunting than the tremendous array which one is likely to encounter on the more developed coral-reefs of the Pacific and Indian Oceans or the Red Sea. It has been estimated that there are around 70 different coral species growing in the Caribbean, with around ten of them accounting for over 90 per cent of the coral cover.

The biological separation of the tropical Atlantic, and in particular the Caribbean, from the Indo-Pacific is best illustrated by the marked difference in coral types on opposite sides of the narrow isthmus of land separating the two great water bodies. Of the hundred or so reef-building coral genera which have been described worldwide, only eight are common to both Caribbean and Indo-Pacific waters. These are *Acropora, Porites, Montastrea, Siderastrea, Madracis, Leptoseris, Cladocora* and *Favia*. A detailed study of those corals living on opposite sides of the Panama isthmus indicated that only one species was common to both sides: *Siderastrea radians*.

The great palm-shaped elkhorn coral with which Caribbean divers soon become familiar is also one of the main reef-building corals of the region. Its scientific name, *Acropora palmata*, indicates its close relationship to the prolific stagshorn and tabular Acroporas of the Indo-Pacific. A recent study of Cuba's coral-reefs listed *Montastrea annularis, Acropora prolifera, Siderastrea siderea, Porites astreoides* and *Agaricia agaricites*, along with *Acropora palmata*, as comprising the main reef-building corals, while the contribution of the coralline hydro-zoan *Millepora complanata* was also noted.

A comprehensive study of marinelife around the tiny coral Carrie Bow Cay, on the Belize Barrier Reef complex, was published in 1982 by the Smithsonian Institution Press. The scientific papers within this 540 page book cover a wide range of biological subjects from the structure of the reefs and the physical factors at play, through the distribution of bottom-living and planktonic communities to de-tailed reports on the species found there and studies of their ecology and behaviour. This whole complex matrix of marinelife owes its existence to the reef-building corals which have created the environ-ment for all the other creatures to live in or among. The study on stony corals at Carrie Bow Cay, written by Stephen Cairns, turned up 37 reef-building corals together with five non-reef-building types. Combining this with the results of other investigations, Stephen Cairns concluded that the stony corals of Belize amount to 39 reef builders and ten non-reef-builders. This total of 49 stony coral species compares with 46 from Jamaica, 41 from Panama and 40 from Bonaire.

Coral identification is based on fine details of skeletal structure and the naming of species (taxonomy) has been built up around descriptions of microscopic features of dead coral skeletons. For a long time after diving became a normal tool for marine-biologists in their field-work, it was almost impossible for them to match the brightly coloured, living corals to the bleached calcareous remains on museum shelves and in monochrome textbooks. Over recent years, however, more and more species have been photographed underwater and their accurate identification later determined in the laboratory. Thus we have created a new data-file based on living corals instead of just their dead skeletons.

Whilst coral genera can now be fairly reliably recognised under-water, slight nuances between many closely related species, together with the great variety of growth-forms which may be exhibited by a single species growing in different places, renders underwater species determination a fairly erratic business, and one would still need to check details under a magnifying glass or low-power microscope to be quite certain about a coral's correct scientific name. From the viewpoint of a diver or underwater photographer, however, generic identification should be sufficient for most purposes. A list of Caribbean coral genera is given in Table 1.

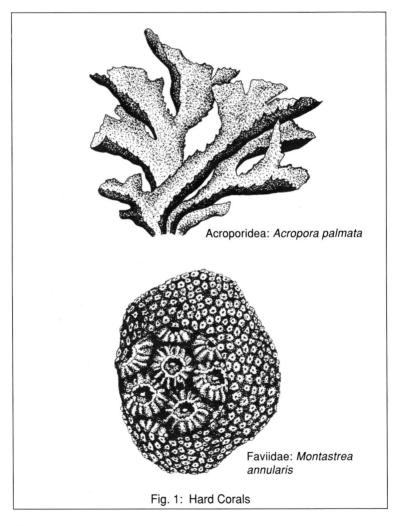

Acroporidea: *Acropora palmata*

Faviidae: *Montastrea annularis*

Fig. 1: Hard Corals

Table 1

CARIBBEAN CORAL FAMILIES & GENERA

SCLERACTINIANS

Family:- ASTROCOENIIDAE
Genus:- *Stephanocoenia*

Family:- POCILLOPORIDAE
Genus:- *Madracis*

Family:- ACROPORIDAE
Genus:- *Acropora*

Family:- AGARICIIDAE
Genus:- *Agaricia*
Leptoseris
Helioseris

Family:- SIDERASTREIDAE
Genus:- *Siderastrea*

Family:- PORITIDAE
Genus:- *Porites*

Family:- FAVIIDAE
Genus:- *Cladocora*
Montastrea
Solenastrea
Favia
Diploria
Manicina
Colpophyllia

Family:- FLABELLIDAE
Genus:- *Gardineria*
Family:- RHIZANGIIDAE
Genus:- *Astrangia*
Phyllangia

Family:- OCULINIDAE
Genus:- *Oculina*

Family:- MEANDRINIDAE
Genus:- *Dichocoenia*
Meandrina
Goreaugyra
Dendrogyra

Family:- MUSSIDAE
Genus:- *Scolymia*
Mussismilia
Mussa
Isophyllastrea
Isophyllia
Mycetophyllia

Family:- CARYOPHYLLIIDAE
Genus:- *Eusmilia*

Family:- DENDROPHYLLIIDAE
Genus:- *Balanophyllia*
Tubastraea

NON SCLERACTINIANS

Family:- MILLEPORIDAE
Genus:- *Millepora*

Family:- STYLASTERIDAE
Genus:- *Stylaster*

Table 2:

COMMON CARIBBEAN CORALS

Family	Species (Common Name)	Comments
Pocilloporidae	*Madracis decactis* (knobby coral) *Madracis mirabilis* (branching coral)	Common, shallows, back-reef Moderate depths, fore-reef.
Acroporidae	*Acropora palmata* (elkhorn coral) *Acropora cervicornis* (staghorn coral)	Dominant shallow reef-builder, windward sides. Common reef-builder in less exposed situations.
Agariciidae	*Agaricia agaricites* (lettuce coral) *Agaricia grahamae* (dotted line coral) *Helioseris cuculata* (cup coral)	Common at moderate depths on fore-reef. Often overgrowing vertical reef walls. Fairly deep on fore-reef.
Poritidae	*Porites porites* (finger coral) *Porites asteroides* (lumpy porites)	Forms large mounds in shallow back-reef and reef-flat, fore reef. Rounded in shallows, plate-like deeper.
Faviidae	*Favia fragrum* (shallow sphere) *Diploria strigosa* (brain coral) *Diploria clivosa* (brain coral) *Diploria labyrinthiformis* (brain coral) *Manicina areolata* (rose coral) *Colpophyllia natans* (grooved brain) *Montastrea annularis* (star coral) *Montastrea cavernosa* (star coral)	Small spherical colonies in shallows. Most widespread brain coral. Shallows to quite deep water. Shallow to deep. Hemispherical colonies up to 2m across. In sea-grass beds and other soft sediments. Forms large mounds or coral plates at moderate depths. Important reef builder in buttress and fore-reef. Reef builder.
Meandrinidae	*Meandrina meandrites* (tan brain coral) *Dichocoenia stokesi* (starlet coral) *Dendrogyra cylindricus* (pillar coral)	On exposed shallows. All diving depths. Distinctive vertical pillars up to 3m. Live in sheltered habitats.
Mussidae	*Mussa angulosa* (giant polyp coral) *Scolymia cubensis* (solitary coral) *Mycetophyllia aliciae* (green coral) *Mycetophyllia lamarckiana* (scalloped green coral)	Polyps up to 5cm across. Steep rock faces. Quiet waters, at moderate depths on fore-reef. Especially at moderate depths on fore-reef.
Caryophylliidae	*Eusmilia fastigiata* (flower coral)	Clustered solitary coral.
Dendrophylliidae	*Tubastrea aurea* (orange clump coral)	Also in Indo-Pacific under ledges

Whilst in the pre-diving days of marine-science, corals were dredged up from the seabed, arriving in something of a tangled mass on the decks of research vessels where scientists attempted to sort out species from species and to note the depth and other basic environmental parameters of the collecting zone, many of the subtle nuances of coral-ecology were lost to these land- or boat-based biologists. Today, however, divers can observe and record how each coral colony is living, its orientation with respect to light, current, wave-surge and its relationship with adjacent coral colonies or other organisms. These *in-situ* studies of coral-biology have been made possible by scuba diving and, whilst we are now much wiser about the ecology of Caribbean reefs and their coral species, a great deal remains to be discovered. This is a field where amateur divers can play an important role.

Reef-building corals are temperature sensitive animals, preferring warm water, and their prolificacy and abundance are thus affected by latitude, with a general reduction in variety and growth towards the northern Caribbean. Southern Caribbean reefs, providing they are well removed from the turbulence, are thus relatively rich in coral-growth.

A diver swimming out from the shore, across the reef-surface, through the shallows, over the reef-top, and down the gradually descending reef-face, passes through a series of zones in which particular communities exist. Each of these can be characterised by dominant coral species and an effort to recognise and differentiate between these underwater zones will greatly help one to recognise key elements of marinelife and to understand something of the reef's ecology. The zones do of course vary in different places but there are nevertheless some generalisations to be made. Let us take a 'typical' example.

Swimming out from the shore on a reef at Bonaire, one passes first of all through a wave-washed, shallow zone with water varying from a few centimetres to about a metre in depth. This has been christened the *Diploria clivosa* zone after the dominant species, a form of brain coral whose encrusting colonies, with irregular protuberances, coat large areas of the shallow seabed. Mixed with these are colonies of the rounded, sub-spherical, similarly convoluted coral *Diploria strigosa*. As we approach the seaward edge of this zone there are dense stands of elkhorn coral, *Acropora palmata*, and a closer look at the area will reveal that smaller colonies of the same *Acropora* are intermingled with *Diploria* throughout the zone. It is only towards the outer edge that they become dominant. Other corals found here include *Acropora prolifera, Porites sp.,* and *Favia fragrum*. Because this is an area in which waves continually shift loose coral fragments, one can find perfectly rounded golf-ball colonies of *Porites* with polyps covering the entire surface, an indication that the colonies are always on the move.

As we have already seen, heading offshore we pass from the zone of braincorals to one of elkhorn *Acropora*. This new *Acropora palmata* zone can be quite impressive with densely packed colonies of elkhorns reaching upwards to form a 'reef-flat' varying in width depending upon location. The species is exceptionally vulnerable to disturbance by strong storms and hurricanes so damage to live colonies has at times been very extensive, causing huge mortalities of *A. palmata*. Dead colonies are quickly covered by calcareous algae which cement the fragments together, increasing the stability of the reef-surface. Despite its vulnerability to hurricane damage, this is a coral which likes strong water-movement, flourishing where wave action is quite heavy, and the best development of its growth is on the outer edge of the zone. Although there appears to be nothing but elkhorn coral growing here, a pause to peer down among the coral stems will reveal patches of the non-reef building (ahermatypic) bright orange coral *Tubastrea coccinea* and perhaps also patches of *Favia fragum* and *Agaricia agaricites*.

As we proceed further offshore, into gradually deepening water (around 4-10m), we may find that a more branching stagshorn coral (*Acropora cervicornis*) predominates. Frequently the coral itself is less obvious in the living form than in the dense pile of rubble from previously existing *A. cervicornis* colonies. An apparently high mortality rate of this coral is as much related to its rather delicate nature as to the severity of attack by various causative agents such as boring organisms or storms. One result is that the zone itself is

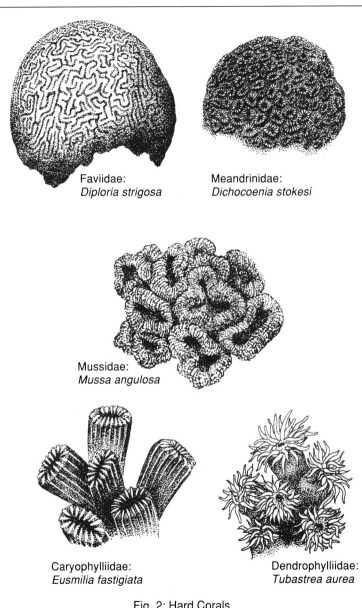

Faviidae:
Diploria strigosa

Meandrinidae:
Dichocoenia stokesi

Mussidae:
Mussa angulosa

Caryophylliidae:
Eusmilia fastigiata

Dendrophylliidae:
Tubastrea aurea

Fig. 2: Hard Corals

less obviously characterised by a single dominant live coral. Indeed, as we move deeper, the definition of coral zonation becomes much less distinct, since there is more gradation between various environmental factors than exists near the surface.

Like the *Acropora palmata* zone, the *Acropora cervicornis* zone is also extremely susceptible to damage by hurricanes and storms but, unlike the shallower one, this is a zone where a great deal of coral rubble and sand accumulates. The rubble is bound together by a variety of organisms including calcareous algae, calcified bases of sea-fans (*Gorgonacea*), colonies of stinging firecoral (*Millepora*) and encrustations of reef-building corals such as *Diploria* and *Montastrea*. It is this latter genus which gives rise to the fourth and final coral-zone, which we shall discuss next.

Swimming along the descending seabed, across the *Acropora cervicornis* zone, we arrive at around 10m depth and the beginning of a new, more steeply inclined, zone named after the predominating coral found here: *Montastrea annularis*. The trend away from single species dominance, towards an enhanced variety of corals continues to increase so that it is in this zone that we find the greatest number of coral species. Whilst the distinctly patterned *Montastrea annularis*, with its regularly distributed, closely packed polyps, is the main species found here, other well represented species include *Montastrea cavernosa*, *Diploria labrynthiformis* and *D.strigosa*.

While the above example is based on a dive off Bonaire, similar zonations of coral species may be noted throughout the Caribbean, usually with local variations on the same or a similar basic theme. Another example of a straight swim out from the shore, across the shallows, over the reef top, across the crest and down the reef face is described for the Belizean reef at Carrie Bow Cay in a paper dealing with the reef's ecology, published in 1982, as part of the comprehensive survey of that reef complex mentioned above.

Caribbean coral-reefs come in all shapes and sizes, from minute isolated patches to huge barrier reefs. Fringing reefs and patch reefs are the most common forms with many of the islands surrounded by fine examples of these structures – created by the growth of living coral polyps and associated organisms. Barrier reefs are less well

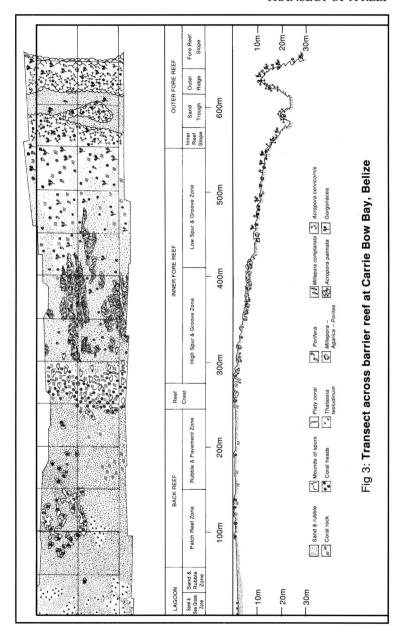

Fig 3: **Transect across barrier reef at Carrie Bow Bay, Belize**

represented but are found off Belize and in the Bahamas, but true atolls do not occur, despite the presence of look-alike sub-circular reefs and semi-enclosed lagoons, referred to as basin or cup reefs.

2.1 (ii): OCTOCORALS – SOFT CORALS

A guide to the octocorals of the Caribbean has been written by Stephen Cairns and published in 1977 under the University of Miami Sea Grant Program (Sea Grant Field Guide Series, 6: 74pp). Thirty-six octocoral species (so named because they have eight tentacles rather than six) were found at Carrie Bow Cay while 43 species have been recorded from around Jamaica. The large sea-fans or gorgonians are a prominent and much photographed feature of Caribbean coral-reefs. Despite the abundance of such forms however, there has been relatively little biological work carried out on them, with the exception of one species. *Plexaura homomalla*, a dark brown bushy gorgonian

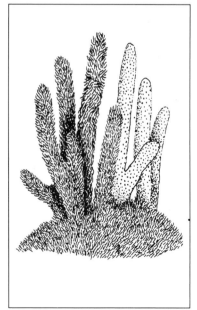

whose distribution is primarily restricted to the shallows and fore-reef zone, has drawn the attention of many scientists as a result of the concentration within its tissues of several commercially important pharmacological compounds, including prostaglandins. It is a soft coral which exudes a brown skin irritating pigment if one inadvertently squeezes it.

Fig. 4: *Briareum asbestinum*

What we refer to as soft corals belong to the order Alcyonacea (class Alcyonaria), all of whose members have polyps with eight pinnate tentacles and skeletons composed of sclerites. Alcyonaceans are much less abundant, in terms of varieties of species occurring on Caribbean reefs, than are the Gorgonaceans. In a study on Carrie Bow reef, Belize, only three such soft corals were recorded, *Erythropodium caribaeurum*, *Iciligorgia schrammi* and *Briareum asbestinum*. Of these, the encrusting soft coral, *Briareum asbestinum* forms extended matting – blue when polyps are retracted or grey-brown when they are extended – or 'dead man's fingers', upright colonies which may be as long as 45cm or so. By contrast, the alcyonacean deep sea fan, *Iciligorgia schrammi*, resembles the true sea-fans or gorgonacea rather than the generally 'clumpy' alcyonaceans. Its prominent deep red to brown delicate lacework colonies form large fans, orientated across the current, along the reef-face from moderate to deep water.

2.1(iii): OCTOCORALS – FAN AND WHIP CORALS

Fan and whip corals belong to the order Gorgonacea (class: Alcyonaria), whose members possess axial skeletons of gorgonin, a collagenous protein. The distribution of these forms is affected by three key factors: the presence of a hard surface on which to attach, the existence of a good current bringing food and removing excretory products, and the presence of adequate light. Thus dive-sites with titles such as 'Sea-Fan Wall' or 'Gorgonian City' are invariably places where a reasonable current sweeps across a hard seabed or sea-cliff. The bright yellow or greeny yellow fan-gorgonian, *Gorgonia flabellum* is typically found in the shallows, often in surge channels, whilst the large sea-fan *Gorgonia ventalina* occurs in deeper water where there is a steady current. One does not tend to find rich growth of these forms in places sheltered from current or water movement.

Among the gorgonians, the sea-whips include the scratchy sea-whip (*Muricea muricata*) and the bushy sea-whip (*Plexaurella*). The former has protuberant calices which render it quite scratchy to

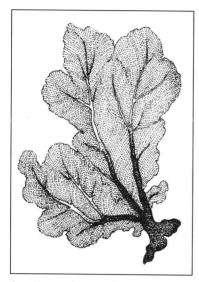

Fig. 5: *Gorgonia ventalina*

touch, in contrast to the bushy sea-whip whose branches are smooth when the polyps are retracted. Generally, they may be seen at moderate depths in daytime with their long polyps extended, giving them their bushy appearance. Sea-plumes, members of the genus *Pseudopterogorgia*, have the appearance of large feather shaped colonies, up to 2m or so in height. True sea-fan *Gorgonia ventalina* or the greeny yellow sea-fan (*Gorgonia flabellum*), are distinctly fan-shaped in appearance with their fans orientated perpendicular to the water current. One of the most distinctive sea fans, characteristic of fairly deep water and less well lit rock surfaces, is the slender orange *Ellisella*.

Underwater photographers, with their eyes set on locating good close-up subjects, could do worse than to take a close look at sea-fans, since several small molluscs and fish can be associated with them. For example, the flamingo-tongue snail, *Cyphoma gibbosum* is regularly found browsing on the swaying fans of *Gorgonia ventalina*.

2.1 (iv): HYDROZOAN CORALS

Fire coral, that bright yellow stinging coral which is the bane of many a snorkeller's first experience on coral-reefs, is not actually a true coral, but a hydroid, or sea-fern, with a hard calcareous skeleton. The family Milleporidae, to which these forms belong, has three west Atlantic species: the branching or encrusting *Millepora alcicornis*; *Millepora complanata* whose colonies form thin vertical plates

Fig. 6: *Millepora alcicornis*

(united only at their bases); and *Millepora squarrosa* also characterised by vertical plates, but with linked lateral extensions, forming a honeycombed complex. Another hydrozoan coral (a member of the Stylesteridae) is found in small cavities in the spur and groove zone on the fore-reef. It has delicate pink or purple, somewhat irregular fans and is *Stylaster roseus*. It has the peculiar habit of actually overgrowing, and thus killing, certain gorgonians.

3.1 (v): HYDROIDS

Also members of the class Hydrozoa are the delicate hydropolyps, sometimes referred to as sea-ferns, which occur in a range of species, each of which shows a particular preference for a combination of light and water movement. Thus some forms, such as *Gymnangium longicauda*, commonly called the feather hydroid, are found in places where low light intensity combines with quite strong water movement; whilst others occur on more illuminated surfaces. The Christmas tree hydroid (*Halocordyle disticha*) is a circumtropical species found at most diving depths. Other commonly observed hydroids include the branching hydroid (*Sertularella speciosa*) which has large tree-shaped colonies often 20cm or so long; and the slender hydroid (*Cnidoscyphus marginatus*) often seen on gorgonians, dead corals or sponges and with filamentous algae attached to its exoskeleton.

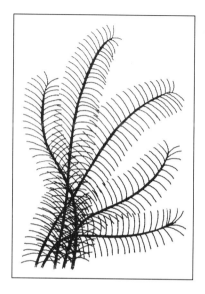

Fig. 7: *Gymnangium longicauda*

2.1 (vi): BLACK CORALS, THORNY CORALS AND CERIANTHIDS

These are all members of the coelenterate class Ceriantipatharia. Black coral is actually not black underwater but usually whitish, yellow or orange. *Antipathes pennacea*, much sought after in some areas for its shiny black axial skeleton which is used in jewellery making, forms large branched colonies, fairly deep on the fore-reef. At least two other species of black coral may be found in similar habitats, at moderate to deep sites.

Closely related to black corals, and a member of the same order Antipatharia, is the spiral whip coral *Stichopathes lutkeni*, whose long 'stalks' protrude from the reef-face in deeper water, generally below 20m.

In the same class, but in a separate order, the Cerianthia, are the cerianthids which are often descibed as tube-dwelling anemones although they are in a completely different class from the true

Fig. 8: *Antipathes pennacea*

Fig. 9: *Arachnanthus nocturnus*

anemones. They live in parchment tubes buried in the sand. Their tentacles are often withdrawn in daytime and are best seen at night. A local example, with brown and white banded tentacles, is *Arachnanthus nocturnus*.

2.1 (vii): SEA ANEMONES (Cl. ZOANTHARIA; orders: ACTINARIA, CORALLIMORPHARIA AND ZOANTHINIARIA).

True sea anemones, like their fellow members of the class Zoantharia, the scleractinian corals, have polyps with six tentacles (or multiples of six). Also like the corals, they include solitary and colonial forms but unlike the corals they do not secrete a calcareous exoskeleton. One result of the absence of a hard calix is that there is less restriction on the size and form of the anemone polyp. Thus some anemones, which are actually single polyps, may be quite large, reaching a metre or so across the base of their 'foot'. These giant anemones with large bulbous tentacles, such as *Condylactis gigantea*, are a prominent feature of reef life, frequently with commensal fish and shrimps. Other anemones on the other hand may be small, with delicate polyps, frequently withdrawn in the day and only visible to night-divers. Colonial anemones create extensive matting over the substrate, superficially resembling true corals.

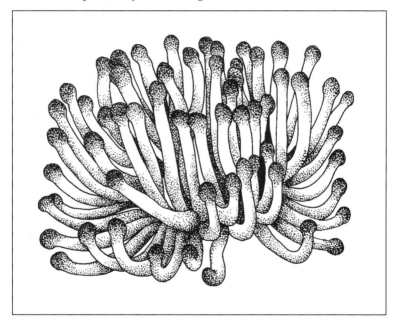

Fig. 10: *Condylactis gigantea*

Regularly encountered actinian species include the knobby anemone (*Heteractis lucida*), the giant anemone mentioned above, the corkscrew anemone (*Bartholomea annulata*) and the sun anemone (*Stoichactis helianthus*) which has quite a powerful sting. Corallimorpharian anemones include *Rhodactis sanctithomas* and

Fig. 11: *Pseudocorynactis caribbeorum*

Fig. 12: *Zoanthus sociatus*

Ricordea florida as well as the red-ball anemone *Pseudocorynactis caribbeorum*. Representatives of the order Zoanthiniaria, include the grey zoanthid, *Zoanthus sociatus* and the white species *Palythoa caribbea*, the former thinly carpeting the substrate whilst the latter forms lumpy, more rounded colonies attached to coral rock. When its polyps are withdrawn it gives the superficial impression of being a stony coral. Other attractive zoanthids include the golden *Parazoanthus swiftii*, usually on red finger sponges, and the bright yellow *Parazoanthus parasiticus* also frequently found on sponges.

2.1.(viii): JELLYFISH

Belonging to the class Scyphozoa, jellyfish are for the most part pelagic coelenterates. One consequence of their ocean-drifting life-style is that they may be very widely distributed geographically. The classic example of this is the moon jellyfish *Aurelia aurita*, which not only occurs in the Caribbean and Indo-Pacific, but also lives in temperate as well as tropical waters. Thus the common jellyfish of the Caribbean may already be familiar to visitors from colder climes. Contrary to popular belief, the moon jellyfish does not give a signifi-

Fig. 13: *Aurelia aurita*

cant sting, but unfortunately the same cannot be said for all local jellyfish. Another widespread species, this time circumtropical in its distribution, is the sea-wasp, *Carybdea alata*. It is a small transparent cube of jelly with four long pink tentacles. At night they swim horizontally, trailing the tentacles behind them. Caution is the watchword here since the tentacles can deliver a powerful sting. One of the most unusual of jellyfish is the upside-down jellyfish *Casseiopea xamachana* which is often found in shallow sheltered areas such as over sea-grass beds or among mangroves. The bell is used more like the disc of a sea-anemone, as a means of loose attachment to the bottom, but if disturbed they are able to swim off, retaining their upside-down (from a jellyfish's viewpoint at least) posture.

2.1 (ix): SPONGES

The traditional practice of diving in the Caribbean owes a great deal to the lowly sponge of the so called 'commercial variety', which supported a whole industry, centred around Nassau in the Bahamas, employing at its peak 265 schooners, 322 sloops and 2,808 open boats together with over 6,000 men and women. The Bahamian sponge industry ran its course, for the most part under full sail, from 1841 – when the shipwrecked French sailor Gustave Renouard recognised the potential for commercial sponge fishing and started exporting to Paris – to 1939 when a mysterious fungal infection virtually wiped out the entire population of commercial sponges from local waters.

There is a vast variety of sponges living in Caribbean waters, but only one or two have any commercial significance. A study of sponges around the Bahamas turned up 82 species.

Among shallow lagoon environments around the Caymans one may find the giant loggerhead sponge *Spheciospongia*. On hard substrata in somewhat clearer water, at depths of 2-4m or so, before the back-reef, one may find the small green sponge *Haliclona viridis*. Sponges are probably most common however in the back-reef and in deeper water along the fore-reef.

Sponges generally compete for space with other sessile reef inhabitants, especially corals. Interestingly enough, the sponge *Mycale laevis* appears to have a mutually beneficial association with the coral *Montastrea annularis*. The sponge grows on the under-surface of the flattened coral plate, causing it to develop upturned peripheral folds above the sponge oscules. The sponge thus achieves a continually expanding substrate on which to grow, whilst the coral is protected from attack along its overgrown underside by boring sponges. *Chondrilla nucula*, an encrusting sponge, frequently overgrows large tracts of the corals *Siderastrea siderea* and *Diploria clivosa*. Cliona sponges inhabit cavities which they excavate in corals by removing small chips of calcium carbonate. On Jamaican reefs, below 30m, they have been shown to be an important element in biodegradation of reef corals. The sponge causes a weakening of the coral's attachment to the substrate, and in consequence coral colonies fall to the seabed where they are smothered by sediment and soon die. Some sponges, such as *Siphonodictyon*, actually take the attack one stage further, burrowing into the living tissues of massive corals, producing 'chimneys'. Other species grow primarily above the substrate, forming large colourful colonies. Large barrel sponges such as *Xestospongia muta* are favourite foreground subjects for underwater photographers on Caribbean reefs while other smaller sponges, such as the pink tube sponge *Callyospongia plicifera* or the purple vase sponge *Dasychalina cyathina*, form excellent close-up subjects. Sponges come in a wide range of shapes, sizes and colours, and they form an essential element in the creation of the Caribbean's rich marinelife.

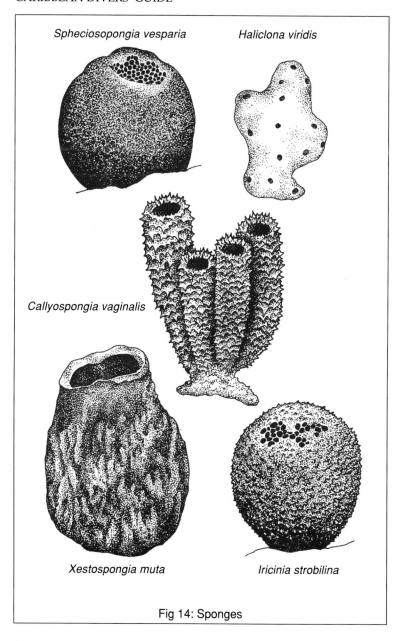

Fig 14: Sponges

Table 3

Some Common Caribbean Sponges

Latin Name (Common Name)	Comments
Leucandra aspera (white cryptic sponge)	In caves and crevices with low water movement.
Leucosolenia canariensis (yellow calcareous sponge)	Small inter-twined yellow tubes. Dark crevices.
Cliona delitrix (orange boring sponge)	Bright orange. Often breaks up large corals.
Siphonodictyon coralliphagum (yellow boring sponge)	Only oscula visible above substrate into which it bores.
Agelas clathrodes (orange elephant ear sponge)	Deep, low light, still water.
Agelas confera (moose antler sponge)	Looks like moose antler. Deep fore-reef and outer edge of buttresses.
Agelas screptrum (lumpy finger sponge)	Symbiotic Parazoanthus in depressions.
Callyospongia vaginalis (branching vase sponge)	Up to 80cm tall and 5cm across. + *Parazoanthus.*
Callyospongia plicifera (azure vase sponge)	On vertical walls. Shallow to deep.
Hemectyon ferox (brown volcano sponge)	Can severely irritate skin!
Mycale laevis (orange encrusting sponge)	Bright orange, undersides of plate corals.
Mycale sp. (red vase sponge)	Deep red but looks purple or black underwater.
Ulosa hispida (orange lumpy sponge)	Shallow to deep and on red mangrove roots.
Haliclona rubens (smooth red finger sponge)	Shallow to deep reefs. Long slender anastomosing upright branches.
Haliclona hogarthi (lavender finger sponge)	Sometimes forms dense thickets.
Dasychalina cyathina (pink vase sponge)	Delicate pink colour. Moderate depths.
Xestospongia muta (giant barrel sponge)	Largest Caribbean sponge. Moderately deep to deep.
Cribochalina vasculum (bowl sponge)	Moderate depths.
Neofibularia nolitangere (irritating sponge)	As its name suggests, do not touch. On level reef, shallow and deeper.
Iotrochota birotulata (green finger sponge)	Usually inhabited by parasitic anemone: *P.swiftii.*
Ircinia strobilina (black ball sponge)	Sub-spherical. All diving depths.
Aplysina fistularis (yellow tube sponge)	Moderate and deep locations.
Aplysina gigantea (giant yellow tube sponge)	Moderately deep zones.
Aplysina archeri (long pink tube sponge)	Up to 2m tall. Deep water.
Aplysina longissima (purple and yellow tube sponge)	Moderate depths.
Aplysina lacunosa (purple tube sponge)	Fairly deep water.
Anthosigmella varians (brown volcano carpet sponge)	Covers rocks in shallow, often silty locations.
Monanchora barbadensis (red encrusting sponge)	Under coral ledges.
Ceratoporella nicholsoni (yellow sclerosponge)	One of the sclerosponges discovered by the late Prof. Goreau in Jamaica. Caves and deep fore-reef. Deep-water reef-builder!

The intricacies of sponge-biology, however, are far beyond the average diver's level of interest. Nevertheless, a general awareness of the competitive struggle silently fought out on the reefs, between many corals and sponges may lend a new element of interest to one's diving and perhaps new insight to underwater photographers in search of pictures with a story to tell.

2.1 (x): WORMS AND WORM-LIKE ANIMALS

Worms are not generally regarded as being of great interest to divers and yet among this group of animals are some of the most beautiful and fascinating creatures inhabiting the sea. On coral-reefs, competition for space and food, and the need to be protected against intense grazing and predation, lead to a wide range of adaptations for survival. Nowhere is this more apparent than among the marine worms and their allies. These adaptations can be structural, in the form for example, of the hard calcareous tube and armoured operculum of *Spirobranchus grandis* (the Christmas tree worm) whose magnificent spiral branchial crowns grace the surface of many corals, ever ready to make a rapid withdrawal into their heavily defended homes at the merest hint of danger. Or they can be behavioural, and there are many examples of such adaptations to survival on the reefs. One interesting association between a worm-like creature known as a sipunculid and coral was discovered by that eminent marine scientist, who spent so much of his life unravelling the secrets of Jamaica's underwater world, Thomas Goreau. Goreau noticed that the unattached reef-building coral *Heteropsammia michelini* was only found growing on mollusc shells which were inhabited by a sipunculid (*Aspidosiphon corallicola*). He guessed, rightly, that this association had essential benefits for both the coral and the sipunculid and was able to demonstrate how this is so. First the sipunculid occupies a dead mollusc shell on the seabed. Using this as a protective home, it crawls along the soft bottom. A larva of the coral then settles on the shell which, unlike other dead molluscs, has been prevented from sinking into the sediment by the inhabiting worm. As the coral grows, it adds further protection to the sipunculid's

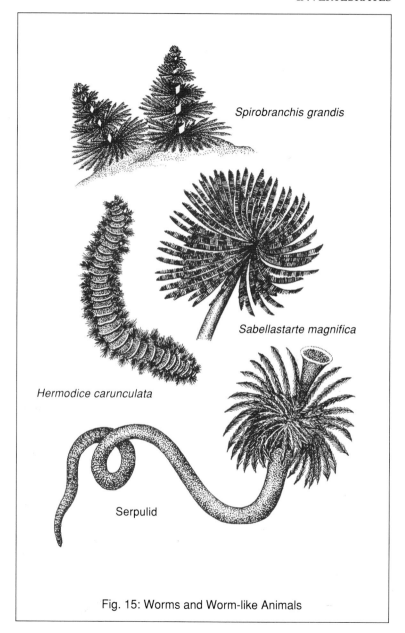

Spirobranchis grandis

Sabellastarte magnifica

Hermodice carunculata

Serpulid

Fig. 15: Worms and Worm-like Animals

home, while leaving a hole for the creature to extend its head region into the sediment. The coral is thus kept from being smothered.

At least one worm actually feeds on corals. *Hermodice carunculata* feeds on *Porites* polyps on Caribbean reefs. Divers may encounter this species at night when it is actively feeding, rather than in the daytime when it is well hidden. If you should find it, take care since its calcareous chaetae can cause severe skin irritations.

Several sabellid worms inhabit parchment like tubes embedded in corals or dead coral rock, including the giant feather duster (*Sabellastarte magnifica*), the spotted feather duster (*Branchioma nigromaculata*) and the yellow fan worm (*Hypsicomus elegans*).

Serpulid fan worms live in hard calcareous tubes rather than the soft ones of sabellids. Apart from the *Spirobranchus* mentioned above, there is a red fan worm, *Pomatostegus stellatus* and the small colonial serpulid *Filograna implexa*.

2.1 (xi): MOLLUSCS

Sea-shells or molluscs have attracted the attention of beachcombers, swimmers, snorkellers and divers since earliest times. Initially used for food or utensils, and later for jewellery or ornaments, they have been avidly fished and collected around all the islands of the Caribbean. In some cases, as with the conch, *Strombus gigas*, this exploitation has been so intense that whole stocks have been depleted to the brink of regional extinction. The size of the Caribbean's conch fishery is apparent in many places, but nowhere more so than in Nassau where huge submarine mounds of dumped conch shells have created hazards to navigation! Recent studies indicate that in 1975 alone 1.7 million conch shells were landed and consumed on New Providence Island in the Bahamas. Fortunately the mollusc produces egg masses containing up to half a million eggs, and efforts to rear conch larvae have proved successful so juveniles may now be reseeded for growth on the reefs. The problem is that they are heavily predated by a variety of creatures from hermit crabs eating the juveniles to rays consuming vast quantities of the sub-adults. They even fall prey to molluscs, such as the tulip shell

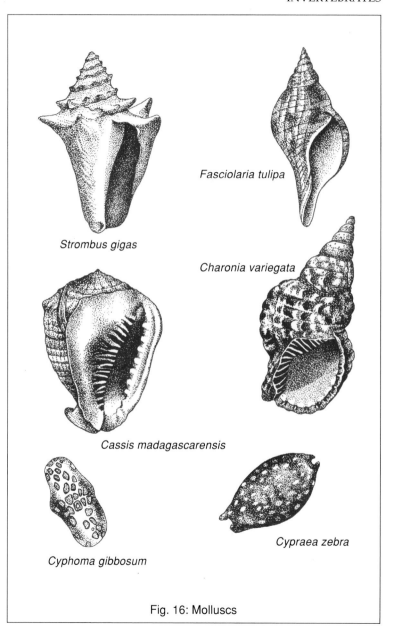

Fig. 16: Molluscs

Fasciolaria tulipa, or the helmet shell *Cassis madagascarensis*, which prey heavily on juvenile conches. Once the conch has reached its formidable adult proportions however, relatively few animals are strong enough to attack it. Two exceptions are the loggerhead turtle and the tiger shark.

Another shell whose numbers have been seriously depleted through over-collection is the trumpet triton, *Charonia variegata*. It is a nocturnal species, emerging at night to feed on sea-cucumbers but generally well hidden during daytime. Many other gastropods share the night and this is undoubtedly the best time to observe them. Among the cowries, one may catch a glimpse of the attractive measled cowrie (*Cypraea zebra*) with its spiky foot lobes partially covering a beautiful shell. Some molluscs, such as the flamingo tongue snail (*Cyphoma gibbosum*) and the less common fingerprint snail (*Cyphoma signatum*) are found on particular invertebrates, in this case gorgonians upon which they feed.

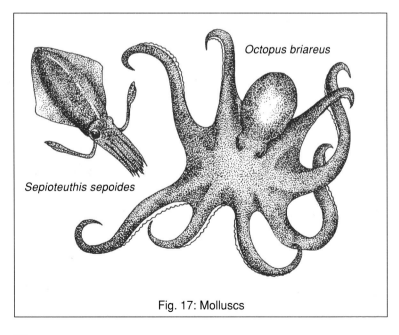

Fig. 17: Molluscs

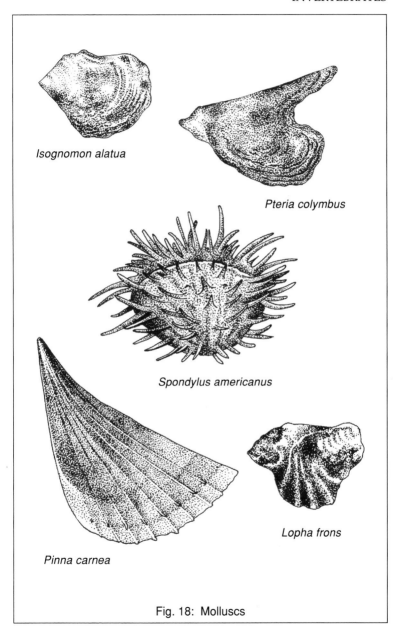

Isognomon alatua

Pteria colymbus

Spondylus americanus

Pinna carnea

Lopha frons

Fig. 18: Molluscs

Among the common bivalve molluscs mention should be made of pen shells (such as *Pinna carnea*) whose shells are always well embedded in sand or coral; wing oysters (e g. *Pteria colymbus*), generally attached to gorgonians; mangrove oysters (*Isognomon alatus*) which attaches itself to red mangrove roots; the frons oyster (*Lopha frons*) whose zig-zag valve edges are highly characteristic; and the Atlantic thorny oyster (*Spondylus americanus*) whose valves are well protected by long spines.

Finally, we must not forget the class Cephalopoda which includes octopus, cuttlefish and squid. Again, the best time to see these is at night. The Atlantic oval squid (*Sepioteuthis sepioidea*) can often be seen swimming in pairs above the reef or sand flats. The common reef octopus (*Octopus briareus*) hunts at night for its food of crustaceans or bivalve molluscs. By day its presence is detectable by the debris of broken shells it leaves near the entrance of its lair.

As a result of widespread interest in sea-shells and their identification, there are many good guides available to Caribbean shells. Divers should note, however, that it is usually prohibited for them to collect shells while underwater, and readers of this book are urged to help in reef preservation by not collecting any living molluscs or indeed any other form of sealife.

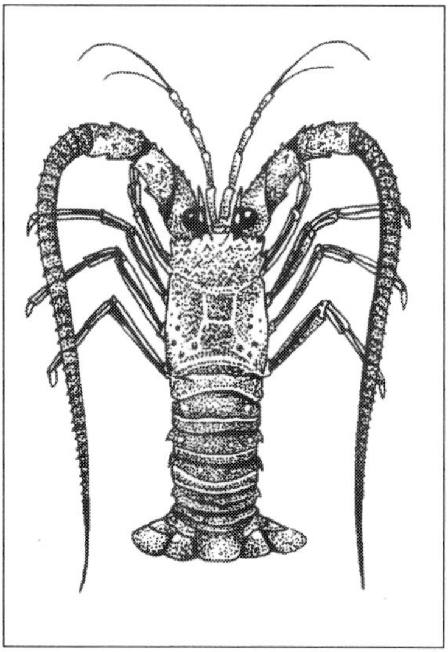

Fig. 19: *Panulirus argus*

2.1 (xii): SHELLFISH: SHRIMPS, CRABS, CRAYFISH ETC

Visitors to the Caribbean invariably praise the crayfish or lobster, a most delicious seafood, and nowhere better presented than Caribbean-style, barbecued over charcoal on the beach or at a restaurant suspended over the tranquil ocean. Sadly, the increase in tourism to the Caribbean has resulted in a very heavy pressure upon the region's naturally rich crayfish resources. The creature in question is *Panulirus argus*, otherwise known as crayfish, crawfish or spiny lobster. Many readers will be familiar with the dramatic photographs of this species migrating in long head-to-tail processions along the seabed, usually along the edge of the Great Bahamas Bank at Bimini. The animal is essentially a nocturnal species, ranging over the reef at night, in search of its food, which may comprise a variety of reef invertebrates, from molluscs to echinoderms. A slightly smaller and less common species is the rock lobster, *Panulirus guttatus*, which may be found in caves during daytime or scavenging over the reef flat at night. There are several other lobster species in Carib-

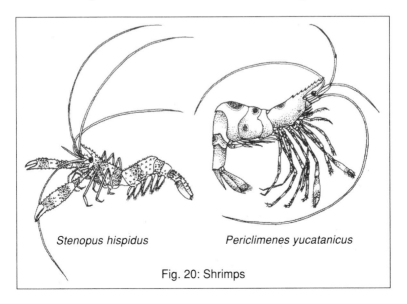

Stenopus hispidus   *Periclimenes yucatanicus*

Fig. 20: Shrimps

bean waters and among these the slipper lobsters are perhaps the most unfamiliar to divers. Rarely observed underwater, they are perhaps more common at greater depths and are frequently trawled off the seabed by fishermen. At least one member of this group, the Spanish lobster, *Scyllarides aequinoctialis*, does occur on reefs but hides deep within the coral during daytime.

Underwater photographers are generally on the look-out for the smaller, highly attractive shrimps and prawns which inhabit the reefs, generally living in some form of close association with other reef organisms. Several of these act as cleaner shrimps, enticing fish to approach their long white antennae, and then climbing aboard the fish to pick parasites from the surface of their scales, from within the gill chambers or even from within the fishes' mouths! Examples of Caribbean cleaner shrimps include the delicately purple spotted Pederson's cleaning shrimp (*Periclimenes pedersoni*) which lives in association with several anemones; the banded coral shrimp (*Stenopus hispidus*) which lives in small crevices or under coral ledges; the less conspicuous yellow shrimp (*Stenopus scutellatus*); and on occasion the sponge shrimp (*Lysmata wurdemanni*). Several other shrimps may occur in association with anemones and are thus loosely referred to as anemone shrimps. These include *Periclimenes yucatanicus* and *Thor amboinensis*, the latter of which frequently occurs in the sun anemone *Stoichactis helianthus* and the giant anemone *Condylactis gigantea*. Before leaving the shrimps, mention should also be made of the pistol shrimp, *Alpheus armatus*, which has the unusual ability to snap its pincer rapidly, resulting in the stunning of its prey or the scaring away of intruders into its territory. It is most often found peeking out from underneath the corkscrew anemone.

Among the crabs, which are well represented on Caribbean reefs, divers are perhaps most familiar with the hermit crabs. It is virtually impossible to night dive without coming across various hermit crabs humping their dead molluscan shells across the seabed. Common hermits include *Dardanus venosus* which usually carries the anemone *Calliactis tricolor* on its shell; the bright red hermit *Paguristes cadenati*, whose vermilion legs and yellow eye-stalks make it unmistakable; and the giant hermit crab, *Petrochirus diogenes*, which is so

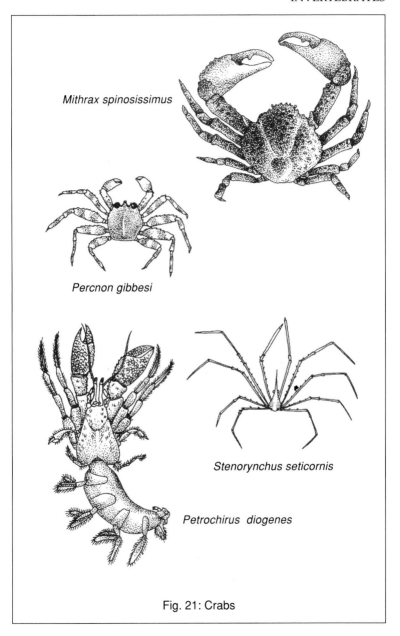

Mithrax spinosissimus

Percnon gibbesi

Stenorynchus seticornis

Petrochirus diogenes

Fig. 21: Crabs

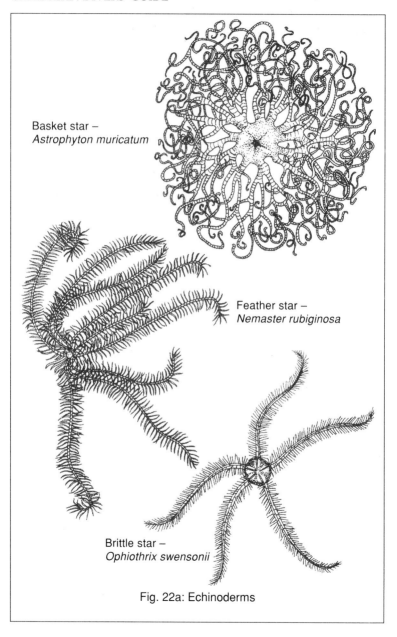

Basket star –
Astrophyton muricatum

Feather star –
Nemaster rubiginosa

Brittle star –
Ophiothrix swensonii

Fig. 22a: Echinoderms

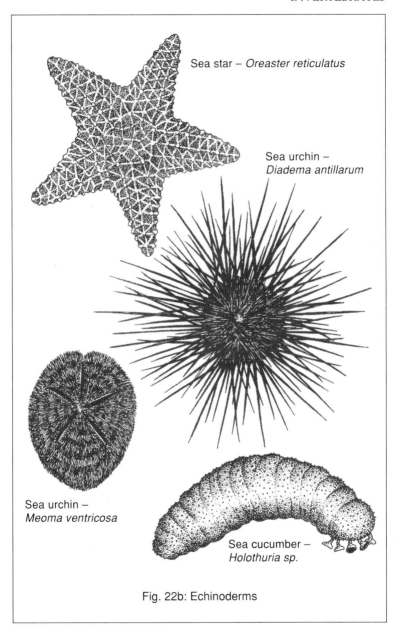

Sea star – *Oreaster reticulatus*

Sea urchin – *Diadema antillarum*

Sea urchin – *Meoma ventricosa*

Sea cucumber – *Holothuria sp.*

Fig. 22b: Echinoderms

big that it generally lives within queen conch shells! Other crabs
frequently encountered underwater are: the flat crab (*Percnon gibbesi*),
often found hiding under the spines of black sea-urchins; the king
crab, *Mithrax spinosissimus*, which is truly a local giant among crabs,
weighing up to 3kg and greatly prized as a food item in some areas;
the swimming crab, *Portunus sebae*, characteristic of shallow areas
such as sea-grass beds; the anemone crab, *Mithrax cinctimanus*, living in association with *Stoichactis helianthus*; and finally the arrow
crab, *Stenorhynchus seticornis*, whose bizarre spider-like form can only
leave one in awe of the incredible variety in form achieved within
the superclass Crustacea.

2.1 (xiii): SEA-STARS, FEATHER-STARS, SEA-CUCUM-BERS, SEA-URCHINS, BRITTLESTARS

The phylum Echinodermata, which includes sea-stars, sea-urchins,
feather-stars, sea-cucumbers and brittlestars is named from the Latin
for 'spiny skinned' – a characteristic which is widely but not uni-
versally held by these varied forms. Most divers are already familiar
with the various classes of echinoderms,but there is some confusion
over the magnificent basket star *Astrophyton muricatum*, which bears
a superficial resemblance to a feather-star when its large light-sensitive feeding net is extended, or to a tangled ball of string when it
is curled up. Many people are surprised to learn that this is actually
a member of the brittlestars (class Ophiuroidea) rather than the
feather-stars (class Crinoidea). Many of the true feather-stars or
crinoids are also light-sensitive, remaining hidden well within the
coral reef during daytime and emerging around dusk to set themselves up on the reef, with their arms extended to create plankton
sieves. Such forms include the golden crinoid (*Nemaster rubiginosa*),
the white crinoid (*Nemaster discoidea*) and the swimming crinoid
(*Analcidometra caribbea*). A feather-star which is often seen fully
extended during daytime is the black-and-white 40-armed crinoid
Nemaster grandis.

Among the brittlestars, we have already mentioned the basket
star which is very rarely seen in daytime but sits prominently attached

to the shallow reef edge at night. Several brittlestars tend to occur in sponges, where they presumably benefit from their hosts' feeding currents. One such species is *Ophiothrix swensonii*, which is often found in the lumen of vase and tube sponges.

There is quite a variety of sea-stars present on the reefs but many of these tend to remain hidden under rocks or in crevices. Divers swimming over sea-grass beds will be hard pressed to avoid noticing the large cushion star *Oreaster reticulatus* which extracts molluscs from the sandy seabed which it inhabits. Sadly, its attractive form has rendered it easy prey for commercial souvenir hunters and its numbers have thus been severely depleted in some areas. A common but reclusive shallow water sea star is the comet star, *Linckia guildingii*, whose juveniles may occur under stones in the intertidal zone.

Sea-urchins are the bane of many a Caribbean bather's life! The villain of the piece in this regard is the long spined urchin *Diadema antillarum*. Since they are often grouped in large numbers in shallow water, they are easy to brush against or even to stand on. Their venom-coated spines can cause a really painful wound, which may also be slow to heal. Having tried many different remedies for sea urchin stings over the years, I have finally discovered the answer. This is to plunge the injured hand or foot into very hot water, just below scorching temperature, as soon as possible after the encounter. On one memorable occasion the excruciating pain, caused by multiple punctures to the palm of my hand, was literally switched off, almost as rapidly as switching off a light, as soon as the hand hit hot water. Furthermore, there was no subsequent pain or infection and the wounds were hardly visible the next day.

Some years ago what appears to have been a viral infection spread through the Caribbean's *Diadema* population, decimating their numbers. Other common sea urchins include the club urchin (*Eucidaris tribuloides*); the jewel urchin (*Lytechinus williamsi*); the edible urchin (*Tripneustes ventricosus*); the boring urchin (*Echinometra lucunter*); the reef urchin (*Echinometra viridis*) and the large red heart urchin (*Meoma ventricosa*).

Sea-cucumbers are frequently a source of fascination to divers

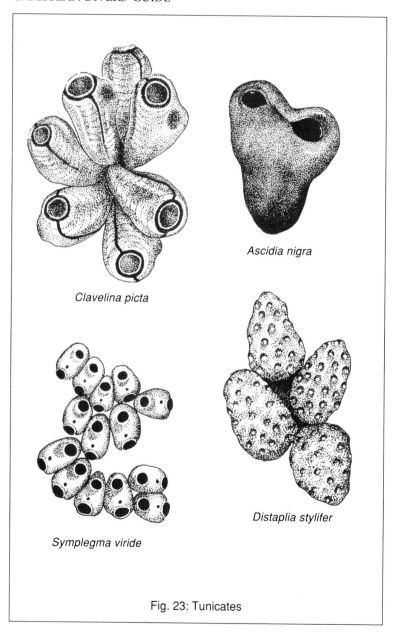

Clavelina picta

Ascidia nigra

Symplegma viride

Distaplia stylifer

Fig. 23: Tunicates

since they may be most closely compared to mobile sausages! The evidence of their feeding behaviour on sand is often the presence of neat cylindrical sand pellets, the remains of sand which has passed through the digestive tract of *Astichopus multifidus*, having had any nutrients extracted from it. The tentacular tube-feet of *Holothuria mexicana*, on the other hand, actively range across sand or coral rock, feeding on filamentous algae or other organic material. One of the strangest sea cucumbers is the tiger's tail (*Holothuria thomasae*) which can extend and retract its body length and has a spiky, sinuous form.

2.1 (xiv): ASCIDIANS OR TUNICATES

Despite their primitive appearance, more like sponges than phylogenetically advanced forms, the ascidians or tunicates are actually members of the phylum Chordata – a grouping to which the vertebrates also belong! The basic form familiar to many people is that of a translucent gelatinous, tubular sessile animal attached at its base with two openings at its opposite end. There is a wide variety of forms within the class, ranging from the conspicuous tubular form described above to thin encrustations of some compound ascidians which may cover very large areas. Some local forms which divers are likely to encounter include the reef tunicate (*Ascidia nigra*), reddish-black in colour; the yellow tube tunicate (*Ascidia sydneiensis*); the light-bulb tunicate (*Clavelina picta*); the strawberry tunicate (*Distaplia stylifer*) and the green social tunicate (*Symplegma viride*); as well as other common forms such as a purple form of *Clavelina*.

2.2 : FISH

Nine hundred and forty-nine species of fish, belonging to 143 families have been recorded from the Caribbean area. There are no doubt others which have escaped the biologist's collecting jar; thus the total number almost certainly exceeds a thousand. Not all of these are closely associated with coral-reefs however and the number of species likely to be observed by divers is much less than this. In the following necessarily brief account we have concentrated on those forms most likely to be of interest to Caribbean divers.

There are 44 recorded species of sharks present, together with two guitarfish and two sawfish species. If one adds to that the 22 species of rays, one can see that the Elasmobranchs are well represented here. From the diver's viewpoint sharks are not generally easy subjects for photography, difficult to approach and quick to flee if alarmed. There are of course exceptions, but it is true to say that the vast majority of shark photographs have been set-up using

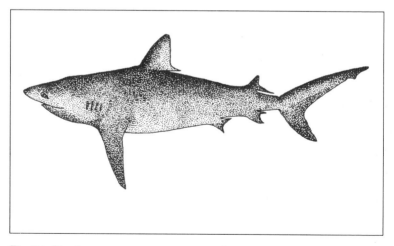

Fig. 24: Shark

Above: Reef scene in Cuba, *Plexaurella* in foreground and
Pseudopterogorgia in background (Pat McCoole).
Below: Coral scenery in Caymans (John Murray).

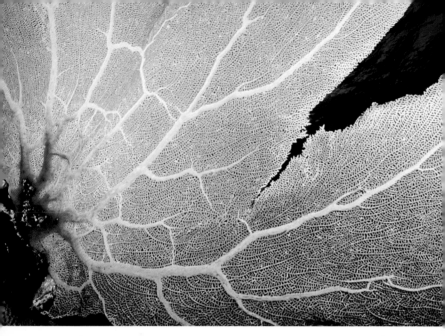

Above: Gorgonian fan coral (F. Busonero).

Below: Coral close-up (John Murray).

Above: Orange cup coral on shaded overhang (W. Gregory Brown).

Below: Anemones and gorgonians on reef at Saba (Joan C. Bourge).

Above left: iridescent vase sponge in St Lucia (Chris Huxley). Right: Carpet anemone in Bonaire (W. Gregory Brown). Below left: Wave-cut channels and diver (W. Gregory Brown). Right: Sponge-dominated reef in Caymans (John Murray).

Above: *Hermodice carunculata* bristle worm (W. Gregory Brown). Below left: *Spirobranchus sp.* or Christmas-tree tube-worms (W. Gregory Brown). Below right: Fan-worms, *Sabellastarte sp.* (John Murray).

Above left: Hermit crab (W. Gregory Brown). Right: Anemone shrimp at
Bonaire (W. Gregory Brown).
Below: Isopod parasite on creole fish (W. Gregory Brown).

Above: Arrow crab, *Stenorrynchus seticornis* (W. Gregory Brown).

Below: Hermit crab, *Paguristes cadenati* (W. Gregory Brown).

Above: Brittle-star at night on a reef at Bonaire (W. Gregory Brown).
Below: Caribbean basket-star at night. This is a member of the brittle-star family (Chris Huxley).

Divers with southern stingrays, *Dasyatis americana,* in the Cayman Islands. (Four pictures by John Murray).

Above: Horse-eye trevally, *Caranx latus* (W. Gregory Brown).

Below: Tang shoal over an algal encrusted reef platform (John Murray).

Above: Goldentail moray, *Gymnothorax miliaris* (W. Gregory Brown).

Below: Green moray, *Gymnothorax funebris* (W. Gregory Brown).

Above: Spotted scorpionfish (W. Gregory Brown).

Below: Coney, *Cephalopholis fulva* (W. Gregory Brown).

Above: Pygmy filefish photographed with Nikon F3 and 55mm macro lens (W. Gregory Brown).
Below: Head of stoplight parrotfish in close-up (John Murray).

Above left: Diver and brain coral (Chris Huxley). Right: Hawksbill turtle in Caymans (John Murray). Below left: Red sponges growing from shaded coral underhang (W. Gregory Brown). Right: Wall dive in Bonaire (W. Gregory Brown).

Gorgonian garlanded slopes, overhanging walls and mysterious caves...
all part of underwater conditions around the island of Dominica.
Photographer: Paul Janosi of Dive Dominica Ltd.

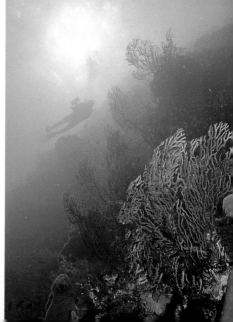

Above: Snorkelling in the shallows (W. Gregory Brown). Below: Dive boat landing on Turtle Beach at Peter Milburn Diving base on Grand Cayman Island (John Murray).

dead fish as a scent-bait. Barracuda heads are a favourite among shark photographers but almost any fish-offal works. At sites where divers regularly feed sharks the sharks show a feeding response as soon as divers enter the water, even if they are not carrying bait. Once the sharks realise that there is no food being offered, they usually lose interest in the divers. If, on the other hand, fish-offal has been carefully deposited on the seabed (always taking care to keep it and its smell away from one's own wet-suit or skin) the sharks tend to swim directly up the current-born scent-trail – i.e.they approach the diver from down-current, heading straight into the current. If they pass the bait without locating it they often turn straight back, swim with the current for a short distance and then turn again as they pick up the scent. Needless to say a strong note of caution should be sounded with regard to divers 'playing', in this or any other way, with sharks. Experienced dive guides will know how local sharks behave and may be willing to give divers a chance to observe these magnificent predators at quite close quarters, but one still needs eyes in the back of one's head! It is really a case of being able to interpret shark behaviour correctly, and to know when to get out! That said, some of my most thrilling moments underwater have been spent observing sharks, the most elegant creatures in the ocean!

Among the rays, the southern stingray, *Dasyatis americana*, deserves special mention as the star of David Doubilet's ballet in words and pictures, published in National Geographic (January, 1989). Performances run daily, admission free, in the shallows at North Sound, off Grand Cayman. Divers Jay Ireland and Pat Kenney have created a unique attraction with the large and potentially dangerous rays feeding from their hands.

There are many other interesting rays which divers are likely to observe underwater, such as the spotted eagle ray, *Aetobatus narinari*, the lesser electric ray, *Narcine brasilensis*, and the common electric ray *Torpedo nobiliana*. The one species which everyone hopes for a glimpse of however, is that most serene of the Elasmobranchs, *Manta birostris*, otherwise known by a host of epithets such as Atlantic manta, blanketfish, sea devil, devilfish, giant devil ray, devil ray,

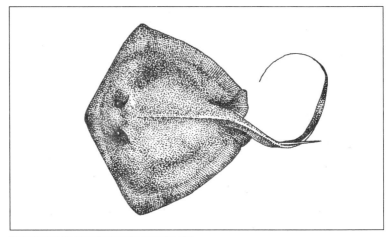

Above, Fig. 25: Ray

Left, Fig. 26: Seahorse

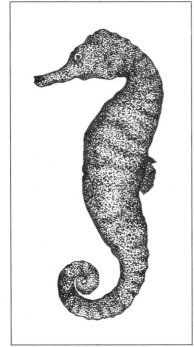

and just plain manta-ray. Here is a creature whose grace and beauty underwater render it worthy of a more endearing title. Whilst one can imagine how sailors were frightened by their strange form and their great displays of power when leaping out of the sea, divers have gained a quite different and less fearsome impression of these gentle giants.

Just as the giant rays create an awesome reaction in divers because of their size and strange forms, the diminutive sea-horses evoke a similar degree of wonder, seeming to pack so much fascination into their tiny bodies.

Needless to say, they are a favourite subject for underwater photographers and in many senses just as challenging as sharks, for what they may lack in speed and mobility they make up for in their camouflage. It is quite common indeed for a photographer to be focussed on a sea-horse, then to take his eye off it in order to adjust his camera, and to turn back again and have great difficulty in locating the animal! There are actually five sea-horse (*Hippocampus*) species recorded from the Caribbean – *H. erectus*, *H.hudsonius*, *H. punctulatus*, *H. reidi*, and *H. zosterae*.

Of the barracudas, the great barracuda, *Sphyraena barracuda* can be seen, normally swimming as a lone fish, often haunting a particular reef site or wreck, while the three other species are smaller and often in schools. Despite their reputations, barracudas are not generally a threat to divers unless some confusion has arisen due to spearfishing.

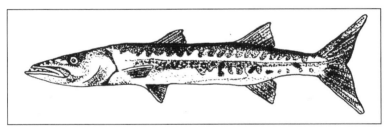

Fig. 27: Barracuda

One of the largest families on the reefs, in terms of species numbers, if not in actual abundance of fish, is the Serranidae which includes the sea-basses and groupers, also referred to as butterfishes, jewfishes or hinds. Fifty-four species are recorded. Among these, the species most commonly encountered by divers are probably: the coney (*Cephalopholis fulva*), a species which may confuse divers with its distinctly different colour phases; the red hind (*Epinephelus guttatus*); the rock hind *(Epinephelus adscensionis)*; the Nassau grouper (*Epinephelus striatus*); the harlequin bass (*Serranus tigrinus*); the tobacco fish (*Serranus tabacarius*); the barred hamlet (*Hypoplectrus puella*); the yellow-bellied hamlet (*Hypoplectrus aberrans*) and possibly also the shy hamlet (*Hypoplectrus guttavarius*). The massive jewfish,

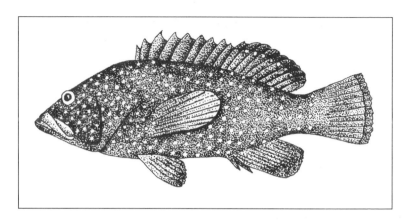

Fig. 28: Sea Bass

Epinephelus itajara, which can grow to over 2.5m long and weigh more than 300kg, is much less likely to be encountered but exceedingly impressive when seen in the flesh!

If the Serranidae are the dominant predatory family living close to the coral, and usually resident on a particular reef, then the Carangidae, or jacks, scads and pompano, are the dominant roving

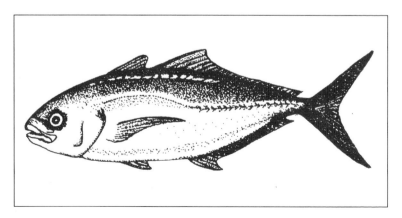

Fig. 29: Jack

predators, more associated with the neritic forms of the water column, but with many species darting in among the reef life to catch their prey. Thirty-three Carangidae species are recorded from the Caribbean area, but once again the diver is likely to encounter primarily those species closely associated with the reefs. Bar jacks (*Caranx ruber*), are roving predators, usually seen in large schools, and easily distinguished by their striking dark bands. Many of the larger predatory Carangidae, such as rainbow runners, (*Elegatis bipinnulata*) tend to lie off the deep sides of reefs, in open water, almost out of sight of the reef-crawling diver. They are more easily approached in fact by breath-hold snorkellers, rather than by bubble generating scuba divers.

Another group of reef-associated predators is the snappers or Lutjanidae of which 19 species are present. Frequently shoaling, and with many species typical of deep water, the snappers tend to hang in the water-column, maintaining their position, facing into the current, and snapping at food items which come their way. They are fished commercially throughout the Caribbean and in consequence, the gigantic schools which were once seen are less frequently encountered. Nevertheless, snappers are among the dominant members of reef-associated fish-life in the Caribbean.

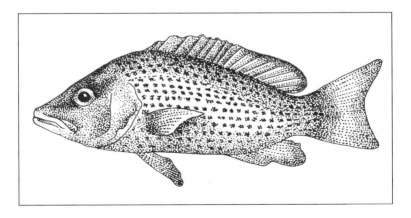

Fig. 30: Snapper

Fig. 31: Grunt

Similar in general body form to snappers, but generally more closely associated with the reef-face, are the grunts or Pomadasyidae, with 22 Caribbean species. These include the familiar French grunt (*Haemulon flavolineatum*) and small-mouth grunt (*Haemulon chrysargyreum*). Both species occur among coral-heads, or over wrecks, frequently in mixed schools, and they are among the first species to colonise artificial reefs. Their common name results from the sound they make when alarmed. Whilst they live in tightly packed schools during daytime, never far from cover, at night they spread out over sand and sea-grass beds where they feed. Whilst the two species mentioned above are relatively small, averaging around 15cm or so in length, the white grunt (*Haemulon plumieri*) can grow up to 40cm long.

The most characteristic fish on coral-reefs, wherever they may be, are of course the butterfly-fishes, members of the family Chaetodontidae. In the Greater Caribbean area there are six species: the parche or *Chaetodon ataeniatus*, which occurs on reefs around Cuba; the four-eye butterfly-fish, *Chaetodon capistratus*; the spotfin butterfly-fish, *Chaetodon ocellatus*; the reef butterfly-fish, *Chaetodon sedentarius*; the banded butterfly-fish, *Chaetodon striatus*; and the long-snout butterfly-fish, *Prognathodes aculeatus*. Of these the commonest

Fig. 32: Butterfly-fish

species on most reefs are the banded and four-eye butterfly-fish, two species exceedingly easy to identify underwater, and perfectly described by their common names.

Angel-fish, once grouped in the same family as butterfly-fish, now have a family of their own, the Pomacanthidae. There are six local species represented: the cherub-fish (*Centropyge argi*); the queen angel-fish (*Holocanthus ciliaris*); the blue angel-fish (*Holocanthus isabelita*); the rock beauty (*Holocanthus tricolor*); the black angel-fish (*Pomacanthus arcuatus*) and the French angel-fish (*Pomacanthus paru*). Of these, the cherub-fish is a small, elusive, blue fish looking more like a damsel-fish than an angel-fish; while the rock-beauty is distinctly angel-fish-shaped with adults primarily black with a bright yellow head and fin margins. The queen angel-fish is mainly blue in its adult form but with a speckling of yellow and bright yellow tail-fin. It can be distinguished from the blue angel-fish by the presence of a dark blue 'crown' on its forehead, as well as by its all-yellow tail. The French angel-fish, by contrast, is much darker, with body scales rimmed in yellow in the adult. Juveniles seem to be more frequently observed, perhaps because of the three bright yellow vertical bars conspicuously marking their flanks.

Fig. 33: Angel-fish

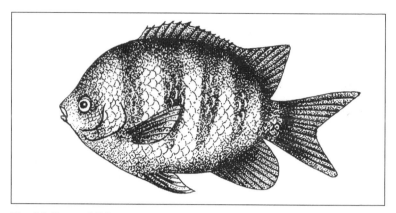

Fig. 34. Damsel-fish

Damsel-fish are common on all shallow reefs, hiding among the coral and darting out to graze on algae, or shoaling close to the reef surface, picking at the plankton, always ready to dart back under cover at the approach of a predatory jack or grouper. The family name for these small fish is Pomacentridae and thus they are commonly known as pomacentrids. Fourteen are recorded from the Caribbean area, and divers are likely to encounter the majority of these. The blue chromis (*Chromis cyaneus*) usually prefers to live among stagshorn coral, often around offshore reefs, below about 6m. The yellow-edge chromis or brown chromis (*Chromis multilineatus*) schools all over the reef, from the shallows to relatively deep. They can be recognised by their distinctive white spot at the rear axis of their dorsal fin. The sergeant major (*Abudefduf saxatilis*) is a fish which many people will be familiar with if they have dived Indo-Pacific or Red Sea reefs for it occurs all over the globe in coral seas. They lay their eggs in round patches, creating pink mats on the shallow reef platform. These they guard quite aggressively. Other species commonly encountered include the cocoa damsel-fish (*Eupomacentrus variabilis*), bicolor damsel-fish (*Eupomacentrus partitus*); dusky damsel-fish (*Eupomacentrus fuscus*); yellow-tail damsel-fish (*Microspathodon chrysurus*) and the yellow damsel-fish (*Eupomocentrus planifrons*).

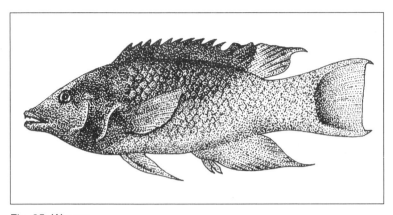

Fig. 35: Wrasse

Among the prime scavengers of the reefs are wrasses, members of the family Labridae, of which 19 species are recorded. Here is a family whose social behaviour is full of surprises for the males rule the roost (or harem) but should a dominant male get eaten by a roving jack, leaving the family of females without a leader, one of the females in the group changes sex to become male, taking over the dominant role. In some species of wrasse there is a further twist to this tale, for the dominance of males over larger groups of females leaves many young males without a safe place on the reef. As soon as they enter a family group they are chased away by the dominant male who is unwilling to allow other males into his group. The solution is for some of the young males to take on female coloration, pretending to be females, and thus become accepted into the family group without the dominant male recognising the deception. Caribbean wrasses are often brightly coloured, frequently shoaling species, in which colour patterns are different for males and females as well as for adults and juveniles. Among the common species, the spanish hog-fish, *Bodianus rufus*, is one of the larger species, growing up to 37cm. Most are smaller than this, closer to 15cm or so in length. Near offshore reefs the creole wrasse, *Clepticus parrae*, swims in schools, often in midwater while the yellowhead wrasse (*Halichoeres garnoti*) is more of a loner, weaving among coral heads, rubble or the debris of old wrecks. One of the most frequently observed wrasses is the clown wrasse (*Halichoeres maculipinna*) which swims all over the shallows. It is the first on the scene if a sea-urchin is broken open. Two other equally abundant wrasses are the bluehead (*Thalassoma bifasciatum*) and slippery dick (*Halichoeres bivittatus*). The bluehead exhibits a further degree of complexity in its social life for a few of the males (possibly including sex-reversed females) become 'super-males' referred to (since this is the final phase of sexual development) as 'terminal phase super-males'. These grow larger than their colleagues, and each mates with a single female instead of courting a whole harem.

Parrot-fish belong to the family Scaridae, and are closely related to the wrasses. It is not surprising therefore that we find a similar, and at times equally confusing, array of colour variations between males and females and between young and old. A perfect example is provided by one of the commonest parrot-fish in the Caribbean, the stop-light parrot-fish (*Sparisoma viride*) in which the female is brown and orange with white patches whilst the male is bright green with patches of blue, brown, pink and yellow! Fourteen species are recorded from the Caribbean area and among the other common species, mention should be made of the striped or mottlefin

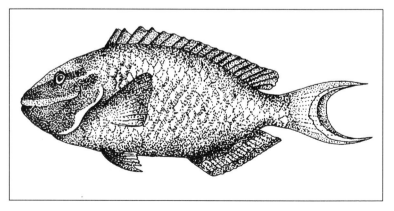

Fig. 36: Parrot-fish

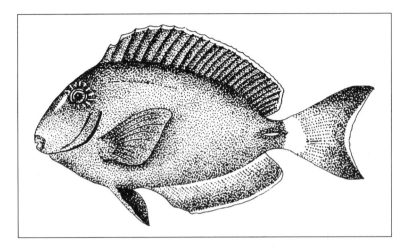

Fig. 37: Surgeon-fish

parrot-fish (*Scarus croicensis*); the princess parrot-fish (*Scarus taeniopterus*) and the red-band parrot-fish (*Sparisoma aurofrenatum*). The parrot-fish feed on algae contained in coral rock, and thus break up large quantities of coral, grinding it in their powerful jaws, and thus extracting their food. In the process they produce huge quantities of recycled coral-sand!

Surgeon-fish, so named because they carry a scalpel-sharp re-tractable blade in their tail, are agile swimmers, generally favouring surge zones or areas of good water movement. They are herbivores, intensively grazing the reef-surface. The family Acanthuridae to which they belong is represented by three Caribbean species: the ocean surgeon-fish (*Acanthurus bahianus*); the common surgeon-fish (*Acanthurus chirurgus*); and the blue tang (*Acanthurus coeruleus*).

While a cut from a surgeon-fish scalpel would be an exceedingly rare occurrence for divers to experience, the possibility of becoming stung by a scorpion-fish such as the spotted scorpion-fish (*Scorpaena plumieri*) should perhaps be taken more seriously. There is no chance of the fish actually attacking a diver since they sit motionless on the

Fig. 38: Scorpion-fish

seabed waiting, in their highly camouflaged state, for the appearance of a tasty morsel to wander close enough to their concealed jaws so that a lunge forward with jaws agape is all that is required to ensure their meal. They are however so well camouflaged that it has been known for divers to place their hands on them, believing them to be inanimate! This would result in rapid erection of the poisonous spines and a very painful sting! The scorpion-fish family, Scorpaenidae, has seven Caribbean species, all of which are more common than one would imagine from underwater sightings, but this need not discourage divers who take reasonable care. Incidentally, should you be stung by this, or indeed almost any other marine creature, the quickest first aid is to plunge the affected part of the body in water as hot as you can stand without actually scalding yourself. This denatures the protein in the venom and can have a dramatic effect in relieving the pain.

Trigger-fishes, members of the family Balistidae, are so named because they carry a strong retractable spine which is held erect by a small trigger spine behind it. The combination of spines makes it almost impossible to pull a triggerfish from a hole into which it has

Fig. 39: Trigger-fish

swum to seek refuge. The spine is used as a wedge to hold it safe, and the only way it will bring down its first spine is if one depresses the trigger-spine. Seven trigger-fish species are recorded from the Caribbean. Of these, the queen trigger-fish, *Balistes vetula* is undoubtedly the most regal despite its other common name of 'old wife'. One reason for the contrast in names is possibly the fish's ability to change colour rapidly from a brilliant blue-green and yellow with vivid blue stripes to a much paler drab phase in a matter of seconds. Young queen trigger-fish are often abundant on seagrass beds and they eat sea-urchins and other invertebrates.

File-fishes, members of the Monacanthidae, are often difficult to distinguish since they have a habit of hanging almost motionless in the sea, and are exceedingly thin if seen 'edge-on'. The slender file-fish, *Monacanthus tuckeri*, is a case in point. It often swims in pairs, among sponges, gorgonians or coral-rubble, and its colour frequently enables it to merge into the background. File-fish have a habit of blowing jets of water into the sand, excavating the sediment, and thus revealing food items. Eleven other species are known from the Caribbean.

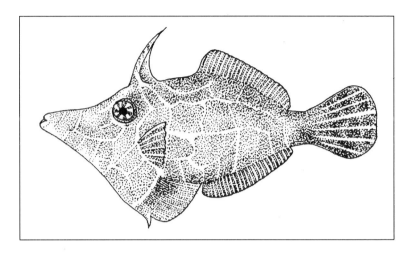

Fig. 40 File-fish

Finally, we must mention the puffers (Tetraodontidae) with nine species, sharp-nosed puffers (Canthigasteridae) represented only by *C.rostrata*, and the porcupinefish (Diodontidae) with eight species.

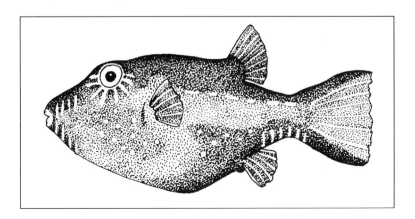

Fig. 41: Puffer

3 : COUNTRYFILES

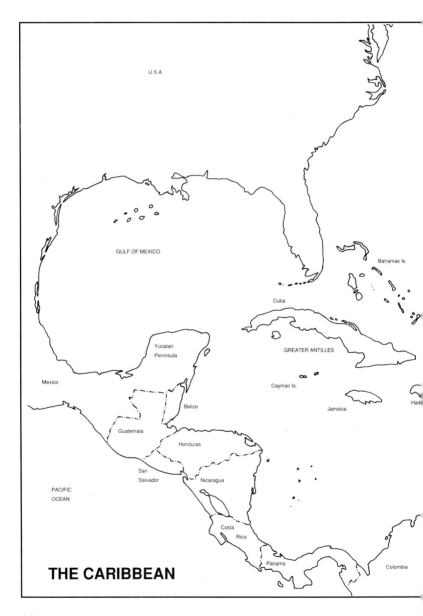

THE CARIBBEAN

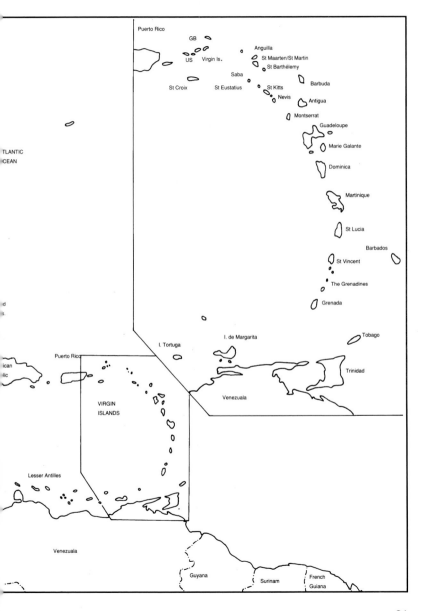

Puerto Rico

GB

Anguilla

US   Virgin Is.

St Maarten/St Martin

St Barthélemy

Saba

St Croix   St Eustatius   St Kitts

Barbuda

Nevis

Antigua

Montserrat

Guadeloupe

Marie Galante

Dominica

Martinique

St Lucia

Barbados

St Vincent

The Grenadines

Grenada

Tobago

I. de Margarita

I. Tortuga

Puerto Rico

Trinidad

VIRGIN
ISLANDS

Venezuala

Lesser Antilles

Venezuala

Guyana

Surinam

French
Guiana

ATLANTIC
OCEAN

3.1 : ANGUILLA

Location: 18°15'N, 63°W. Most northerly island of the Leeward chain. Nearby islands include the Virgin islands to the west; St Croix to the south-west; St Martin/St Maarten, St Barthélemy, St Kitts and Saba to the south. Barbuda lies roughly south-east. The capital is The Valley.

Physical Description: Low island (maximum height 62m); 26km long by 5km wide (area: 90 sq.km). Gained its name from the Spaniards who were commenting upon its long narrow, sinuous, eel-like form. Possesses 20km of beautiful beaches. Limestone and marls on volcanic rock. Situated on the same submarine shelf as St Barthélemy and St Maarten/St Martin. Includes several uninhabited sand cays such as Dog Island, Prickly Pear Cays, Seal Island, Sandy Island and Sombrero Island. Anguillita is a small island lying at the western end of Anguilla.

Climate: Dry tropical marine climate. Mean monthly temperature is 80°C. Dry season January-April; wet season August-November. Average annual rainfall – 889mm. Winds quite steady in form of brisk easterly tradewinds. Tropical storms most prevalent in August and September. Hurricanes occur every few years with recent memories of Klaus in the mid eighties and Hugo and Gabrielle in 1989. Hugo blew from the south and did not cause much damage to Anguilla's dive-sites except for some broken elkhorn coral on Sail Reef and some silting up of corals which showed good signs of clearing by late in the same year.

Electricity Supply: 110 volts at 60 cycles.

Visitor Accommodation: Anguilla is a particularly attractive small island where tourism has not spoilt the character of the place. The following accommodation is available: Carimar Beach Club (497-

6881); Casa Nadine (497-2358); Coccoloba (497-6871; fax: 497-6332); Covecastles (497-6801); Ferry Boat Inn (497-6613); Harbour Lights Apartments (497-4435); La Sirena (497-6827; fax: 497-6829); Lloyds Guest House (497-2351); Malliouhana Hotel (497-6111); The Mariners (497-2815; fax: 497-2901); Rainbow Reef Villas (497-2817); Rendezvous Bay Hotel (497-6649); Sea Feathers Resort (497-2038); Shoal Bay Resort (497-2011); Shoal Bay Villas (497-2051); Spindrift (497-4164); Queen Sago Apartments (497-2107); View Fort Cottage (497-2537). In addition, there are a good range of budget priced guest-houses including Camora (497-6556); Casa Nadine (497-2358); Flemings (497-2234); Florencia's (497-2319); Inter Island (497-6259); Lloyds (497-2351); Maybern (497-6350); Norman 'B' (497-2242); and Yellow Banana (497-2626).

Diving Centres: Tamariain Watersports is a PADI 5-star diving centre, the only one operating as such at the time of writing. It is owned and operated by Scottish-born Iain Grummitt and his American partner Thomas Peabody. The centre has a series of guided boat dives and offers full PADI instruction (PO Box 247, The Valley, Anguilla, British West Indies; 497-2020).

Marine Environment, General: While southerly reefs seem to have been affected by hurricanes, with vast quantities of broken fragments of *Acropora palmata*, northerly reefs have some well preserved beds of this elkhorn coral, together with its relative *A. cervicornis*. Underwater visibility is generally good and diving can be excellent.

Recommended Dive-Sites: The sinking of the *MV Sarah* by Hurricane Klaus in November 1984 has created an interesting dive-site, particularly at night (Depth 3-8m). Tamariain Watersports have themselves sunk the *MV Ida Maria* to create a 12-18m dive where many fish can be hand-fed; and also the *MV Commerce*, a 40m freighter which offers a somewhat deeper wreck dive (12-24m). Dog Island, West Prickly Pear Island and Scrub Island are centres for underwater activities. Scrub Island has a dive-site at Deadman's Cay. Grouper Bowl dive site is on the Sail Reef, an area where some

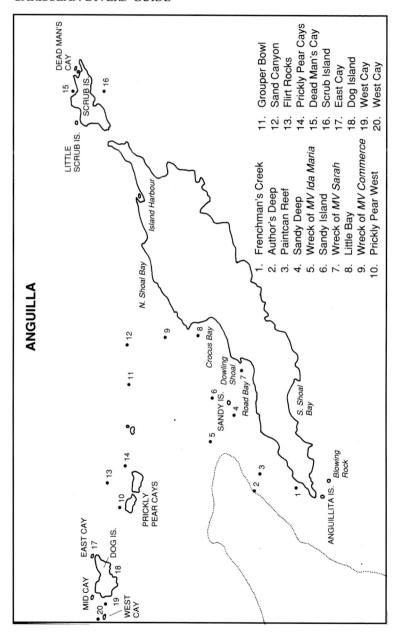

ANGUILLA

DEAD MAN'S CAY

SCRUB IS.

LITTLE SCRUB IS.

Island Harbour

N. Shoal Bay

Crocus Bay

Dowling Shoal

Road Bay

SANDY IS.

S. Shoal Bay

Blowing Rock

ANGUILLITA IS.

PRICKLY PEAR CAYS

EAST CAY

DOG IS.

MID CAY

WEST CAY

1. Frenchman's Creek
2. Author's Deep
3. Paintcan Reef
4. Sandy Deep
5. Wreck of MV Ida Maria
6. Sandy Island
7. Wreck of MV Sarah
8. Little Bay
9. Wreck of MV Commerce
10. Prickly Pear West
11. Grouper Bowl
12. Sand Canyon
13. Flirt Rocks
14. Prickly Pear Cays
15. Dead Man's Cay
16. Scrub Island
17. East Cay
18. Dog Island
19. West Cay
20. West Cay

of Anguilla's finest coral formations are to be found and where large groupers lurk among the numerous overhangs. At the easterly extremity of the same reef system lies Sand Canyon, a 27m dive-site where a winding, steeply sided canyon has walls coming to within 8m of the surface. East of West Cay there is a particularly attractive seascape consisting of a groove and spur reef. The steep drop-off on the west side of the same cay is adorned with clumps of the colourful, non-reef building coral, *Tubastrea coccinea*. There are good snorkelling and shallow dive-sites north of Prickly Pear Cay East, on the seaward edge of a reef surrounding a lagoon, especially towards the north-west. Little Flirt Rock, off Prickly Pear North, is at the western extremity of a bank reef dominated by *Acropora cervicornis*, *Montastrea annularis* and *Porites porites*. The rock area itself abounds with caves and tunnels where one may be fortunate enough to see large nurse sharks resting on the sandy seabed. Between Crocus Bay and Little Bay, along the north coast there are no true coral-reefs but sea-grass beds are well developed and sea-fans prominent; many have flamingo tongue gastropods (*Cyphoma gibbosum*) together with a good variety of other invertebrates. The Little Bay dive-site is usually sheltered and offers underwater photographers some very interesting subjects. The shallows around Sandy Island, a popular venue for yachts and pleasure boats, have a good population of the queen conch, *Strombus gigas*. The shallow reef along the north-west side of the island is good snorkelling territory while in the range of 10-20m there are many sea-fans and soft corals. Slightly to the south-west is a deeper hole known as Sandy Deep where the reef drops quite sharply from 5 to 18 metres. A great deal of marinelife, including lobsters and a good variety of fish, are found along the 'mini-wall'. Paintcan Reef offers a dive to 24m where several acres of lush coral can be enjoyed in usually excellent visibility. The dive-site known as Author's Deep consists of a deeper reef at around 34m where black coral trees and large pelagic fish can be seen. (See also list of areas proposed for protection under Legal Aspects.)

Special Interest: Lagoon floor in west Forest Bay where an unusual zoanthid sea anemone zone exists. Sombrero Island, 48km north-west of the main island of Anguilla, is a raised-reef island circled by cliffs extending from above water to around 15m underwater, offering interesting photographic opportunities. (See also under Other Wildlife below.) Anguilla is a favourite venue for marriages and honeymoons.

Other Wildlife: Nesting seabirds on Anguillita Island and several other small islands such as Mid Cay, West Cay, East Cay, West Prickly Pear Cay and Seal Island. Species include: red-billed tropic-bird, masked booby, brown booby, brown pelican and magnificent frigate-bird. Green and hawksbill turtles nest on Dog Island and Prickly Pear Cays. Leatherback turtles nest on Scrub Island.

Conservation Issues: Nesting seabirds. Turtles include green, loggerhead, hawksbill and leatherback. Fishing areas for lobster, fin-fish and conch are rotated on a fairly regular basis. Coral damage can be locally quite serious as a result of careless boat anchoring and use of fish-traps. An unfortunate effect of hitting corals with anchors is that they become vulnerable to bacterial infection in the form of blackline disease, which can kill large colonies and spread through whole reef systems. There have been proposals for marine parks at Sandy Island, Crocus Bay, Shoal Bay and Seal Island. (See also under Legal Aspects below.)

Legal Aspects: In September 1988 the Government of Anguilla enacted a Marine Resources Law which will provide a framework for the development of marine parks and reserves around the island. Tamariain Watersports forbid all divers to take any form of marinelife. Spearfishing is illegal throughout Anguilla. IUCN recommendations for the proposed reserves included control of access through permits, with all spearfishing, shell-collecting, coral-collecting, placement of fish-traps, anchoring, standing, resting and walking on coral, breakage of coral, littering of reefs or cays and beaches forbidden around Sandy Island, Dowling Shoal, north and west of Dog Island and its cays, north of Prickly Pear Cays and east to the end of Seal Island Reef, over the Shoal Bay-Island Harbour reef complex, around Little Scrub Island and Deadman's Cay, between Crocus Bay and Flat Cap Point to a distance of 50m offshore and around the grottoes and caves at the western end of the island. In November 1989 the Government announced a complete ban on the issuing of cruising permits to visiting yachtsmen. All boats must now anchor in Road Bay, the main harbour, and will not be allowed to sail in the neighbouring cays and islands. This is partly in response to damage caused to the marine environment by careless anchoring and the disposal of waste from visiting yachts.

Medical Facilities: There is one cottage hospital on the island, staffed by expatriate doctors, and there are also clinics in all the island villages. At the time of writing a completely new hospital is under construction. The nearest recompression chamber is on Saba, a short journey by low-flying aircraft, should the need arise. There is a first-class dental clinic on the island.

3.2 : ANTIGUA AND BARBUDA

Location: Antigua (17°N, 61°50'W) and Barbuda (17°40'N, 61°50'W) together with the uninhabited Redonda (16°56'N, 62°20'W) are under a single administration based on Antigua. The islands form part of the eastern Leeward chain with St Kitts and Nevis off to the west of them and open Atlantic on their easterly side. To the south lies the French island of Guadaloupe, a short hop on an inter-island flight. Barbuda lies 35km due north of Antigua, separated by a stretch of water averaging 27-33m, forming part of a submarine shelf, approximately 80km long by 25km wide, surrounded by deep water and closely bounded by the 183m depth contour.

Physical Description: These attractive and relatively unspoilt islands are formed from coral limestone with a volcanic outcrop on Antigua (280sq. km) forming the south-westerly mountains reaching 402m. Elsewhere the island has gently undulating hills while Barbuda (174sq. km) is essentially a low coral island (maximum height 45m). Whereas Antigua tends to have a deeply indented coastline, that of Barbuda is relatively smooth, but surrounded by a more extensive reef system.

Climate: The islands are heavily influenced by their presence within the Easterly Trade wind zone. The season for tropical storms is primarily August and September. Hurricanes occur on average once every 20 years. Dry season January to April; wet season August to November. Barbuda is a particularly dry island (mean monthly rainfall 8.2mm).

Electricity Supply: Supply is not standardised. Both 110 volts and 220 volts are used. Double check before plugging-in!

Visitor Accommodation: The main town on Antigua is St John's. The only settlement on Barbuda is Codrington. Suitable accommodation there ranges from small comfortable guest houses to hotels such as The Sunset View Hotel, Thomas Guest House, the Earl's Cottage and Pink Sands Beach Hotel.

Diving centres: The Antigua and Barbuda Dive Club, established in 1984, meets on the first Thursday of every month at 8pm at the Bucket Club in Coolidge. Dive Runaway (462-2626) is a PADI diving centre and training facility located at Runaway Beach Club. Aquanaut Diving Centres in Antigua are based at St James's Club (463-1113) and the Galleon Beach Club (463-1024), both close to good sea-cliff dives off the rugged south-eastern tip of the island. The Ramada Rennaissance Royal Antiguan Resort on the more sheltered west coast is also an Aquanaut Diving Centre (462-3733) on the more sheltered west coast. Instruction, certification and a wide range of facilities are offered.

Marine Environment, General: The North Equatorial current affects local marinelife, with the surface current flowing NWW and sea temperature steady at around 28°C. Tidal range is low, around 3m. Visibility underwater is good, estimated up to 40m. Between the two islands it has been estimated that there are 25.45sq. km of coral reef, most of it fringing reef. Along the north coast of Antigua a 20km bank-barrier reef formed primarily by elkhorn coral stretches from Mercer's Creek to Diamond Bank. The 40m depth contour circles both islands, generally less than a few hundred metres from the shore, effectively restricting the development of shallow reefs.

Recommended Dive Sites: Barbuda possibly offers the better dive-sites of the two islands, with well developed reefs in pristine condition. Try the south end, near Cocoa Point. The huge reef system protecting the exposed easterly coast is formed primarily from calcareous algae and the hydrozoan fire coral, *Millepora*, while reefs to the north and south are dominated by elkhorn coral. Diving at either of the Reef Marine Parks is rewarding. Palaster Reef Marine Park lying approximately 3km south-east of Cocoa Point, near Spanish Point on Barbuda, consists of a group of patch reefs, dominated

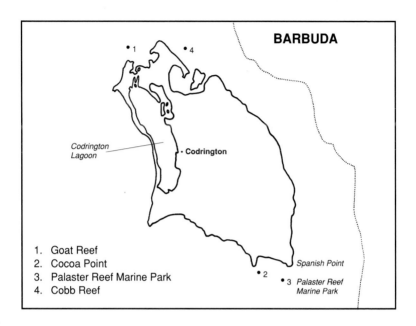

BARBUDA

Codrington
Lagoon

• Codrington

1. Goat Reef
2. Cocoa Point
3. Palaster Reef Marine Park
4. Cobb Reef

Spanish Point

• 2
• 3 Palaster Reef
Marine Park

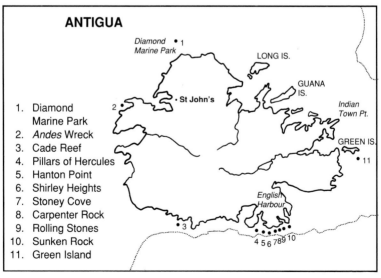

ANTIGUA

Diamond • 1
Marine Park

LONG IS.

GUANA
IS.

Indian
Town Pt.

• St John's

GREEN IS.

• 11

1. Diamond
   Marine Park
2. *Andes* Wreck
3. Cade Reef
4. Pillars of Hercules
5. Hanton Point
6. Shirley Heights
7. Stoney Cove
8. Carpenter Rock
9. Rolling Stones
10. Sunken Rock
11. Green Island

English
Harbour

• 3

4 5 6 789 10

by elkhorn coral, with surrounding waters of roughly 50m. The intricate nature of the reefs has long been a danger to shipping with the result that several interesting wrecks occur here. Diamond Marine Park, 5km off the north-west coast of Antigua, consists of an extensive area of shallow coralline banks and patch reefs surrounded by clear water of up to 100m in depth. Cade Reef, off the south coast of Antigua is also reported to be a protected area. 'One of the best dive sites in Antigua is between Blue Heron Hotel and Curtain Bluff Hotel. Lobster, queen, helmet and milk conch abound. There is even a friendly barracuda... There is no report of any shark attack in Antiguan waters.' (Marine Guide, 1985-1986). Green Island, along the south-east coast of Antigua, has good diving off Man O' War Point where calm weather conditions are necessary. The Sunken Rock dive site, just off the mouth of Indian Creek, bottoms out at 37m and is one of the best dives in Antigua. The Pillars of Hercules at the entrance of English Harbour are, along with dive-sites such as Nanton Point, Shirley Heights, Stoney Cove, Carpenter Rock and Rolling Stone, the most interesting and spectacular areas one could dive on Antigua's south coast. Beautiful cliff and drop-off over-hangs together with huge boulders, are encrusted with all forms of marinelife. Regular sightings of stingrays, barracudas, schooling mackerel and kingfish, together with occasional nurse sharks, dolphins and manta rays add to the fun!

Special Interest: The marine areas around Antigua and Barbuda are especially productive in lobsters and conch. IUCN recommendations for special conservation efforts on Antigua and its surrounding waters emphasise Great Bird Island, including the associated islands to the south-west, and the submerged reef stretching north towards Long Island, together with the southerly section, through Indian Town to Green Island.

Other Wildlife: Green, hawksbill and leatherback turtles nest on both Antigua and Barbuda. Important seabird sites exist along the entire reef system 'north of Guana Island, through Bird Island Reef, including Exchange, Lobster, Rabbit, Red Head, Hell's Gate, Gallery, Grey and Little Bird Islands' (IUCN, 1988). The rare Antilles wood duck nests among mangroves at Guana island and Bull Hole on Barbuda with the former location containing the only recorded nesting site of the West Indian mockingbird.

Conservation Issues: Recent studies on the state of reefs around the islands have found them to be in a relatively undisturbed condition. Antigua and Barbuda have recently been recommended as marine sites to be included in a Lesser Antillean Biosphere Reserve. Hurricane David, in 1979, did cause severe damage to certain reefs such as Goat Head Reef which was totally destroyed. Fishery activities are controlled by various regulations (see comments under legal heading below) affecting lobster and turtle harvesting. Leisure activities in the sea are also controlled by a Marine Parks Act (see below).

Legal Aspects: Fisheries Regulations of 1978 define closed season and minimum size limits for lobsters. The Turtle Ordinance, 1927, is still in force for the control of turtle harvesting. At the time of writing conch fishing is not covered by legislation. The Marine Parks Act (the Marine Area Preservation and Enhancement Act, No.5, 1972) was followed by a series of regulations and schedules (e.g. SRO Nos. 25 and 47 of 1973). These established Palaster Marine Park and Diamond Marine Park.

Medical Facilities: A trained medical advisor for divers is normally based at the Beachcomber Hotel (VHF 68; 462-3100). Also refer to Dr Kelvin Charles (office: 462-4973; home: 462-3994). The nearest recompression chambers at the time of writing are reported to be at Guadaloupe, St Almason and Barbados.

3.3 : ARUBA

Location: (12°30'N, 70°W). Situated in the southern Caribbean, 29km off the coast of Venezuela.

Physical Description: This 186sq. km island has a dry climate and it shows in the flourishing cacti which form a prominent feature of the vegetation. Eleven kilometres of palm-fringed beach along the south-west coast are particularly attractive. The north-east coast on the other hand is formed by rugged rocks against which the full force of the ocean's waves crash.

Climate: Dry, sunny and warm just about sums it up. Average rainfall is 500mm per year, primarily falling from October to December. Aruba is not in the hurricane belt.

Electricity Supply: Approx 127 volts.

Visitor Accommodation: Listed hotels are as follows: Americana Aruba Hotel and Casino (297-8-24500); Aruba Beach Club (297-8-24595); Aruba Caribbean Hotel and Casino (297-8-22250); Aruba Concorde Hotel and Casino (297-8-24466); Aruba Palm Beach Hotel and Casino (297-8-23900); Atlantis Apartahoteles and Villas (297-8-24343); Best Western Manchebo Beach (297-8-23444); Best Western Talk of the Town (297-8-23380); Bushiri Beach Hotel (297-8-25216); Divi Divi Beach Hotel (297-8-23300); Dutch Village (297-8-32300); Holiday Inn Aruba (297-8-23600); Playa Linda Beach Resort (297-8-31000) and Tamarijn Beach Hotel (297-8-24150).

Diving Centres: Pelican Watersports (297-8-31228; fax: 297-8-32655) has a dive store, air-filling station and pier at the Holiday Inn (297-8-23600) together with dive shops at the Concorde Hotel (297-8-24466) and the Golden Tulip (297-8-33555). This is a PADI certified centre offering resort courses, certification and rental of equipment.

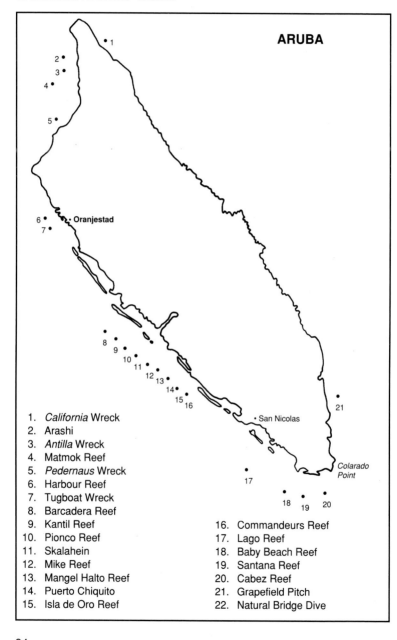

ARUBA

1. *California* Wreck
2. Arashi
3. *Antilla* Wreck
4. Matmok Reef
5. *Pedernaus* Wreck
6. Harbour Reef
7. Tugboat Wreck
8. Barcadera Reef
9. Kantil Reef
10. Pionco Reef
11. Skalahein
12. Mike Reef
13. Mangel Halto Reef
14. Puerto Chiquito
15. Isla de Oro Reef
16. Commandeurs Reef
17. Lago Reef
18. Baby Beach Reef
19. Santana Reef
20. Cabez Reef
21. Grapefield Pitch
22. Natural Bridge Dive

Scuba Aruba at the Aruba Palm Beach Hotel (297-8-23900, fax: 297-8-21941) is also a PADI base offering resort courses and equipment rental; Hallo Aruba Dive Shop at the Surfside Beach has similar courses.

Marine Environment, General: Since it is situated on the continental shelf, Aruba does not have the drop-offs into dramatically deep water that can be found at Curacao and Bonaire. The south-east coast has some of the best developed reefs.

Recommended Dive-Sites: The following summary of dive sites around Aruba was recently compiled by the diving organisations around the island (see map for relevant locations).

California Wreck: 9-13m. Experienced divers only. Moderately exposed. Ship, almost 100 years old is the one that received but did not respond to Titanic's SOS. Arashi: 11-12m. Good coral development with plentiful fish. *Antilla* Wreck: 18m. 120m long German freighter scuttled in 1940. Good for penetration dives. Malmok Reef: 21m. Meeting ground for rays. Giant barrel sponges and large brain corals. Large lobsters. *Pedernalis* Wreck: 8m. Oil tanker torpedoed by German submarine in Second World War. Sliced into three by US navy divers. Centre piece left on seabed while bow and stern sections towed to USA and welded together creating a new ship which took part in Normandy invasion! Wreck dive suitable for beginners; many groupers and angel-fish. Harbour Reef: 6-12m. Boulders and brain corals together with soft corals and sponges. Good beginners dive. Tugboat Wreck: 12-27m. Coral, green morays and old tug make an interesting dive. Good for photography. Barcadera Reef: 6-24m. Sandy sea-bed with brain corals and sea-fans. Kantil Reef: 12-34m. Drop-off dive. Good for fish and rays including mantas. Plonoco Reef: 6-30m. Many green morays. Good for spiny lobsters. Skalahein: 5-37m. Rich coral. Barracudas. Some current. Mantas occasionally. Mike Reef: 8-27m. Prolific coral and good invertebrate life. Mangel Halto Reef: 34m. Good slope from 5m to 34m. Good variety of species. Puerto Chiquito: 6-24m. Abundant snappers. Accessible by car. Possibility of mantas and turtles.

Isla de Oro Reef: 27m. Good for morays, invertebrates and fish, especially snappers. Commandeurs Reef: 12-27m. Abundant marinelife including some big fish. Lago Reef. 37m. Deepest dive around Aruba. Deepwater gorgonacea, sponges, sea anemones and other invertebrates. Abundant variety of fish. Baby Beach Reef: 6-18m. On relatively exposed southerly end of island. Large elkhorn coral patches; lobsters. Santana Reef: 6-18m. Exposed reef. Rich marinelife. Entry is somewhat rough. Accessible by car. Cabez Reef: 15m. Rough seas, strong currents. Experienced divers only. Shore entry. Good schools of pelagics. Virgin territory! Natural Bridge Dive: 6-34m. Boulders and brain corals make for dramatic underwater scenery. Exposed site. Strong currents at times. Abundant black coral and giant barrel sponges. Advanced divers only. Grapevine Pitch: On exposed coastline, between Rincon and Boca Grandi.

Conservation Issues: Unfortunately pollution has affected some of the southern reefs of Aruba, the prime culprits being nitrates and phosphates from sewage effluent, the island's main rubbish dump, the rum factory, and also oil spills. Toxic metals have also been released from the paint factory. High levels of sewage bacteria were found in the sea along the south coast of Aruba. The Government is actively seeking to improve the situation and these are not likely to remain as serious factors for long.

3.4 : BAHAMAS

Location: Stretching from just off the east Florida coast of America to the Turks and Caicos, near the south-easterly tip of Cuba, almost as far as Haiti and the Dominican Republic, the Bahamas represent huge system of low islands, coral reefs and banks in the open Atlantic. The archipelago covers 260,000sq.km and is situated on two extensive submarine plateaux, the Little Bahama Bank to the north and the Great Bahama Bank in the south. Between mainland America and the two shallow banks there is an 80km wide deep rift through which flows the Florida Current, an offshoot of the Gulf Stream.

Physical Description: All the 2,750 islands, cays and outcropping rocks are low-lying (highest elevation in the whole group is Mount Alvernia on Cat Island, rising to 63m), and many hardly rise more than a few metres above sea-level. They are formed of coralline rubble, frequently surrounded by mangroves and fringed by algal or coral-reefs. Total land area is 11,400sq.km. The two main islands of Grand Bahama and Great Abaco are situated on the more northerly Little Bahama Bank whilst the largest island in the entire group is Andros which is situated on the westerly side of the Great Bahama Bank. The shelf on which the islands are situated slopes gradually on its easterly (ocean) side, to depths of around 18m-45m, approximately 1.5km offshore, then it plunges steeply into the real depths of the ocean so that there are locations where soundings as great as 3,658m can be found as close as 3km from the shore.

Climate: Mild subtropical climate. Wet season is May-October (average annual rainfall varies according to location between 1,020 and 1,520mm). Easterly trade winds blow for most of year and the islands are occasionally affected by hurricanes. Occasional low winter temperatures tend to limit the growth of some corals.

Electricity Supply: 120 volts at 60 cycles.

Visitor Accommodation: The Bahamas receive over two million visitors per year. The most populated island is New Providence. Small Hope Bay Lodge (US Mailing Address: PO Box 21667, Ft Lauderdale, Florida, 33335, USA; PO Box N 1131, Nassau, Bahamas; 368 2014; fax: 368 2015) on Andros Island is the oldest diving base in the Bahamas. Comprising 20 hand built coral-rock cottages and other facilities, this informal people resort was built by the Birch family about 30 years ago and has acquired a reputation as one of the friendliest and best run diving centres in the Bahamas. Equally professional in its approach to diving, and a very popular location with visiting scuba enthusiasts, is the 60-room Stella Maris Inn on Long Island (PO Box SM 105, Long Island, Bahamas or 750 SW 34th St #215, Ft Lauderdale, Florida, 33315, USA).

Diving Centres: The following dive operators are present in the Bahamas:

ABACO: On Green Turtle Cay: Brendal's Dive Shop, (c/o Island Services, 750 SW 34th St #105, Ft Lauderdale, Florida 33315, USA; 367-2572; (305) 522-6918); At Hope Town: Island Marine Dive Shop, (PO Box G, Hope Town, Abaco, Bahamas, 366-0828, fax: (305) 359-3080); Marsh Harbour: Dive Abaco Ltd (PO Box 555, Marsh Harbour, Abaco, Bahamas; 367-20140); Dive Odyssea (Great Abaco Beach Hotel, PO Box 511, Marsh Harbour, Abaco, Bahamas, 367-2158); Treasure Cay Beach Hotel (US contact: 2301 S. Federal Hwy, Fort Lauderdale,Florida 33316, USA; 367-2570, fax: 367-2577); on Walker's Cay: Walker's Cay Undersea Adventures (PO Box 21766, Ft Lauderdale, Florida 33335-1766, USA; (800) 327-8150, (305) 763-2188).

ANDROS: At Fresh Creek (Andros Town), Small Hope Bay Lodge (PO Box 21667, Ft Lauderdale, Florida 33315, USA; (800) 327-223-6961, 368-2014, (305) 463-9130, fax: 368-2112) on Andros has been a favourite base for divers for many years. One and a half kilometres offshore is the 228km long Andros Barrier Reef, the third longest in the world. Dive-sites include coral gardens and caverns, wreck dives, ocean blue holes, and wall dives down to 56m! The facilities of this centre include two flat-top dive boats (15- and 28-passenger carriers) and an efficient air filling system. There is equipment for hire and dive-boats cover two dive-sites each morning and one in the afternoon. Apart from the diving, it is also a delightful place to stay. At Nicholl's Town: Andros Undersea Adventures (Andros Beach Hotel and Villas, PO Box 21766, Ft Lauderdale, Florida 33335-1766, USA; (800) 327-8150, 329-2582, (305) 395-0065, fax: (305) 359-0071).

BERRY ISLANDS: Chub Cay Undersea Adventures (Chub Cay Club, PO Box 21766, Ft Lauderdale, Florida 33335-1766, USA, (800) 327-8150, 407-655-2822, (305) 359-0065, fax: (305) 359-0071).

BIMINI: Bill and Nowdia Keef's Bimini Undersea Adventures (PO Box 21766, Ft Lauderdale, Florida 33335-1766, USA; (800) 327-8150, 347-2089, (305) 359-0065, fax: (305) 359-0071).

CAT ISLAND: Greenwood Inn, Tabaluga Diving Island Services Inc. (750 SW 34th St #105, Ft Lauderdale, Florida 33315, USA; (800) 825-5099, (305) 522-6918).

ELEUTHERA: On Harbour Island: Romoroa Bay Club (PO Box 7026, Boca Raton, Florida 33431, USA; (800) 327-8286, (305) 760-4535, 333-2324/5); Valentine's Dive Centre (US office: 3928 Shelbyville Road, Louisville, Kentucky 40207, USA 502-897-6481, (800) 662-2255); Spanish Wells Beach Island Services Inc. (750 SW 34th St, #105, Fort Lauderdale, Florida 33315, USA; (800) 825-5255, 332-2645, (305) 522-6918, fax: (305) 463-7532).

EXUMA: At George Town: Exuma Divers (PO Box 110, George Town, Exuma, Bahamas, 336-2710; (800) 468-9876, (305) 359-3066, (305) 359-3080).

LONG ISLAND: Stella Maris Inn. On Long Island Jorg Friese and Peter Kuska operate the Stella Maris Inn (US contact: (800) 426-0466 or (305) 467-0466; PO Box SM 105, Stella Maris, Long Island, Bahamas, 336-2106. US office: 750 SW 34th St., Suite 215, Ft. Lauderdale, Florida, USA; 33315, (305) 467-0466, (800) 327-0797), a PADI affiliated centre which offers Resort Course and Open Water certification. E6 film processing is available. The hotel is near the north end, and the best dive-sites on Long Island. It is famous as the location of Shark Reef where sharks are regularly fed. Visitors in winter months should note that Stella Maris has the advantage of offering leeside and Atlantic side diving, as well as regular visits to Rum

Cay. Diving vessels include the 8.5m *Enterprise* (8 divers); the 9.4m *Sol Mar II* (12 divers) and the magnificent 20m *Sol Mar III* which can carry up to 40 divers and still not feel overcrowded! Stella Maris is a good base for diving at both Long Island and other reefs in the area, including Exuma Reefs, Rum Cay (with its famous walls) and Conception Island. Apart from being a great diving base, it is also a great place to stay

RUM CAY: Rum Cay Undersea Adventures (PO Box 21766, Ft Lauderdale, Florida 33335-1766, USA; (800) 327-8150, (305) 763-2188).

SAN SALVADOR: Riding Rock Inn (Out Island Service Co. Inc., 750 SW 34th St, Suite 206, Ft. Lauderdale, Florida 33315, USA; (800) 272-1492, (305) 761-1492, 332-2631).

GRAND BAHAMA ISLAND: At East End: Deep Water Cay Club (PO Box 1145, Palm Beach, Florida 33480, USA; 407-684-3958); at Freeport/Lucaya: Sunn Odyssey Divers (Atlantic Beach Resort, PO Box F-4166, Freeport, Grand Bahama, 373-1444, ext 203; Underwater Explorers Society (UNEXSO) (PO Box F-2433, Freeport, Grand Bahama, 373-1244, US Office: PO Box 5608, Ft. Lauderdale, Florida 33310, USA; (800) 992-DIVE (US), (305) 761-7679, US fax: (305) 760-9629, Bahama fax: 373-8956); and at the West End: West End Diving Centre (c/o UNESO as above).

NEW PROVIDENCE ISLAND: Nassau: Dive, Dive, Dive, Ltd. (PO Box N-8050, Nassau, Bahamas, 362-1143, (800) 328-8029, ext 246, 362-1401, fax: 362-1994); Peter Hughes Diving at Divi Bahama Beach Resort and Country Club (54 Gunderman Road, Ithaca, NY 14850, 362-4394, (305) 987-1791, 607-277-3484, fax:607-277-3624; Stuart Cove's Nassau Undersea Adventures (PO Box CB-11697, Nassau, Bahamas, 362-4171, 327-7862); Sun Divers Ltd (British Colonial Beach Resort (PO Box N-10728, Nassau, Bahamas, 322-3301, ext 364, 325-8927); and Sun Skiff Divers Ltd (PO Box N-142, Nassau, Bahamas, 809-362-1144, (800) 548-8570, 809-328-4075, 804-838-2218).

PARADISE ISLAND: Bahama Divers Ltd (PO Box SS-5004, Nassau, Bahamas, 393-5644); and Sea & Ski Ocean Sports (affiliated with Grand Hotel) (PO Box 9141, Nassau, Bahamas, 326-2011, 326-3370).

Marine Environment, General: From a biological and geological viewpoint the Bahama Bank is exceptionally interesting since it is one of the few examples in existence today of the warm, shallow, calcium/lime-depositing seas which were characteristic of earlier periods in the Earth's evolution. For divers, the Bahamas still contain many areas which have hardly been explored. Since the sediment consists of very fine calcareous silt or 'ooze', it is easily stirred up into suspension in shallow lagoonal areas and underwater visibility may therefore be quite badly affected in these areas. Diving conditions on the outer side of the Banks are often superb, providing that some shelter can be found, with very clear water. Hurricanes, particularly Betsy in 1965, have caused considerable damage to some northern Bahamian reefs.

Divers with a penchant for the the bizarre might care to go in search of the spiny-lobster procession, part of the species' annual migration, which takes place down along the western side of Bimini and has been well reported by William Herrnkind who published his findings, along with pictures by Rick Frehsee and Bruce Mounier, in National Geographic (June 1975). Hurricanes seem to trigger mass migrations with huge aggregations reported to have marched across the Bahama Bank after Hurricane Betsy in 1965 and on other occasions since then.

Recommended Dive-Sites: Grand Bahama: Peterson Cay, is 1km off Barbary Beach on the south shore of Grand Bahama and about 10km east of Freeport; Peterson Cay National Park, including Hydrolab site; Theo's Wreck and Treasure Reef, west of Peterson Cay, which can be reached in less than an hour, by car or boat, from Freeport. Abaco Island: Fowl Cay Preserve, Fowl Cay reef and adjacent Abaco barrier reef; Pelican Cays Park, especially the reef at Sandy Cay, one of the most popular diving areas of the Bahamas, with considerable legal protection which appears to have benefited marinelife. Berry Islands: Mamma Rhoda Reef. New Providence: Athol Island; Rose Island Rocks to Pimlico Cays. Bimini: Around Turtle Rocks on west side of islands, where clear deep water occurs; also west of Rabbit Cay and Round Rock. Andros, North: Barrier reef, regarded as one of the finest in the Caribbean with a spectacular vertical drop-off or underwater cliff-face. Here is also the location of the famous Blue Holes including Uncle Charlie's, Stalactite, Cousteau's and Church's. Other sites around Andros include Stafford Creek Reef, Small Hope Bay Reef, Andros Beach Hotel Reef, Big Wood Cay Reef, Las Palmas Hotel Reef, and South Driggs Hill Settlement Reef. Eleuthera: Preacher's Cave; Devils Backbone; north of Spanish Wells and areas along this reef-edge including Current Cut; Corrie Sound, which is a proposed national reserve. On South Eleuthera, Starve Creek is a proposed reserve. Cat Island: outer reef. Conception Island: Southampton Reef including an unnamed wreck and extended reef of stagshorn and elkhorn coral (proposed national park). Great Exuma: Elizabeth Harbour is a proposed national reserve and Pigeon Cay has been proposed as a protected area. Little Exuma: south, White Cay. Exuma Cays Land and Sea Park, 80 kms south-east of Nassau, was established in 1958, and has the best diving along the north and east side of Park. Crooked Island: Plana Cays to the east of Crooked Island have been proposed as a National Park, while Samana Cays to the north are a proposed National Reserve; Acklins Island reefs. Long Island (see map for this and adjacent islands with marked dive sites): northern tip, close to where Columbus landed on his first trip in 1492. Mayaguana Island: Booby Cay. Hogsty Reef north of Great Inagua, south of Acklins Island and west of Little Inagua is 64km from the nearest land and is one of most exposed and isolated areas of Bahamas. It is one of the very few true atolls in the western Atlantic, with two small sand cays, a lagoon, and with surrounding depths exceeding 1,800m. From a scientific viewpoint it is virtually unexplored. Cay Sal Bank, north of Cuba, is another atoll or pseudo-atoll structure. Inagua National Park: off Union Creek. San Salvador: fringing reef, from Riding Rock Inn south, around French Bay, Fernandez Bay (including Telephone Pole Reef and Snapshot Reef) and Graham's Harbour. See also list of Diving Centres.

Special Interest: Blue Holes on north Andros. Lucayan Cavern is the most extensive underwater cave system known to Man. It is protected as Lucayan National Park. Abaco reef barrier is 'the only extensive reef development in the Bahamas found seaward of the

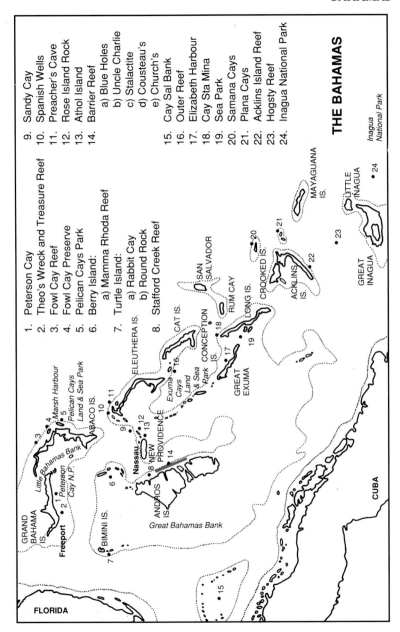

BAHAMAS

THE BAHAMAS

1. Peterson Cay
2. Theo's Wreck and Treasure Reef
3. Fowl Cay Reef
4. Fowl Cay Preserve
5. Pelican Cays Park
6. Berry Island:
   a) Mamma Rhoda Reef
7. Turtle Island:
   a) Rabbit Cay
   b) Round Rock
8. Stafford Creek Reef
9. Sandy Cay
10. Spanish Wells
11. Preacher's Cave
12. Rose Island Rock
13. Athol Island
14. Barrier Reef
    a) Blue Holes
    b) Uncle Charlie
    c) Stalactite
    d) Cousteau's
    e) Church's
15. Cay Sal Bank
16. Outer Reef
17. Elizabeth Harbour
18. Cay Sta Mina
19. Sea Park
20. Samana Cays
21. Plana Cays
22. Acklins Island Reef
23. Hogsty Reef
24. Inagua National Park

103

submarine ridge and the line of cays. It contains, particularly at Hopetown on Elbow Cay, the sequence of zones expected in an ideal coral reef area, and may be the only example in the Bahamas of a typical self-built reef' (IUCN, 1988).

Other Wildlife: Allen's Cay rock iguana (*Cyclura cyclura inornata*) on Bush Hill Cay and Sandy Cay, south end of Exmore; and the Bahamian hutia (*Geocapromys ingrahami*) on Little Wax Cay (both in north Exuma Cays Park area). Approximately 50,000 roseate flamingos (*Phoenicopterus ruber*) 50 pairs of spoonbills (*Platalea leucrodia*); together with nesting reddish egrets and parrots are found on Great Inagua Island. Turtles occur throughout the Bahamas.

Conservation Issues: Local developments resulting in coastal pollution and maritime activities such as intense fishing and coral or shell collecting have caused a deterioration in some marine areas of the Bahamas during recent decades. Over-fishing of conch, spiny lobster and grouper remains a problem. Divers have themselves placed certain reefs under pressure, both through their own activities and through regular anchoring of boats causing coral damage. Spearfishing has also been a problem on many north Bahamian reefs, depleting stocks and making those which remain shy of divers. New legislative measures (see below) are aimed at combating the deterioration of reefs.

Legal Aspects: Fisheries Resources (Jurisdiction and Conservation) Regulations, 1986, control fishing and diving activities and are aimed at protecting marine resources. Spearfishing is now prohibited within 1.6km of the coast of New Providence, the southern coast of Freeport, Grand Bahama and within 183m of the coast of other islands in the Bahama group. All commercial spearfishing and spearfishing competitions are forbidden. Coral collecting is prohibited without special ministerial permission. The closed season for fishing spiny lobsters extends from 1 April to 31 July. All collection of these crustaceans by scuba divers and spearfishermen is prohibited. Hawksbill turtles are totally protected. Only adult conch (i.e. those with a well formed lip) may be taken. Sponges are also totally protected and stone crab may not be fished within 3km of the shores of Bimini and Grand Bahama. The same act deals with controls on sport-fishing and fish-farming.

Marine parks are under the jurisdiction of the Bahamas National Trust, with new bye-laws passed on 13 February 1986. Apart from their aim of protecting and creating tourist attractions the parks are also being regarded as 'marine replenishment and nursery areas'.

Medical Facilities: The nearest recommended recompression facilities are in Miami. Unofficially, emergencies may be made treated at the American military facilities on Andros, but this should not be taken for granted.

3.5 : BARBADOS

Location: 13°15'N, 59°30'W. Somewhat isolated from the main chain of islands forming the Lesser Antilles, situated approximately 150km east of St Vincent.

Physical Description: Occupying a land area of approximately 430sq.km, the island is roughly 30km long with an average width of around 14km. Highest point on the limestone island is 339m. Coastline is regular, lacking any deep indentations, and there are no offshore islands.

Climate: Dominated by north-east trade winds so that the westerly coast is generally sheltered. Wet season is from September to December (average annual rainfall varying, depending on location, between 1,100-1,250mm in the coastal regions and 1,750-2,120mm in the interior).

Electricity Supply: 110 volts at 60 cycles.

Visitor Accommodation: The Barbados Tourist Department lists 60 hotels, 11 guest houses and 51 apartments or cottages. Les Wooten's diving centres operate out of the Coral Reef Club, Cunard Paradise at Black Rock and Sandy Lane Hotel.

Diving Centres: At the time of writing there are at least a dozen professionally managed diving centres in Barbados. These are as follows: Blue Reef Water Sports (Alston Fergusson, 422-3133); Dive Barbados/Jolly Roger Marine Charter Watersports Shop (Dave Farmer, 432-7090); Explore Sub Barbados (formerly Peter Hughes Underwater Barbados), the only 5-Star PADI facility on the island (Mike Seal, 435-6542); Station Break, Hi Tech Watersports (Winston Mitchell, 436-9502); Pakis Watersports (Paki Degia, 426-9947); Shades of Blue Diving (Andrew Routley, 422-3215); Paradise Pirates

Watersports Club (424-5299); two branches of Willie's Watersports (Willie Hassel, 425-1060 and 422-4900); Club Mistral Windsurfing Club Hotel (Paul Rapson, 428-9095). Dive Boat Safari, Barbados (427-4350 or 426-0200, ext 395), at the Hilton International Hotel at Needham's Point, specialises in taking divers to interesting shipwrecks and reefs off the west coast of Barbados.

Marine Environment, General: Lying along the route of the North Equatorial Current, surface seawater ranges from 26°C to 29.5°C and salinity can fall as low as 32ppt, apparently due to the effects of outflows from the Orinoco and Amazon rivers. Tides are semi-diurnal with a range of around 1.1m. The constant wave-battering generated by the north-easterly trades results in shallow-water coral-reefs being restricted to the more sheltered westerly coastline (see map). An extensive submerged (fossil) barrier reef with prolific coral growth forming a 100m wide terrace (the only one of its kind in the entire Caribbean), reaching 12-20m below the surface, runs parallel with the westerly shoreline, roughly 700m offshore. Below this, at around 65-70m there is a second fossil reef terrace, providing evidence of considerably lower sea levels in earlier times. Listed marine resources include sea-urchins; queen conch (*Strombus gigas*), spiny lobster (*Panulirus argus*), black coral and flying fish. The fringing coral reef along the west coast has been much studied and nine distinct zones have been identified, from the sandy rubble zone in the shallows to an outer reef slope (40-50m) dominated by sponges, black corals and soft corals together with a few reef-building corals.

Recommended Dive-Sites: The map identifies 17 of the most popular dive-sites found on the island. The accompanying key records depth profiles and site names. The wreck of the *MV Stavronikita*, 6km south of the main Barbados Marine Reserve, lies in 40 or so metres depth, off Prospect, and is a fascinating dive for more advanced divers.

Fringe and patch reefs, averaging in depth 6-12m, are numerous along the south and west coasts. Offering good shallow dives, these reefs abound with schooling bait fish and an abundance of tropical

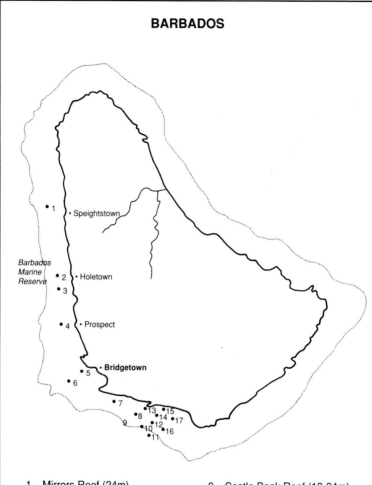

BARBADOS

- 1 • Speightstown
- Barbados Marine Reserve
- 2 • Holetown
- 3
- 4 • Prospect
- 5 • **Bridgetown**
- 6
- 7
- 8
- 13
- 14
- 15
- 17
- 12
- 9
- 16
- 10
- 11

1. Mirrors Reef (24m)
2. Dottins Reef (12-24m)
3. *S.S.Stavronikita* (15-30m)
4. Clarke Bank (3-24m)
5. *Berwyn* (wreck) (6-12m)
6. The Gut (Bottle Dive) (3-30m)
7. *Friar's Craig* (wreck) & Asta Reef (3-21m)
8. Fork's Reef (18-24m)

9. Castle Bank Reef (18-24m)
10. The Muff Reef (18-24m)
11. Mount Charlie Reef (18-24m)
12. Trotters Reef (18-24m)
13. The Boot Reef (9-24m)
14. Church Point Reef (9-21m)
15. Southwinds Fringe (9-21m)
16. Graeme Hall Shallows (18-24m)
17. Carl'n Point Reef (12-24m)

reef-fish. Although it is possible to reach many of these inshore locations from the shore, in general boat diving is the recommended practice. Barrier reefs, averaging 18-30m at their 'crests', themselves signs of earlier lower sealevels, are locally called Bars, and run parallel to the shore. Their position relative to one another is designated by terms such as 'inner bar', 'middle bar' or 'outer bar'. Dropping away from both the inside and outside of these 'bars' the reefs appear as mountains rising from the depths. They are densely adorned with soft corals, gorgonians and sponges while visibility is always in the 18-30m bracket, making them an attractive place to dive throughout the year.

Wreck diving around Barbados is very attractive. Among the major wreck dive-sites, of which there are at least ten, the Greek freighter *Stavronikita* is among the most impressive. This 111m long vessel, gutted by fire in the 1970s, was deliberately sunk by the Barbados government in 1978. She now stands upright on her keel in 43m of water, with her top-deck cabins as close as 17m to the surface. In contrast to this huge wreck, the *Berwyn* is a small French tug, lying with her keel in 6m of water and coming to within 2m of the surface. It is an ideal place for beginners to familiarise themselves with the thrills and skills of wreck diving. An added bonus is that two other wrecks lie near by and all three can be taken-in on a single bottle dive. The general environs of the Berwyn are also attractive for underwater photographers and the marine fauna frequently includes some attractive species such as frogfish, seahorses and flying gurnards. As a regular diving/feeding station, the fish are also extremely tame, including one or two pet morays. The site is also popular as a night-diving location.

An extra dimension to diving in Barbados is hunting for old bottles underwater. Finds range from Hamilton & Codd torpedo bottles to hand blown black and brown beer bottles dating back to the seventeenth century!

Special Interest: Bellairs Research Institute of McGill University has carried out considerable local marine research. Barbados is headquarters for ECSDA, the Eastern Caribbean Safe Diving Association, whose president (Martha Gilkes) and secretary (Major Florence Gittens) are both contactable at Barbados Defence Force Headquarters (127-8819).

Other Wildlife: Barbados Wildlife Reserve offers an opportunity for visitors to see Barbados's wildlife in a protected environment. Visits may be arranged by telephoning 422-8826.

Conservation Issues: Barbados, with a population of almost 300,000 is one of the most densely populated islands in the world, a fact which places tremendous pressures on its wildlife. Coastal erosion has been partially attributed to damage caused to coral-reefs and previously fringing mangrove stands. Barbados Marine Reserve, comprising 250ha of protected reef, is situated on the west coast, between Sandy Bay and Heron Bay, roughly 1km offshore, near Holetown. The marine environment here is seriously affected by local rainfall and subsequent siltation.

Legal Aspects: Legislative instruments for the protection of local marinelife include: Marine Areas (Preservation and Enhancement) Act, 1976; Marine Areas (Preservation and Enhancement) Designation of Restricted Areas Order, 1981; Marine Areas (Preservation and Enhancement) Barbados Marine Reserve Regulations, 1981.

Medical Facilities: Barbados has a hyperbaric chamber unit, situated at Barbados Defence Force Headquarters, St Ann's Fort, The Garrison, St Michael. The unit operates a 24 hour emergency service. This centre was recently visited by Diver Alert Network (DAN) and received high praise, both for the facilities offered and for the personnel involved with the unit. The chamber has also been used with a high degree of success in non-diver related illnesses. The senior diving doctor is Dr Michael Brown MBBS, telephone 427-8819 (chamber) or 436-6215 (office).

3.6 : BELIZE

Location: Belize (formerly British Honduras) lies south of Mexico and to the east of Guatemala (approx 16°-18°N and 89°W). The coral reefs forming Belize's extensive barrier reef system are in line with a southerly extension of the Yucatan peninsula.

Physical Description: Inland, Belize consists of dense jungle, cultivated land and riverine communities whilst its coastline has long narrow sandy beaches and extensive mangrove stands. The outstanding marine feature is the country's 257km long barrier reef, the second largest such reef structure in the world.

Climate: Subtropical (10°C-32°C); easterly winds predominate for most of the year. Dry season is from March to the beginning of June and this is followed by a hurricane season running from June to November or even later. Average rainfall on the cays and islands along the barrier or inside the lagoon is around 1,780mm.

Electricity Supply: Both 110 volts and 220 volts at 60 cycles so check before plugging in.

Visitor Accommodation:
Ambergris Cay: Over 20 hotels are situated on Ambergris Cay (see list of diving centres), which is the largest and most developed of the islands. It is easily accessible by local airline or boat service. The nearby Hol Chan Marine Reserve is particularly well endowed with a rich variety of marinelife.
St George's Cay: The barrier reef at St George's Cay is only 14km from Belize City, making the island extremely accessible and yet featuring excellent underwater visibility and abundant marinelife. The north end of the island is a small residential enclave of mostly private weekend and holiday retreats. St George's Lodge, owned and operated by Fred Good, is toward the southern end of the island and is

hand-built with beamed cathedral ceilings. The main lodge, which sits among 4ha of tropical foliage and faces seaward, consists of ten rooms surrounding a central dining room and bar. Six cottages to the rear of the property are built on stilts overlooking a mangrove lagoon. The fleet includes four outboard powered skiffs in the 6-8m range.

Caye Caulker: Caye Caulker has become very popular with budget travellers. College students have discovered the island and have brought a perpetual mini-spring break atmosphere to the place. Accommodation is unpretentious but clean and living is relatively inexpensive. The cay features an immense cave system which should only be penetrated by the most experienced cave divers.

Lighthouse Reef: Only eight miles from the famous Blue Hole, Lighthouse Reef Resort will have 20 cabanas and operate as a full service dedicated diver base. Contact: Lighthouse Reef Resort (PO Box 26, Belize City, Belize, CA; US contact: (409) 291-6111).

Glover's Reef: Glover's Reef Resort has operated for a number of years. It has recently been augmented by Manta Reef Resort (US reservations: (800) 324-0053). Glover's Reef Atoll is regarded as one of the world's most spectacular dive locations.

Caye Chapel: The only commercial development on this private island is the 32 unit Pyramid Island Resort (Peg and Bob Huffstutler, PO Box 192, Belize City, Belize CA; 501-244409; US contact: Pyramid Island Resort, PO Box 1545, Ashland, Kentucky 41105; (800) 325-3401). It has the unusual honour of hosting the country's biggest beach party on the last Sunday of each month when 500 or so people descend on the tranquil island for barbecues and live music.

Moho Caye: Moho Caye is a private island only 365m from the mainland. There are two luxurious Topsider resort villas, each with its own dock and guests have the use of a custom 8m *Shamrock* diesel dive boat. The villas are completely self-contained. The Belize Aggressor fleet sails from a protected marina at this Maya Landings development. Sail and Dive Belize is also based here (PO Box 997, Belize City, Belize, CA; radio ch. 78; 501-245798; US contact: Dive/Sail Belize, PO Box 9182, Treasure Island, Florida 33740, USA; (800) 237-DIVE; (813) 367-1952).

South Water Caye: Situated virtually on top of the barrier reef, 56km south-east of Belize City, South Water Caye provides visitor accommodation at 10 room Blue Marlin Lodge (PO Box 21, Dangriga, Belize, CA; 501-278007; US contact: (800) 798-1558). The lodge arranges all transfers and utilises a 9m Mako with twin 225 hp outboards to cover the 23km between the island and the mainland. Several new cabanas are presently under construction, thus expanding the available accommodation.

Diving Centres: At the time of writing air-filling (compressor) facilities, together with equipment rental and other diving facilities, are available at Moho Caye, South Water Caye, St George's Cay, Caye Caulker, Caye Chapel, San Pedro on Ambergris Cay, and Rum Point Inn, Placencia.

Ambergris Cay: The traditional services are via local dive guides operating from their own island built skiffs, 7-8m long, powered by twin outboards. There are approximately 100 dive guides registered with the Ambergris Dive Association and at any one time perhaps half of these are actively operating. Single-tank, one-location dives are generally scheduled for both morning and afternoon with occasional night dives. Dive guides collect guests from the hotel dock. A few hotels have added dockside dive shops complete with tank-filling and gear rental facilities. Most resorts have resident instructors and nowhere on the island is far from some form of diving facilities. San Pedro is so small that all you have to do is ask!

Dive operations on Ambergris Cay are listed as follows:
Captain Morgan's Retreat (San Pedro, Belize, CA; contact Magnum America Tours, PO Box 763, Detroit Lakes, Michigan 56501, USA, (800) 447-2931); Coral Beach Hotel (Allan Foreman, PO Box 116, San Pedro, Belize, CA; 501-26-2013); House of the Rising Sun Apartments (contact: Mary Taylor, 16730 El Camino Real, Houston, Texas 77062, USA, (713) 484-6993); Island Photos (Middle Street, San Pedro, Belize, CA; 501-26-2343); Journey's End Caribbean Club (PO Box 13, Ambergris Caye, Belize, CA; 501-26-2173). La Joya Resort & Beach Club (San Pedro, Belize, CA; 501-26-2050); Out Island Divers (Ray Bowers, PO Box 7, San Pedro, Belize, CA; 501-26-2083); Paradise

Resort Hotel (San Pedro, Belize, CA; 501-26-2083); San Pedro Holi-
day Hotel (Celi McCorkle, PO Box 1140, Belize City, Belize, CA; 501-
26-2014); Sunbreeze Hotel (Ambergris Cay, Belize, CA; 501-26-2191);
The Belizean (San Pedro, Belize, CA.; 501-26-2138); Ramon's Reef
Resort (Ramon Nunez, San Pedro, Belize, CA; 501-26-2071); Royal
Palm Inn (PO Box 18, San Pedro, Belize, CA; 501-26-2148); Victoria
House (PO Box 22, San Pedro, Belize, CA; 501-26-2067).

St George's Cay: St George's Cay Lodge (Fred Good, PO Box 625,
Belize City, Belize, CA; 501-244190).

Caye Caulker: Belize Diving Services Ltd (PO Box 667, Belize City,
Belize, CA; 501-245937, ext 143).

Lighthouse Reef: Contact Lighthouse Reef Resort (PO Box 26, Belize
City, Belize, CA; US contact: (409) 291-6111).

Glover's Reef: Glover's Reef Resort has been operating as a diving
base for a number of years. This has recently been augmented by the
Manta Reef Resort which accommodates its guests in pleasant thatch
roofed cabanas and runs a V-hulled fibrelass Chris Craft. (Manta
Reef Resort, US reservations: (800) 324-0053).

Caye Chapel: Courtesy of the Pyramid Island Resort (see under Visitor Accommodation), the centre has a 15m vessel, the Offshore Ex-
press; an 11m Ensign and an 11m narrow fast boat capable of 88km/
h; and some 6-8m outboard powered skiffs. It is a fully equipped,
self sufficient, dive base.

Moho Caye: The *Belize Aggressor* (contact the Aggressor Fleet, PO
Drawer K, Morgan City, Louisiana 70381, USA; fax (504)384-0817;
tel.: (800) 348-2628), a modern live-aboard dive-boat, gives visiting
divers an excellent opportunity to visit the world's second largest
barrier reef, 185 miles of superb diving with many deepwater drop-
offs and an extensive system of atolls and cays. The boat regularly
takes divers to Lighthouse Reef, Glover's Reef and the Turneffe
Islands. The Blue Holes of Belize are also on the diving agenda. On
board facilities include an underwater camera rental department
with an E6 processing laboratory and a helpful and experienced
crew. Cabins and lounge are air conditioned, and the latter has
video viewing facilities. Dive Belize (PO Box 997, Belize City, Belize,
CA; radio ch. 78; tel. 501-245798).

South Water Caye: Blue Marlin Lodge (South Water Caye, PO Box 21, Dangriga, Belize, CA; 501-278007; US contact (800) 798-1558) operates several fast and efficient V-hulled boats and provides full equipment rental.

Marine Environment: Tidal range is 0.6m. Sea temperatures are 25-29°C; salinity 36ppt. The Belize shelf-edge barrier reef system is one of the largest of its type in the world. A measure of the extreme water clarity which can occur here is given by the fact that reef building corals and even the green calcareous alga, *Halimeda*, have been found as deep as 100m, considerably more than their usual depth range. Commercial fishing by local boats concentrates on spiny lobsters, conch, grouper and snapper. Reefs are prone to serious damage by hurricanes such as Hattie (1961), Laura (1971), Fifi (1974), and Greta (1978).

Recommended Dive-Sites:
Ambergris Cay: There are seven cuts through the barrier reef with the seaward side of these, close to the cuts, representing the main dive sites. Hol Chan is the most famous of these and has recently been designated a marine reserve. A good current through the pass promotes healthy marinelife.

Dozens of other sites are frequented by the San Pedro dive-guides. Most are spur and groove surge channels running to seaward, perpendicular to the barrier reef. These are characterised by good stands of hard corals punctuated by azure vase and yellow tube sponges. Socorrita Point is famous for its rays and schooling horse-eye jacks; the Caverns for swim-through caves populated by iridescent copper sweepers; and Mexico Rocks for shallow reef inhabitants, inside the barrier.

St George's Caye: This is only 14km from Belize City and yet on the barrier reef and as such offers some excellent diving.

Caye Caulker: This features an immense cave system. The main entry shaft is just offshore and is currently being explored by divers from the Smithsonian Institute. This cave system has claimed a few lives over the years so extreme caution is needed; only experienced and trained cave divers should consider penetrating it!

Lighthouse Reef and the Blue Hole Area: This provides numerous dive-sites allowing divers to experience vertical walls commencing from as shallow as 11m. The walls of Lighthouse reef feature exceptional underwater visibility and are colourfully adorned with huge yellow tube-sponges, orange elephant's ear sponges, black coral and deepwater gorgonians.

Made famous by a Cousteau documentary some years ago, the Belize Blue Hole is an almost perfectly circular 300m diameter cylinder in the midst of a shallow reef area. The Cousteau underwater vehicles took the team to a depth of 126m in order to explore the bottom of this huge cavern, but sports divers today do not descend below about 40m, where they may view the immense stalactites which hang suspended from what was once the roof of a cave. Towards the cave base, at around 120m, are corresponding stalagmites, providing incontrovertible evidence of a much lower ancient sealevel.

Glover's Reef: This is an oval shaped coral atoll, 45km offshore, featuring an almost continuous narrow reef encircling a 200 sq.km lagoon. The outer walls of the encircling coral-reef create vertical walls, starting from 9m and dropping to around 600m! Needless to say, the diving is super!

Caye Chapel: Most diving from this base takes place around the island itself which has an extensive spur and groove reef complex along the barrier reef. Drop-offs at St George's Cay and Long Cay are also visited from here and plans are afoot to take divers to further destinations such as Turneffe Atoll and Lighthouse Reef.

South Water Caye: Situated where it is, right on the Barrier Reef, far from the population centre, this offers some of the finest diving in Belize.

Special Interest: Barrier Reef, including Blue Holes. 'The Belize coral reef system is unique in the Western Hemisphere on account of its size, its array of reef types and the luxuriance of corals thriving in such a pristine condition.' (IUCN, 1988). Moray eels abound in Hol Chan Cut, off Ambergris Cay. Spawning aggregations of Nassau

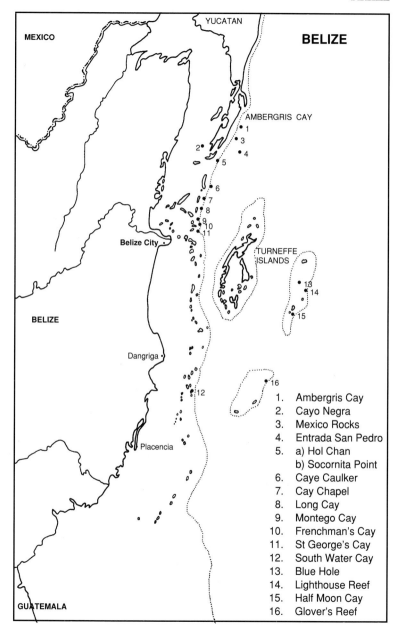

1. Ambergris Cay
2. Cayo Negra
3. Mexico Rocks
4. Entrada San Pedro
5. a) Hol Chan
   b) Socornita Point
6. Caye Caulker
7. Cay Chapel
8. Long Cay
9. Montego Cay
10. Frenchman's Cay
11. St George's Cay
12. South Water Cay
13. Blue Hole
14. Lighthouse Reef
15. Half Moon Cay
16. Glover's Reef

grouper (*Epinephelus striatus*) and yellow-fin grouper (*Myteroperca interstitialis*) may be observed off Rocky Point, off Ambergris Cay. 'Lighthouse Reef is surrounded on all sides by a well defined reef-flat; the reef plunges steeply to abyssal depths on the seaward sides, and there are living coral pinnacles on the lagoon floor.' (IUCN, 1988). Above water, the centuries old ruins of Mayan Indian civilisation at Altun Ha are definitely worth a visit.

Other Wildlife: Loggerhead and hawksbill turtles nest on offshore cays and along the southern beaches. The American crocodile (*Crocodylus acutus*) occurs along the coast, particularly within sheltered lagoons. The Caribbean manatee (*Trichechus manatus*) occurs wherever there are sea-grass beds, along the shore and around cays offshore.

The Cockscomb Basin Wildlife Sanctuary, established in February 1986, is situated in southern Belize, below the jagged peaks of the Maya Mountain's Cockscomb Range. It is home to a significant number of wild jaguar. In addition the reserve is an ornithologists paradise with over 290 species recorded, including the scarlet macaw, great curassow, keel-billed toucan and king vulture. In addition it is rich in plants, reptiles and many other faunal groups.

The Crooked Tree Wildlife Sanctuary, just 53km north-west of Belize City and 3km off the Northern Highway, provides visitors with an excellent opportunity to learn about Belize's rich natural heritage.

Conservation Issues: The main cause of damage to reefs has been hurricanes, which have been known to wipe out 80 per cent of the live corals in areas which they hit (e.g. between Rendezvous Cay and English Cay on the barrier reef). An indication that all may not be well with the marine environment was a recent mass mortality of the black-spined sea-urchin *Diadema antillarum*. There are fears of the possible effects on reefs of increased agricultural activities on shore (releasing fertilisers and herbicides), but there have not so far been any noticeable effects on the barrier-reef system, which remains in extremely good condition. The clearance of mangroves and the dredging of sea-grass beds are potentially serious issues, however, which are bound to have consequences for coastal marinelife, especially for turtles and manatees (which have already suffered heavily from being hunted).

Legal Aspects: Coral reefs within areas designated as national parks receive general protection under the National Parks System Act, 1981. The Fisheries Regulations, 1977, place controls on the taking of crayfish, lobsters (closed season from 15 March to 14 July), conch (closed season from July to September), and manatee, porpoise and turtles, which are protected at all times. The coastal marine tract, within 5km of Belize, is protected as a marine reserve under the Fisheries Regulations (Amendment), 1982. It is forbidden to use scuba gear to take conch or lobster.

Medical Facilities: Recompression chamber facilities are available at Sub Aquatic Safety Services of Belize Ltd, San Pedro Airstrip, Ambergris Cay, Belize (501-026-2425). They have a multi-double lock hyperbaric chamber and run a 24 hour emergency evacuation service via helicopter.

3.7 : BONAIRE

Location: Forming part of the Netherlands Antilles, the main island of Bonaire together with its small offshoot of Klein Bonaire (12°02'-12°18'N, 68°12'-68°25'W) are in the Windward Islands of the Lesser Antilles (confusingly referred to as the Leeward Islands of the Netherland Antilles!)

Physical Description: The island has a parched, dry, almost desertic appearance with some blanched mounds of white salt piled at the edges of salinas. Its major redeeming feature is its wildlife in the form of exotic birds and reptiles together with its surrounding coral-reefs and their abundant marinelife (the entire island is surrounded by a marine park). The island's northern section is hilly with quite steep cliffs along much of its coastline, which lacks sandy beaches; whereas the southern section is flat with a low coastline merging in places into coral rubble or beachrock and sand beaches.

Climate: Sea breezes, primarily from the north-east, temper an otherwise uncomfortably hot climate. What little rain does fall here is most likely to occur between November and December. Very occasionally short bouts of torrential rain occur, carrying freshwater and mud into the surrounding ocean and thus affecting underwater visibility.

Electricity Supply: 127 volts at 60 cycles; 220 volts in some diving centres

Visitor Accommodation and Diving Centres: Since the prime focus of tourism in Bonaire is for divers, and most hotels incorporate diving facilities, these two sections have been combined to provide a single listing.

The following symbols have been used in the entries:
SP = Swimming pool on premises; OF = Ocean front property; DS =

Diving shop; I = Diving instruction given; PADI = PADI diving centre; DG = Diving guides available; A = Accommodation especially for divers; A(20) = Accommodation, with the number of rooms in brackets; Ac = Airconditioned; B = Diving boat or boats available; E = Diving equipment available for rent; WS = Other watersport facilities available; UP = Specialises in dives for underwater photographers; MB = Special focus on and knowledge of marine-biology; RT = Round-trip packages offered; BD = Beach diving. ***=Special recommendation.

- Bonaire SCUBA Centre *** (US Sales Office, PO Box 755, Morgan, New Jersey 08879, USA; 599-78978; fax: 599-78846)

SP;OF;DS;I;PADI;DG;A;Ac;B;E;WS;UP;MB;RT;BD.

An SSI-, PADI-, and YMCA- affiliated centre providing full diving shop and facilities for 14-24 divers on assorted boats with its local headquarters at Black Durgon Inn.

- Black Durgon Inn (599-8866)

OF;DS;I;PADI;DG;A;A(6);Ac;B;E;BD.

- Bonaire Beach Hotel and Casino (566-78448)

148 units.

- Buddy's Dive Resort (PO Box 231, Bonaire, Netherlands Antilles; 599-78647, telex:1200)

OF;DS;I;PADI;DG;A;A(20);Ac;B;E;BD.

Facilities for 12 divers.

- Touch The Sea (Dee Scarr)***, (PO Box 369, Bonaire, Netherlands Antilles) DG;I;B;UP;MB.

Specialises in boat dives for underwater photographers to locations with diver-familiar marine creatures. Dive leader, Dee Scarr, is extremely experienced and sensitive towards marinelife.

- Captain Don's Habitat & Hamlet, (PO Box 88, Bonaire, Netherlands Antilles; US Office:Maduro Travel, 1080 Port Boulevard, Miami, Florida 33132, USA (800)327-6709)

OF;DS;I;PADI;DG;A(43);Ac;B;E;WS;UP;MB;RT;BD.

- Carib Inn Dive Resort (599-78819)

SP;OF;DS;I;PADI;DG;A(10);Ac;B;E;WS;UP;BD.

Facilities for 20 divers.

- Divi Flamingo Beach Resort/Casino Diving Centre (599-78285)

SP;OF;DS;I;PADI;DG;A;A(150);Ac;B;E;WS;UP;RT;BD.
Bookings via Divi Hotels Marketing Inc., 54 Gunderman Road, New York 14850, USA.
• Dive Inn, Parnassia, (599-78761)
SP;OF;DS;I;PADI;DG;A;B;E;WS;UP;BD.
Facilities for 16 divers.
• Peter Hughes Dive Bonaire (599-78285). Operates two dive shops, situated at Divi Flamingo Beach Hotel and Casino, together with ten diving boats. Facilities for 185 divers (see Divi Flamingo Beach Resort and Casino).
• Sand Dollar Condominiums, (US contact: 50 Georgetown Road, New Jersey 08505, USA; 599-78738)
SP;OF;DS;I;PADI;DG;A(38);Ac;B;E;WS;UP;BD.
Facilities for 52 divers.

In addition there are several live-aboard dive vessels which cruise waters not normally dived by the land-based operations. Among these the Antilles Aggressor is well established and belongs to the Aggressor Fleet (US contact: (800) 348-2628).

Marine Environment, General: The entire 104km long coastal marine tract of Bonaire and Klein Bonaire is incorporated into a marine park which extends from high tide to 60m deep. Sea water is exceptionally clear and with stable surface temperatures around 26°C to 28°C. Lying outside the hurricane belt, the north-easterly trade wind blows with great regularity and persistence at an average velocity of 7.2m/sec, resulting in an exposed north and east coast and a calm sheltered westerly coastline.

Bonaire, formed by a series of volcanic eruptions 70 million years ago, is particularly attractive to divers since it is surrounded by deep, clear oceanic water. A continuous fringing coral-reef circles the islands, followed by a gently inclined terrace which turns, at around 10m depth, into a drop-off whose slope varies from overhung or near vertical to a less precipitous 30° angle. This deep reef-face extends to around 50-60m. The distinction between terrace and drop-off is, however, lost along much of the windward coast where the reef slopes down into deep water at a fairly steady angle.

Recommended Dive Sites: Bonaire is one of the most popular diving locations in the Caribbean. Most diving takes place along its more sheltered westerly side. Klein Bonaire is probably the most frequently dived area with the reef in front of the Flamingo Beach Hotel running a close second. Scuba diving is prohibited in two coastal zones: from Karpata to Goto, and from Playa Frans to Boca Slagbaai. A novel approach to marine-park management and conservation research is the 'hands-off' dive-site where only experienced but *non-camera-carrying* divers are permitted access. The object of this is to compare the damage thus caused by their activities with that on those reefs which are regularly visited by underwater photographers, and to monitor the effects of novice divers on the reef. Thirty moorings at dive sites around Bonaire greatly reduces the damage caused by boats anchoring over coral. The Pike in front of Captain Don's Habitat is a popular diving venue.

Scuba diving on the eastern side of the island is difficult at the best of times since 2.5m waves are the rule rather than the exception! While some diving does take place here it is only for the most experienced of divers since currents can also be strong and entry and exit points generally involve scaling down and up cliffs!

Almost all the diving takes place along the sheltered western side of Bonaire. Divers who visit here may wish to obtain a copy of the Bonaire Marine Park Guide which gives an excellent summary of what they are likely to discover along this fascinating section of coastline. The Director of the Marine Park, Eric Newton, recommends snorkelers to head for Nukove, Playa Funchi, Playa Benge or Klein Bonaire. There was a special underwater trail marked out but many of the corals on this were destroyed by bad weather a few years ago. Scuba divers may refer to the listed dive-sites in the Bonaire Marine Park Guide, summarised below.

Off Bonaire:

Pink Beach, off the south-west coast of the island, near the solar salt pans, is accessed by boat and a mooring buoy marks the beginning of the dive. There is a good variety of fish, including some large ones. Salt Pier and Salt City provide diving beneath the salt pier to study the myriad forms which live among the heavily encrusted pilings. About 450m south of the pier is a group of small patch reefs, about 18m deep, forming a focal point for various reef-fish. Angel City is a good dive-site at moderate depth enhanced by the wreck of the *Hilma Hooker*, a 1,000 ton freighter seized for carrying drugs, and deposited here on 12 September 1984. Punt Vierkant is a west-facing promontory along the south-west coast of the island. It is a good site for congregating reef and pelagic fish. Windsock is the name given to the shallow reef-area just offshore, at the end of the airport. Calabas reef is one of the most popular diving areas around the entire island. It has an abundance of marinelife and a well-garlanded wreck. Town Pier provides an easy but interesting dive, especially good for close-up photographers. Swim under the pier. Access to Something Special by boat, is between the Marina and the Bonaire Beach Hotel. There are gardens eels on the sand at 18m. Avoid the boats. Other sites are: Front Porch, offshore from Bonaire Scuba Centre, with the wreck of a tug in 20m; La Machacha with a wreck at 11m, a slope to 37m and garden eels at base; Small Wall, a steep drop-off, with gorgonians and soft corals, from 12-20m; Petrie's Pillar, a shore dive, named after the pillar-coral (keep clear of the seawater intake); Thousand Steps, with access by land or sea – good for reef-fish; Ol' Blue just north of Thousand Steps, good for coral; and Rappel, one of the best dives on the island.

Off Klein Bonaire:

The island of Klein Bonaire, cradled within the westerly bay bight of Bonaire proper, only a 1.5km offshore, is recommended as one big dive-site. Different locations offer different features and attractions, but wherever one dives the experience is likely to be a memorable one. A few of the more popular locations are: Southwest Corner, with luxuriant corals and abundant fish in clear water, and an old anchor at 23m; Carl's Hill, which offers a good variety of underwater scenery and marinelife; Jerry's Jam, named after underwater photographer Jerry Greenberg, which has good stands of elkhorn coral; Sampler, a hand-feeding station where the fish have become over-tame, creating difficulties for underwater photographers, and the eels tend to be somewhat boisterous; and Ebo's Reef which has black corals – look but don't touch!

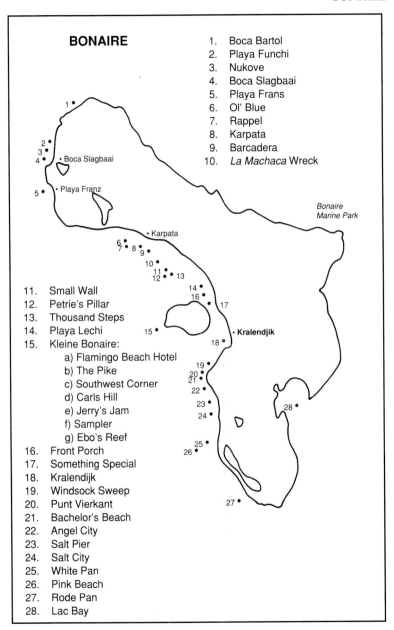

BONAIRE

1. Boca Bartol
2. Playa Funchi
3. Nukove
4. Boca Slagbaai
5. Playa Frans
6. Ol' Blue
7. Rappel
8. Karpata
9. Barcadera
10. *La Machaca* Wreck

Bonaire
Marine Park

11. Small Wall
12. Petrie's Pillar
13. Thousand Steps
14. Playa Lechi
15. Kleine Bonaire:
    a) Flamingo Beach Hotel
    b) The Pike
    c) Southwest Corner
    d) Carls Hill
    e) Jerry's Jam
    f) Sampler
    g) Ebo's Reef
16. Front Porch
17. Something Special
18. Kralendijk
19. Windsock Sweep
20. Punt Vierkant
21. Bachelor's Beach
22. Angel City
23. Salt Pier
24. Salt City
25. White Pan
26. Pink Beach
27. Rode Pan
28. Lac Bay

Special Interest: Hand-feeding of green and moray eels is a popular pursuit among Bonaire's seasoned divers. Nursery grounds exist among the sea-grass beds at Lac which is also an important site for birds. Karpata Ecological Centre provides basic research and residential facilities for visiting naturalists. The Washington/Slagbaai National Park is a 6,000ha game reserve in the north-west of the island.

Other Wildlife: Over 150 species of birds, including flamingoes. Iguanas are common.

Conservation Issues: In 1979, the Netherlands Antilles National Parks Foundation (STINAPA) received a grant from the Worldwide Fund for Nature (then known as the World Wildlife Fund) to help create the Bonaire Marine Park. Supported by legislation and sound management, the stability of one of the world's most flourishing and breathtaking seascapes has been assured.

Legal Aspects: Marine Environment Ordinance, 1985, is the most recent legislation incorporating the provisions of earlier acts banning spearfishing, protecting turtle eggs and controlling lobster harvesting as well as legislating against any potentially damaging activities in Bonaire Marine Park.

3.8 : BRITISH VIRGIN ISLANDS

Location: The British Virgin Islands (BVI), forming part of the Greater Antilles, incorporates over 40 islands and small cays or rocky outcrops. They are situated approximately midway between the easterly tip of Puerto Rico and the small island of Anguilla.

Physical Description: The total land area is 15,281ha and the four largest islands are Tortola, Virgin Gorda, Anegada and Jost Van Dyke. The islands are situated on a marine platform known as the Puerto Rican Shelf whose surface is roughly 65m below sea level in this area. Formed from volcanic debris, the major islands tend to be hilly, rugged in places, and relatively well vegetated, whereas the offshore cays are lower, much drier and more arid. Many of the islands are bordered by attractive white sand beaches. Road Town on Tortola (population 9,000) is the only town of note, while the main activity on Virgin Gorda can be found around its marina. The highest land is the 542m peak forming part of Mount Sage National Park. The islands are some of the most attractive in the Caribbean, creating an overall impression of mountains capped by jagged peaks descending through slopes resplendent with frangipani, oleander, and in places traces of primeval rain-forest, to powder-white sand beaches and rocky sea-cliffs surrounded by azure blue water.

Climate: The wettest months are October and November with average annual rainfall at around 1,143mm with less on the offshore cays. Easterly to north-easterly trade winds predominate. Winter temperatures range between 22°C and 28°C whilst the summer ranges between 25°C and 32°C.

Electricity Supply: 110 to 120 volts at 60 cycles.

Visitor Accommodation: Hotels serviced by Baskin In The Sun diving centre include the beautifully situated and charming Frenchman's Cay Resort Hotel (495-4844); the extensive development and varied accommodation at Long Bay Beach Resort (PO Box 433, Road Town, Tortola, British Virgin Islands; 495-4252; fax 495-4677); the romantically situated Peter Island Resort and Yacht Harbour (PO Box 211, British Virgin Islands; 494-2561); Prospect Reef Resort (494-3311); The Sugar Mill Hotel (PO Box 425, Tortola, British Virgin Islands; 495-4355 and Treasure Isle Hotel (US contact: (800) 233-7938). In each case a full dive plus accommodation package is offered. Whichever way you look at it, there is a wide selection of good land-based accommodation in BVI, with 37 hotels and 35 guesthouses throughout the islands.

Diving Centres: At least seven dive centres are based in BVI. Alan Baskin and Eva Cope run Baskin In The Sun (PO Box 108, Tortola, British Virgin Islands; standing by on channel 16; US contact: (800) 233-7938; in Tortola: 494-2858), a well-established 5-star PADI diving operation (the only one with this rating currently operating in BVI), which has been operating since 1969. The centre, with facilities at Prospect Reef Resort and Long Bay Beach Resort, employs 14 certified instructors/dive-guides and offers full facilities for visiting divers including hire of underwater video and camera gear and custom underwater video productions in PAL format. All PADI courses are offered for certification of divers. An advantage of this centre for underwater photographers is that film processing is offered at the centre and special beginners', intermediate and advanced courses are offered in underwater photography. The centre, which is open all year, also offers yacht charters and facilities for professional film makers. Baskin dive boats include the 9m *Apache*, the 11m *Tejas*, and the 17m *Narcosis Too*. Photography and video services are carried out through Rainbow Visions Photography and Video (PO Box 680, Road Town, Tortola, British Virgin Islands; 494-2749 and PO Box 5181, St Thomas, US Virgin Islands 00803). It is owned by Jim and Odile Schneider, and is the largest and most complete underwater photography facility in the Virgin Islands, used by Baskin in the Sun, Dive BVI, Blue Water Divers, and other dive operators. Kilbrides Underwater Tours (PO Box 40, Road Town, Tortola, British Virgin Islands; 494-2746) is owned and managed by Bert and Gayla Kilbride who have been running the Saba-based centre, in the North Sound of Virgin Gorda, since 1963. Divers are picked up from Bitter End Yacht Club and taken on either the *Shah* or *Sea Trek* (both 13m long boats). In addition to the ever popular resort course, Kilbrides offers PADI speciality courses such as those for wreck diving, deep-diving, night-diving, underwater hunter, equipment repair, underwater navigation and underwater photography.

Blue Water Divers (PO Box 437, Road Town, Tortola, British Virgin Islands; 494-2847) operate two dive boats and offer holidays in conjunction with Nanny Cay Ramada Hotel. Other diving centres include: Anegada Reefs Hotel Dive Shop (776-8242); Dive BVI (PO Box 1040, British Virgin Islands; 495-5513 or 495-7328) at the Virgin Gorda Yacht Harbour; Island Divers (494-3878) located in down town Road Town; and Underwater Safaris (PO Box 139, Road Town, Tortola, British Virgin Islands; 494-3235 or 537-7032) one of the largest facilities in BVI, situated at the Moorings Mariner Inn on Road Town Harbour, and offering dive packages with Treasure Isle and a number of other hotels, using their vessels, a 13m *Mako*, 8m *Underwater Safaris I* and 9m *Rendezvous II*.

In addition to the land-based diving facilities some Caribbean live-aboard diving organisations exist in BVI. One of the most comfortable is the huge Trimaran, *Cuan Law*, whose 32m length and 13.5m beam accommodate divers in real style. For information call (800) 648-3393 in the USA or write to PO Box 4065, St Thomas, US Virgin Islands.

Marine Environment, General: The islands, although situated on the narrow Puerto Rican Shelf, are surrounded by deep water. The most developed reefs are on the more sheltered southerly coastlines. In places, isolated rocky outcrops, such as Santa Monica Rock off Norman Island, provide dramatic diving venues.

Recommended Dive-Sites: Dive boats from Baskin In The Sun regularly visit Santa Monica Rock, west of Norman Island. This is a doughnut-shaped formation, 18m at the centre, 12m around the rim,

129

and back down to 21m on the outside. Treasure Island has some nice shallow caves good for snorkelling. Ring Dove Rock lies just outside the bight of Norman Island. It is a submerged rocky pinnacle surrounded by tame butterfly-fish and coated with magnificent purple tunicates. Alice's Wonderland and Devil's Kitchen are both popular sites adjacent to Ginger Island. Other sites include Shallow Dry Rocks and Sergeant Major City.

The wreck of the *Rhone*, site for underwater filming in a recent movie: *The Deep*, consists of an intact bow section lying in 24m of water while the stern lies in pieces at around 6-15m. Fish are tame for hand-feeding and it is a particularly rewarding night-dive. The area is now designated as a marine park. A Korean refrigeration ship, the *Chikuzen*, is a completely intact steel-hulled, 75m long vessel, sunk in 1981, lying on sand in 24m of water, 14km out into the Atlantic off Tortola's north shore. It is a classic wreck dive surrounded by pelagic fish, numerous barracuda and an occasional shark. Horseshoe Reef, Anegada, is famous for its 300 plus wrecks dating from 1600 to 1929 (about 80 of which are visible!); the wreck of the *Rocas*, at end of Horseshoe Reef, in a 15m deep pass (near the White Horse) is especially worth a dive. The Baths is south-west of Virgin Gorda. The Dogs include a gorgonian garden at north Great Dog and the north-west tip of George Dog. West Green Cay has an especially attractive shallow gorgonian garden in its lee. Other sites are north of Green Cay, the four rocks known as The Indians lying west of Pelican Island and Treasure Point on Norman Island.

Other Wildlife: Hawksbill, green and leatherback turtles nest in BVI. Flamingo Pond Bird Sanctuary. The humpback whale's migration route passes near Horseshoe Reef.

Conservation Issues: Tourism and development activities in BVI are dominated by the yacht chartering and recreational boating business, closely followed by diving, with at least 30,000 scuba dives made annually. Marina and breakwater construction, boat anchoring, run-off from land development, pollution from yachts and antifoulants are all affecting local marinelife. One of the most unfor-

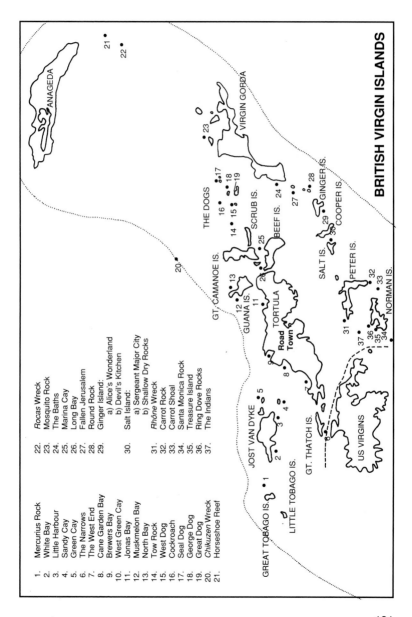

1. Mercurius Rock
2. White Bay
3. Little Harbour
4. Sandy Cay
5. Green Cay
6. The Narrows
7. The West End
8. Cane Garden Bay
9. Brewers Bay
10. West Green Cay
11. Jonas Bay
12. Muskmelon Bay
13. North Bay
14. Tow Rock
15. West Dog
16. Cockroach
17. Seal Dog
18. George Dog
19. Great Dog
20. *Chikuzen* Wreck
21. Horseshoe Reef

22. *Rocas* Wreck
23. Mosquito Rock
24. The Baths
25. Marina Cay
26. Long Bay
27. Fallen Jerusalem
28. Round Rock
29. Ginger Island:
    a) Alice's Wonderland
    b) Devil's Kitchen
30. Salt Island:
    a) Sergeant Major City
    b) Shallow Dry Rocks
31. *Rhône* Wreck
32. Carrot Rock
33. Carrot Shoal
34. Santa Monica Rock
35. Treasure Island
36. Ring Dove Rocks
37. The Indians

BRITISH VIRGIN ISLANDS

tunate consequences of development has been serious erosion, caused by sand extraction, of the leatherback turtle nesting beach at Josiah's Bay on the north-east coast of Tortola. Black coral is collected for jewellery and ornaments, and there is inadequate control of this activity.

A Parks and Protected Areas System Plan was published in September 1986, which recommended management planning for already protected and newly proposed areas, including the wreck of the Rhone, The Baths, Horseshoe Reef, the north sound of Virgin Gorda, the bight at Norman Island, The Dogs, Sandy Cay, Green Cay, Sandy Spit, and a portion of Little Jost Van Dyke, Cane Garden Bay, Fat Hogs Bay at Tortola, as well as many of the other small cays.

Legal Aspects: Fishing is controlled, or in theory controllable, by the Fisheries Ordinances (18/1979 and 12/1980) which require the licensing of fishermen and establishes a framework for issuing statutory rules such as that controlling the legal size and breeding condition of spiny lobsters (i.e. female lobsters with eggs may not be taken by any means and the use of spear or hook for lobster fishing is forbidden). Turtles, except leatherbacks, enjoy *de jure* (if not *de facto*) protection under the Turtle Ordinance (1969) which prohibits capture throughout the year and permits egg harvesting only in July and August. The legal framework for the protection of areas as marine parks is established by The Marine Parks and Protected Areas Ordinance (8/1979). This ordinance empowers the Governor in Council to proclaim any area to be a marine park or protected area, so long as part of the area is submarine within the territorial sea of BVI and the remaining area, which may be adjoining land or swamp, forms with the submarine area a single ecological entity or complementary ecological units. It bans specific activities within marine parks and sets fines for offences. Beaches are protected under the Beach Protection Ordinance, 1985, which prohibits the removal of sand or gravel from beaches.

Medical Facilities: The nearest recompression chamber is located at St Thomas General Hospital in Charlotte Amalie, St Thomas, US

Virgin Islands, just 19km from Tortola. A Medivac helicopter is available to transport injured divers from BVI to the chamber where an operator and doctor are on 24-hour call. Jana Downing MD is a diving doctor with offices in Road Town, Tortola, and is certified in diving medicine.

3.9 : CAYMAN ISLANDS

Location: The three Cayman Islands, Grand Cayman, Cayman Brac and Little Cayman (19°15'N-19°45'N, 79°44'-81°27'W) rise out of the ocean as the eroded peaks of three submarine mountains, 770km south of Miami and roughly WNW of Jamaica.

Physical Description: Grand Cayman (197sq.km) is a low (maximum height 20m), slightly concave, arid limestone island. From the viewpoint of divers a significant element, contributing to very clear coastal waters, is the fact that there is no direct run-off from the island to surrounding waters, since any rain falling on the island drains towards its centre and then filters through the calcareous rock, rubble and sand, before seeping back into the ocean. There has been substantial development on the island. Little Cayman (25sq.km) is situated 117km ENE of Grand Cayman and, with a maximum height of only 14m, is even lower in profile than its larger cousin. Despite this it has a remarkably rugged terrain. Its pitted surface is covered by tangled vegetation and scattered saline ponds. It has been described as 'one of nature's last outposts in the Caribbean'. Only 20 people live there permanently. Cayman Brac, 19km long by 3km wide has a tilted profile with 30m cliffs at the east end while the west end slopes into the sea. Approximately 1,100 permanent residents live here and the island retains more of its old-world charm than its larger, more sophisticated neighbour.

Climate: Winter has steady north-easterly trades whereas these veer to south-easterlies in summer. North-westerly storms may occur from December to April. The hottest period is May to November which is also the wet season (average annual rainfall on Grand Cayman is around 13,300mm).

Electricity Supply: 110 volts at 60 cycles.

Visitor Accommodation: On Grand Cayman there are at least 20 hotels and more than 50 condominiums and guesthouses together with three live-aboard dive boats. Luxury class hotels catering for general tourism, not excluding diving, but not dedicated towards it either, include the Hyatt Regency Grand Cayman, the Treasure Island Resort; the Holiday Inn Grand Cayman and the Grand Pavilion Hotel. Divers wishing to stay in accommodation focussed more directly on their needs have a wide choice of venues with facilities on site, enabling visitors to enjoy their diving with no problems. Some of the major dive-resorts on Grand Cayman are Sunset House, Coconut Harbour, Cayman Diving Lodge, Tortuga Club and Spanish Cove. Divers seeking smaller, and possibly less expensive, accommodation may stay in the more modest hotels or guesthouses distributed in the west end, near Georgetown, Seven Mile Beach or West Bay. There is also the option to stay at a 'condo' (in English parlance a holiday-flat). These are managed by resident companies and are generally privately owned. Major condominiums for divers are at Plantation Village, London House, Victoria House, Villas of the Galleon, Tarquynn Manor, The Christopher Columbus, Pan Cayman House, Silver Sands, Tamarind Bay, Sundowner, Coral Reef and Plantana. Several 'condos' are actually on the shore-front and adjacent to, or very near, diving centres, including Spanish Bay Villas, Cayman Kai, The Retreat and Bonnie Arch. Those who prefer to live on the water instead of next to it, may choose one of the live-aboard dive-boats such as, at the time of writing, the 20m *Gulfstream* (14 divers) or the *Cayman Aggressor II* and *III*: each 34m long and able to accommodate 18 divers.

Accommodation for divers on Cayman Brac includes the highly popular and successful Divi Tiara Beach Resort, the largest diver dedicated resort in the Caymans (and base for Peter Hughes Dive Tiara). Photo Tiara, an underwater photography specialist centre offering film processing, underwater photography classes and equipment rental is situated within the Divi Tiara complex. Brac Beach Reef Resort is also a diver-dedicated centre, smaller and perhaps more intimate than its larger neighbour. A locally based live-aboard boat, the *Little Cayman Diver*, a 20m vessel with eight private cabins, runs one-week excursions around Little Cayman.

Little Cayman, at the time of writing, remains a really undeveloped island but there are moves afoot to bring new tourism projects here. Accommodation may not be up to the standards of luxury found on other islands, but the place and its natural wonders more than compensate for that. Each of the three hotels have associated diving facilities. Pirates Point and the Southern Cross Club are on South Hole Sound while Sam McCoy's Diving Lodge is a family run business on the north coast, just east of Bloody Bay.

Diving Centres: The Cayman Islands, with more than 40 professional diving operations, ranks in the top three dive destinations for American divers, for whom it is a mere one hour flight from Miami. The whole island of Grand Cayman seems to revolve around diving and, with around 20 diving operations, running 50 or so diving boats, there is no shortage of facilities or lack of choice! The recommended diving centres are as follows:

Grand Cayman:
• Bob Soto's Diving (PO Box 1801, Grand Cayman, Cayman Islands; 949-2022) is a major centre with seven big dive boats ranging from 16m to 5m in length.
• Cayman Aggressor (PO Box 99, Grand Cayman, Cayman Islands; 949 5551) operates the two 34m long live-aboards, *Cayman Aggressors II* and *III* with onboard film-processing.
• Cayman Diving Lodge (331 Washington Avenue, Marietta, Georgia 30060, USA; (404) 424-7500; local 7-7555) operates three diving boats.
• Cayman Diving School (PO Box 1308, Grand Cayman, Cayman Islands; 949-4729) is a shore diving base offering unlimited diving at any time.
• Cayman Kai Resort (PO Box 1112, Northside, Grand Cayman, Cayman Islands; 947-9556) runs two flat-tops.
• Clint Ebank's Scuba Cayman (PO Box 746, Grand Cayman, Cayman Islands; 949-3873) has the 14m *Queen Angel.*
• Coconut Harbour/Quabbin Dives (PO Box 157, Grand Cayman, Cayman Islands; 949-5597) has 11m and 14m dive boats.

- Don Foster's Dive Cayman (PO Box 151, Grand Cayman, Cayman Islands; 947-7025; local 9-5679) has seven diving boats ranging from the 18m flat-top Skindiver to the 8m flat-top *Adventure Diver*.
- Eden Rock Diving Centre (PO Box 1907, Grand Cayman, Cayman Islands; 949-7243), a shore diving base.
- Fisheye Photographic (PO Box 2123, Grand Cayman, Cayman Islands; 947-4209), an underwater photography diving centre operating two dive-boats, the 8m *F-stop* and 7m *Focus*, both providing in-house film-processing.
- Gulfstream Charters (3547 Forest Edge Drive, Conyers, Georgia 30208, USA; (404) 483-2770; local 9-4456) has the 20m live-aboard *Gulfstream* with full facilities, including onboard film processing.
- Peter Milburn's Dive Cayman (PO Box 596, Grand Cayman Cayman Islands; 947-4341) has three dive boats, the *Champs I*, *II*, and *III*. (See also Personal Insight).
- Parrots Landing (PO Box 1995, Grand Cayman, Cayman Islands; 949-7884; local 9-7884) has the 8.5m *Genesis* and 9m *Calypso*.
- Red Sail Sports (PO Box 1588, Grand Cayman, Cayman Island; 949-7965; local 9-8745) runs two flat-tops of around 14m in length, the *Coral Spirit* and the *Reef Spirit*.
- Rivers Sport Divers (PO Box 442, Grand Cayman, Cayman Islands; 949-1181) has a 10m flat-top, the *Blue Horizon*.
- Seasports Ltd (PO Box 431, Grand Cayman, Cayman Islands; 949-3965) runs the *Cayman Lady*, a 7m dive boat.
- Spanish Cove (PO Box 637, Grand Cayman, Cayman Islands; 949-3765) has the 12m V-hull *North Wall Diver* and a 10m flat-top, the *Shuttle Diver*, and offers in-house film processing.
- Sunset Divers (PO Box 479, Grand Cayman, Cayman Islands; 949-7111) has three custom dive-boats in the 10-11m range, the *Eagle Ray*, the *Leopard Ray* and the *Sun Diver*. It also offers in-house film processing.
- Surfside Ltd (PO Box 891, Grand Cayman, Cayman Islands; 947-7330) has two V-hulls, the 11m *Surf Diver* and 13m *Down Under* together with a 12m flat-top, the *Galleon Diver*.
- Surfside Rum Point (PO Box 891, Grand Cayman, Cayman Islands; 947-9098) specialises in diving the North Wall and has an

excellent 11m V-hull dive boat, the *Rum Point Diver* together with the 8m *Dolphin I.* (see also Personal Insight below).

• The Tortuga Club (PO Box 496, East End, Grand Cayman, Cayman Islands; 947-7551) runs the 10m *Tortuga Diver*.

• Treasure Island Divers (PO Box 157, Grand Cayman, Cayman Islands; 949-4456) has three 14m vessels, the *Twitty Diver*, the *Gattin Diver* and the *Milsap Diver*.

Cayman Brac:

• Brac Aquatics Ltd (PO Box 89, Stake Bay, Cayman Brac, Cayman Islands; 948-7429) runs three boats, the 17m *Reef Runner*, 14m *Brac Runner* and the 10m *Bogue Runner*, and has in-house film processing.

• Peter Hughes Dive Tiara (PO Box 238, Stake Bay, Cayman Brac, Cayman Islands; 948-7313) has five 12m vessels, *Brac Fever*, *Cayman Fever*, *Tiara Fever*, *Ocean Fever* and *Reef Fever*, together with the 11m *Island Fever*, and also offers in-house film processing.

• Little Cayman Diver (PO Box 89, Stake Bay, Cayman Brac, Cayman Islands; 948-7429) is a 20m live-aboard carrying up to 16 divers.

Little Cayman:

• Pirate's Point (Pirates Point, Little Cayman, Cayman Islands; 948-4210) has two small dive boats, a 5.5m inflatable, the *Porpoise I*, and a 5m flattop, *Porpoise II* together with an 8.5m Delta craft.

• Sam McCoy's Diving Lodge (14 Rochambeau Ave.,Ridgefield, Connecticutt 06877, USA; (203) 438-5663) runs two vessels based in Little Cayman, the 9m *Cayman AK* and a 6m fibreglass boat suitable for four divers.

• Southern Cross Club (South Hole Sound, Little Cayman, Cayman Islands; 948-3255) operates two vessels, the 8m *Miss Southern Cross* and a 5.5m Boston Whaler called *Outrage*.

PERSONAL INSIGHT:

The editor is indebted to diving colleague John Murray from Dublin, Ireland, who filed the following personal summary report on a recent diving trip to the Caymans. In view of the large number of diving companies based there, and the confusing array of promotional literature available to visiting divers, the publishers feel that these first-hand observations may be of some help to visiting divers.

• West Side: Most of the boats and the tourist diving is concentrated on the southwest and west side of Grand Cayman. Most means 90 per cent. Why? Because all the hotels and condos (excepting three or four) are on that side and that is where the diving is easy. You get out of bed, stroll 50m down the beach into the boat, and five minutes later are rolling in over the side! There are hundreds of good sites along the west side, including a number of wrecks such as the *Oro Verde*, *Balboa*, and the *Cali*. For those more experienced and well travelled divers who seek the unexpected, however, many of the west side dive sites are too heavily dived and the coral shows all the symptoms of diver damage. Nevertheless, the reef here does have its attractions, with plenty of arches and caves on the wall. The boats of the major operators are somehow reminiscent of buses, ferrying divers in and out to dive sites. Along this west side the drop-off is approximately 500-700m offshore and starts in about 20m of water. It is steep, but perhaps not quite as steep as on other sections of the island. The west side is usually quite well protected from prevailing winds and bad weather. Georgetown, the capital, is a thriving business centre and it is strange to watch people jumping into the sea, right off its shoreline! Needless to say, the coral here shows a fair degree of 'wear and tear' but the diving is shallow, safe, and with some nice arches and grottoes. The Eden Rock Dive Centre serves the area and has the Eden Rocks just offshore, together with their interesting grotto caves and arches.

In town are Bob Soto's and Surfside, both providing boats and shore diving. South of town is Parrot's Landing and Sunset House (including Cathy Church's underwater photo centre). North of town is Seven Mile Beach which stretches up to the north-west tip. It is very built up, with shops, many hotels, condos on the beach, and dive centres, and comes complete with morning and evening traffic jams! The beach is lovely, and even in the high season seems uncrowded. All the major dive operators are along here, together with lots of smaller ones. Most of the major dive sites are along Seven Mile Beach. (On a personal note, I dived with Peter Milburn Diving run, not surprisingly, by Peter Milburn. He has three boats and his staff were genuinely pleasant – something I did not find at all the dive centres). Peter sends his boats out at 07.30 for a two-tank morning of diving. It does seem early but has the decided advantage of arriving at the dive sites before the crowd (which starts to arrive in force just as you are getting out of the water). He has regular customers who come back time after time, all seemingly satisfied with the care he takes to ensure that discerning divers are satisfied. He also ensures that numbers on his boats are kept down, thus avoiding overcrowding. I also dived with Surfside who have a down-town dive centre, not as big as Soto's and Foster's, but none the worse for that. Surfside also keeps its numbers down, and they run a very pleasant and efficient operation. A nice touch is their big patio in front of the centre where one can hang around in the sun after diving. It makes a good meeting place. I do not wish to give the impression that the other centres are not as good as these two; they all have their positive and negative aspects, and cater for a wide range of tastes and levels of experience.

• South Side of Grand Cayman: Some of the west-side diving centres bring their boats around to the south-west side of the island. The wall here is up to 600m or so offshore with a sandy bottom and outcrops sloping down to 25m before the drop-off. Coral along this side is much healthier than on the west side and much of the south and east side remains virtually undisturbed. In this sense at least the concentration of divers along the west side is a blessing in disguise! If one wishes to be based down in this area the East End Diving Lodge serves most of the east coast. This, together with the North Wall, is regarded as the best diving on Grand Cayman. The north coast has a relatively new diving operation in the form of the Tortuga Club.

• North Side: Grand Cayman's North Wall is justifiably world famous. A 1,900m drop-off running 200-400m out from the shore provides some of the finest diving on Cayman, including the steepest drop-off, most prolific marinelife and biggest fish! Only two operations are based over here (Surfside Rum Point and Cayman Kai), and the other operations bring their boats the whole way around from the west side which is quite a long trip, or out from north sound, still quite a journey. Cayman Kai have two flat-tops, fine in calm weather, but less than ideal in a chop. *Rum Point Diver* is the 11m V-hulled dive boat of locally based Surfside Rum Point, and was the best diving boat I was on during my trip. Its deep V-hull handles a bit of weather extremely well; and the boat is very comfortable to dive from. Surfside head out to the North Wall from Rum Point itself, making it a very short journey. Apart from being a great place to dive, it is also usually relatively uncrowded here, adding to the enjoyment. Surfside's staff were particularly pleasant and I would have no hesitation in coming back for three weeks diving in Cayman, doing nothing but diving every day with these people! The wall is great and very reminiscent of the Red Sea. We often saw hammerheads, eagle rays and turtles together with plenty of colourful sponges and intriguing crevices. Visibility here is normally in excess of 30m

• Stingrays: There are two sites to dive with stingrays. One is Stingray City, on the western side of North Sound and the other is a place called Sandbar on the east side of the sound. It was from the latter location, incidentally, that David Doubilet is reported to have taken his wonderful pictures of the stingrays which were published in National Geographic. The water here is less crowded and perhaps somewhat clearer than at the more popular venue of Stingray City. Whichever place you choose to dive however, this is a real treat; the stingrays are magical!

The Cayman Watersports Association is a federation of diving companies and divers which has brought some organisation into the Cayman underwater scene. They have a good code of practice with a set of rules including such points as: (a) no tourist diver is taken below 30m; (b) no marinelife of any kind may be taken while diving; (c) divers must be instructed in how to avoid damaging reefs with their fins; (d) gloves are not permitted, thus discouraging divers from gripping live coral; and (e) underwater strobes must be carried on the back of dive boats during night-dives.

A conservation comment: while many of Cayman's professional divers speak proudly of having saved Cayman's reefs and stopped black-coral diving, the same people often wear necklaces made from black-coral harvested not here but in Honduras, and sold locally in an ostrich-like charade in which the real point of conservation seems to have been lost. Despite being protected on Cayman's reefs the trade in black coral jewellery remains big business in Cayman.

Marine Environment, General: Clear seawater is one of the special attributes of diving around the Caymans. On Grand Cayman average horizontal visibility underwater, along the deep reefs, ranges from an average of 41m to 60m while that around Cayman Brac and Little Cayman can be even better than this. Tides are mixed diurnal or semidiurnal, while the range is small, between 12 and 50cm.

The Caymans are surrounded by a narrow shelf on which corals and other marinelife flourish. Outside this are two distinct underwater terraces: indications of previous sea-levels. The lower terrace, at around 20m depth, has an outer edge, reminiscent of a cliff-edge, over which one may peer down an almost vertical wall (the Cayman Wall), into the depths. Shallow fringing-reefs are absent along the west coast but the terraces remain a feature of the undersea environment.

The deep-water environment of Cayman has been explored using underwater submersible vehicles. One such investigation, led by Dr Eugenie Clark, using a 7m long submersible manufactured by Perry Oceanographics, explored the Wall to a depth of 975m! The results of her work, reviewed in National Geographic, divide the Wall into four main zones: the Reef from 0-60m where sunlight plays a key role in the energy budget; the Wall, from 60m to 180m where a 'sponge-belt' dominates the rock-face and where few fish are seen but worms, crustaceans and other invertebrates abound; the Haystacks, from 180 to 300m, created by upright pinnacles of rock, some 30m tall, inhabited by deep-water species and haunted by the wreck of the freighter *Kirk Pride*; and the Deep, below 300m, where a fine 'white-desert', poorly lit, is inhabited by weirdly adapted creatures.

For those who wish to explore the upper reaches of the wall at their leisure, a trip in the submersible, *Atlantis 1*, which may descend to 45m, is a memorable experience.

Recommended Dive-Sites: The Caymans have it all: clear water, magnificent coral reefs, dramatic drop-offs and 326 recorded ship-wrecks! The following list summarises the major features on some of the most popular sites. Locations of the sites are shown on the dive-site map.

The following summary of protected areas will provide an indication of which sites are regarded as worthy of special protection.

Environmental Zones

Grand Cayman: Little Sound.

Marine Park Zones

Grand Cayman: Spanish Cove Resort Jetty
North West Point – West Bay Cemetery
Victoria Cay – Sand Cay Apartments
Bowse Bluff – Rum Point

Cayman Brac: Scotts Anchorage – White Bay
Dick Sessinger's Bay – Beach Point
Jennifer Bay – Deep Well

Little Cayman: Bloody Bay - Jackson Point
Preston Bay – Main Channel

Replenishment Zones

Grand Cayman: Head of Barkers – Flats
West Bay Cemetery – Victoria House
South Sound
North Sound
Bat's Cave Beach
Frank Sound
Cayman Dive Lodge
Radio Mast – Sand Bluff
Spotter Bay – Anchors Point

Cayman Brac: Spot Bay
Salt Water Point – Beach Point
Coral Isle Club

Little Cayman: Mary's Bay – East Point
South Hole Sound

While diving is well organised and information on sites is readily available locally, one should be aware of special conservation legislation in force in the different areas. For an explanation of this see notes on Legal Aspects.

• *Grand Cayman*
GEORGETOWN AREA

Soto's Reef	Shallow. Snorkellers & scuba.
Balboa	114m wreck sunk in 1932 hurricane. 8-11m
Eden Rock	Rock has many caves. Boat or shore-dive. 4-11m.
Devil's Grotto	Tunnel in rock to grotto. Boat or shore. 4-11m.
Anna Marie	Wreck of mini-tug to Atlantis submarine. 17m.
Parrot's Reef	Complex coral reef good to explore. 6-14m.
Parrot's Perch	Boat dive only. Wall dive, 300m off shore.
Sunset Reef	Boat a.m.; from shore p.m.; good night diving.
Waldo's Reef	Named after large green moray, Waldo. 9-15m.
Eagle Ray Rock	Attractive wall dive, and eagle rays. 17-30m.

SEVEN MILE BEACH

Orange Canyon	Orange sponges. Canyon in wall. 23-27m is best.
Bonnie's Arch	Named after long narrow coral arch. 9-18m.
Sentinel Rock	Coral pinnacle rising from 27m on drop-off.
Big Tunnel	Coral archway over drop-off at 32-37m.
Big Dipper	Drop-off from 17m. Large basket sponge at 32m.
Trinity Caves	Wall dive with canyons and tunnels. 18-30m.
Sand Chute	Sand chute splays out from 18 to 36m.
Spanish Anchor	Often second a.m. dive. Tame fish at 15m.
Aquarium	Feeding station with over-tame fish. 12-15m.
Oro Verde	A 55m deliberately sunk wreck. Many fish. 15m.
Royal Palms Ledge	Good for invertebrates and night-diving. 11-17m.

WEST BAY AREA

Hepp's Pipeline	Undercut coral-ledge rich in sponges. 9-20m.
Neptune's Throne	Chair shaped basket sponge. 15m on above site.
Spanish Cove Reef	Off Spanish Cove Resort. Shore-dive possible 8-17m.
Little Drop-Off	For small invertebrates and macro photography.
Grouper Point	Promontory forms vertical reef-face from 21-30m.

NORTH WALL/WEST

Josh's Canyon	Dramatic spur and groove structures along wall.
Stingray City	Convention centre for a dozen or so stingrays. 4m.
Gale's Mountain	Flat-topped mount rises to 12m. Impressive fishlife.
Grand Canyon	Formed by deep indentation in the wall. Dramatic.
No Name Wall	Wall dive with attractive red sponge at 37m.

NORTH WALL/EAST

Neptune's Gallery	Deep ravine cut into wall. Some black coral trees.
Brinkley's Wall	Beautiful area. Sheer wall. Excellent for sponges.
Grapetree Wall	Drops vertically from 11m.
A & W Wall	Dramatic drop-off descending from crest at 11m
Babylon	Brilliant wall dive from rich 12m crest to 34m.

EAST END

Cinderella's Castle	Deeply in-cut reef on exposed side. 9-18m.
Two Wrecks	Two old sailing ships lie here. 4.5-8m.
The Chimney	A funnel goes through reef from 41m on face to 15m.
Grouper Grotto	Deeply indented reef with caves and crevices. 8-18m
Shark Alley	Blacktips, bull sharks and grey sharks in 12-15m.
Ridgefield	Largest shipwreck (188m) on Grand Cayman. 6m.
The Maze	Drop-off with deep indentations. From 17m.
Cayman Canyons	Sheer drop of wall from 15m to 300m or so! Sharks.
Wall Ninety	Stunning vertical drop-off from 18m. Black corals.
Lost Wally	Named after green and yellow tube sponge at 21m
Three Sisters	Pinnacles at edge of drop-off garlanded by sponges.
Tunnel of Love	From 18m on reef top to 38m on face, 3.5m diameter.
Ironshore Gardens	Dense stand of elkhorn coral at 15m. Caves.
River of Sand	Sand chute runs from 14m to 30m. Adjoining corals.

SOUTH SHORE

Pinnacle Rock	Coral pinnacle 24m in height, covered by inverts.
South Sound Wall	Wall deeply indented and begins at 21m.
Palace Wall	Wall dive near shipwreck. Drop-off from 21m.
Teach's Caverns	Live-aboards. Blackbeard's castle and underwater caves.
Paul's Caves	Live-aboards. Named after Paul Humann, caves on reef
Lighthouse Wall	Live-aboards. Dramatic sheer wall from 15m down.
Ruddy's Caves	Live-aboards. Elkhorn coral and caves at 9-15m.
Wahoo Wall	Live-aboards. Unspoilt reef and sheer wall from 15m.

• *Cayman Brac:*

SOUTH SIDE

The Hobbit	Sponges and sheer wall create fairyland from 21m.
Anchor Site	Wall from 20m to aprox. 300m. Deeply indented.

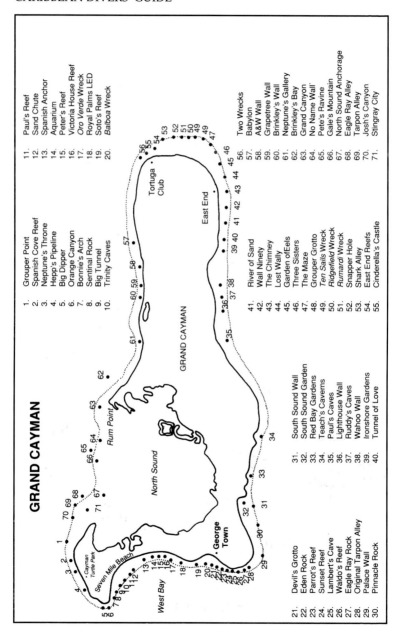

GRAND CAYMAN

GRAND CAYMAN

West Bay

North Sound

George Town

Rum Point

East End

Tortuga Club

Cayman Turtle Park

Seven Mile Beach

1. Grouper Point
2. Spanish Cove Reef
3. Neptune's Throne
4. Hepp's Pipeline
5. Big Dipper
6. Orange Canyon
7. Bonnie's Arch
8. Sentinal Rock
9. Big Tunnel
10. Trinity Caves

11. Paul's Reef
12. Sand Chute
13. Spanish Anchor
14. Aquarium
15. Peter's Reef
16. Victoria House Reef
17. *Oro Verde* Wreck
18. Royal Palms LED
19. Soto's Reef
20. *Balboa* Wreck

21. Devil's Grotto
22. Eden Rock
23. Parrot's Reef
24. Sunset Reef
25. Lambert's Cave
26. Waldo's Reef
27. Eagle Ray Rock
28. Original Tarpon Alley
29. Palace Wall
30. Pinnacle Rock

31. South Sound Wall
32. South Sound Garden
33. Red Bay Gardens
34. Teach's Caverns
35. Paul's Caves
36. Lighthouse Wall
37. Ruddy's Caves
38. Wahoo Wall
39. Ironshore Gardens
40. Tunnel of Love

41. River of Sand
42. Wall Ninety
43. The Chimney
44. Lost Wally
45. Garden of Eels
46. Three Sisters
47. The Maze
48. Grouper Grotto
49. *Ten Sails* Wreck
50. *Ridgefield* Wreck
51. *Rumardi* Wreck
52. Snapper Hole
53. Shark Alley
54. East End Reefs
55. Cinderella's Castle

56. Two Wrecks
57. Babylon
58. A&W Wall
59. Grapetree Wall
60. Brinkley's Wall
61. Neptune's Gallery
62. Brinkley's Bay
63. Grand Canyon
64. No Name Wall
65. Pete's Ravine
66. Gale's Mountain
67. North Sound Anchorage
68. Eagle Ray Alley
69. Tarpon Alley
70. Josh's Canyon
71. Stingray City

146

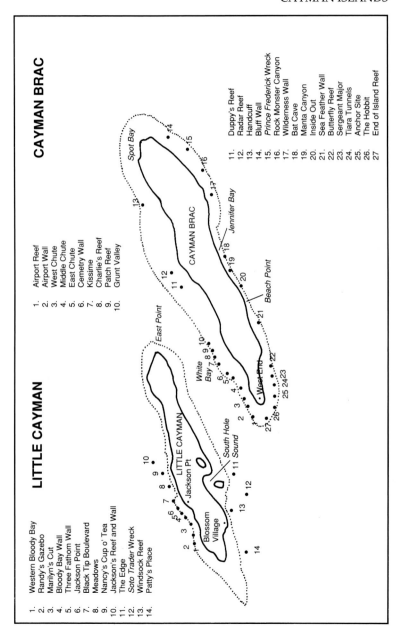

Tiara Tunnels	Wall dive with abundant elephant-ear orange sponges.
Sergeant Major	Shallow reef with tame fish including Nassau grouper 11m.
Butterfly Reef	Shallow reef with some tame angel-fish. 11m.
Sea Feather Wall	Dramatic wall dive, relatively unspoilt.
Inside Out	Spectacular wall dive.
Manta Canyon	Deeply indented wall dive with occasional mantas.
Bat Cave	Wall dive with large cavern in reef face.
Wilderness Wall	Impressive wall dive with great natural vistas.
Rock Monster Canyon	Another great wall dive.
Prince Frederick	Paddlewheeler sank in 1895 and relatively remote.
Bluff Wall	Drop-off starting from 30m. Big fish including sharks.
Handcuff	Named for its proximity to local police station!

• *Cayman Brac:*
NORTH SIDE

End Reef	Well-encrusted drop-off starts at 27m. Gorgonians.
Airport Wall	Sheer reef-face with rich crest starts at 20m.
Airport Reef	Attractive and quite shallow reef, many reef-fish.
East Chute	Wall dive starts at 20m; broad sand-filled canyon.
Cayman Mariner	Wreck, 20m long lies on sand at 17m. Sunk in 1986.
Middle Chute	Similar to East Chute above.
West Chute	Another sand-filled groove in face of steep wall.
Cemetery Wall	Wall starts at only 14m. Many sponges and sea-whips.
Kissime	Shallow attractive reef. 18m.
Charlie's Reef	A popular shallow reef with plenty of fish. 8m.
Patch Reef	Reef isolated by sandy bottom, good fish-life. 8m.
Grunt Valley	Shallow reef. Many yellow-tail snapper, grunts etc.
Duppy's Reef	Shore or boat access to medium depth reef. 8-12m.
Radar Reef	Beach or boat access to high profile reef. Tunnel.

• *Little Cayman:*
JACKSON POINT AREA

Jackson's Reef /Wall	Reef-face with large coral heads from 15m.
Nancy's Cup o'Tea	Reef & wall dive with tame Nassau groupers.
Meadows	Garden eels, Nassau groupers, jacks, stingrays etc.

Labyrinth	Indented wall with sponges, black coral, and jacks.
Blacktip Boulevard	Resident black-tip shark and tame black groupers.
BLOODY BAY AREA	
Three Fathom Wall	Incredible wall from 5m to infinity! Black coral.
Mixing Bowl	Fish gather at crest of wall. Some quite tame.
Marilyn's Cut	Vertical chimney in wall. Nassau groupers and others.
Randy's Gazebo	Wall from 6m to 300m. Cave at 23m. Big fish.
SOUTH SIDE	
The Edge	Dramatic wall from 18m with chimney exiting at 43m.
Patty's Place	Wall from 17m with six chimneys exiting at 34m.
Windsock	Shallow spur-and-groove reef. Rich marinelife. 14m.
Soto Trader	Shipwreck, 37m long in 15m. 50kg jewfish and others.

Special Interest: The Cayman Turtle Farm is government owned and situated north of West Bay on Grand Cayman (see map). Stingray City a recently created diving attraction on the north coast of Grand Cayman has daily visits from around 150 divers who come to gaze in awe as large stingrays literally envelop dive-guides who have been hand-feeding them for several years. Since all this takes place in just 4m of water the experience is open to all comers, including snorkel divers.

Other Wildlife: Colony of 7,100 red-footed boobies (*Sula sula*), together with around 200 pairs of magnificent frigate-birds (*Fregata magnificens*) nests among mangroves adjacent to the salt pond at Blossom Village on Little Cayman.

Conservation Issues: The Caymans are on the path of hurricanes which have wrought their destruction on shallow fringing coral reefs over the years. Development of Grand Cayman, especially over the last decade, has had inevitable consequences for local marinelife, despite the best efforts of the government to minimise the environmental consequences. Sadly, the importance of mangroves as nursery areas and as coastal buffer zones has been realised too late in the day. On the reefs, large fish and spiny lobsters are notably depleted around Grand Cayman with healthier populations around the less accessible Little Cayman and Cayman Brac. Black coral has been intensively harvested around the Caymans, causing a considerable depletion of its population.

Legal Aspects: Spearfishing with scuba equipment has been banned in the Caymans for over ten years (Marine Conservation Law, 1978). Corals and shells may not be taken without a permit. Turtles enjoy partial protection under the Marine Conservation (Turtle Protection) Regulations of 1978. The Marine Conservation (Marine Parks) Regulations 1986 designated marine parks on Grand Cayman, Cayman Brac and Little Cayman. Under this legislation, three categories of protected areas have been established: environmental zones, marine park zones and replenishment zones. In environmental zones, one is forbidden to take any form of marinelife, to use any form of anchor, or to enter or leave the water. A five knot speed limit applies for vessels passing through such zones. In marine park zones one may not take any marinelife (except, under certain circumstances, fish) and anchoring is strictly regulated. In replenishment zones the taking of conch and lobster, together with the use of spearguns, fish-traps and most types of net, are forbidden.

3.10 : CUBA

Location: The main island and the multitude of small islets which constitute Cuba straddle the ocean, forming the northern boundary of the Caribbean Sea proper. Stretching eastwards from its westerly point at Cabo San Antonio (reaching out like a finger directed towards the shores of Mexico), this largest Caribbean nation extends to its easterly headland, Cabo Maisi, pointing across the straits towards neighbouring Haiti. Off its northern shores lie Florida, the Bahamas and the Turks and Caicos, whilst the Caymans and Jamaica lie due south.

Physical Description: With a total land area of 110,922sq. km and a coastline of over 5,000km, this is by far the largest island in the Caribbean.

Climate: Cuba enjoys quite high rainfall and is in consequence a green, well vegetated island. The wettest months are May to October. Hurricanes do occasionally occur, causing damage above and below water.

Electricity Supply: 110 volts at 60 cycles.

Visitor Accommodation: A favourite hotel for divers is El Colony which organises regular promotional diving events. The hotel is also headquarters for the International Scuba Diving Centre in Cuba. It is reached by plane from Havana's Jose Marti International Airport and by hydrofoil from the port of Batabano. (See also Diving Centres below).

Diving Centres: Cuba is one of the less developed diving locations in the Caribbean but offers some excellent diving. The locations of Cuba's diving resorts are indicated on the dive-site map. Isla de la Juventud (Isle of Youth) and Cayo Largo del Sur, both islands in the

Los Canarreos southern archipelago, have diving facilities for visiting Scuba divers. The former of these is now Cuba's main diving centre. Colony Hotel, International Scuba Diving Centre, Treasure Island (Isle of Youth or Isle of Pines), 30 minutes flying time from Havana and 45 minutes by courtesy coach, caters for 80 divers. This is an excellent dive base with good facilities. Hotel Isla del Sur, Cayo Largo Island (to the east of Treasure Island), is reached by air and coach from Havana which is roughly 40 minutes away by air. It tends to cater for smaller groups. Mainland hotels along the north coast, where diving is offered, include the Barlovento and Hemingway Marina, 20 minutes by road west of Havana; the Hotel Kawama, roughly three hours by road east of Havana (caters for 30 divers); Hotel Marazul also east of the capital; Hotel Mayanabo at Santa Lucia, east of Varadero, about 570km from Havana, near Camaguey, with a local airport; and Guardalavaca near Holguin, east of Santa Lucia. Facilities facing south, strung out along the main-island coastline, include Playa Giron in the Cienaga de Zapata, south-east of Havana and the Club Rancho Luna, near Cienfuegos, east of Playa Giron.

Marine Environment, General: The islands are situated on a shelf whose outer boundary approaches the coastline as close as 100m south of the Sierra Maestra and extends up to 140km offshore from Havana in the north or around Isla de la Juventud in the south. The shelf itself has a maximum depth of 100m, whilst immediately off the shelf soundings have indicated depths as great as 7,000m. Surface sea temperatures fall lower than in the mid to south Caribbean, dropping to wet-suit diving temperatures of 20°C in winter and rising to 28°C in summer.

There are different estimates of how many islands there are in Cuba's territorial waters, with figures varying between 1,600 and 4,195! The islands are arranged into four major groups: the two northern archipelagos of Los Colorados and Jardines del Rey (also referred to as Sabana-Camaguey) and the two southerly groups of Jardines de la Reina and Los Canarreos. Extensive coral reefs occur around the coastline: 2,150km along the north coast and 1,816km off

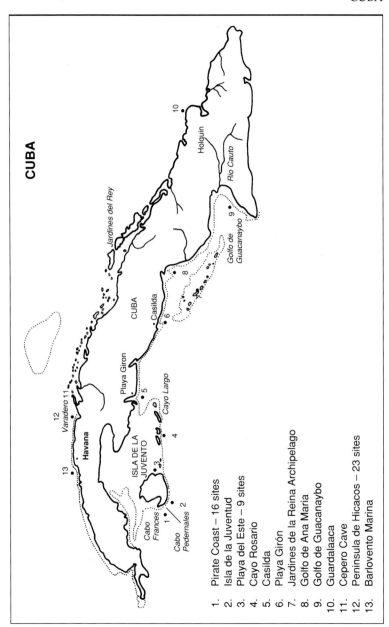

CUBA

Jardines del Rey

Holguin

Rio Cauto

Golfo de
Guacanaybo

9

CUBA

Casilda

8

6

Varadero 11

12

Playa Giron

Havana

13

ISLA DE LA
JUVENTO

Cayo Largo

5

3

4

Cabo
Frances

Cabo
Pedernales 2

1

1. Pirate Coast – 16 sites
2. Isla de la Juventud
3. Playa del Este – 9 sites
4. Cayo Rosario
5. Casilda
6. Playa Girón
7. Jardines de la Reina Archipelago
8. Golfo de Ana Maria
9. Golfo de Guacanaybo
10. Guardalaaca
11. Cepero Cave
12. Peninsula de Hicacos – 23 sites
13. Barlovento Marina

the southern coastline. There are several different kinds of reefs around Cuba, including fringing, barrier and patch reefs and elkhorn coral (*Acropora palmata*) is the main reef-builder.

Recommended Dive-Sites: There is a dramatic drop-off on the south side of Isla de la Juventud which is Cuba's major Scuba diving centre, and a marine reserve. In addition, there are 16 marked dive-sites, each with a mooring buoy, along the Pirate Coast of the same island, between Cabo Frances and Punta Pedernales. Cayo Rosario off Cayo Largo del Sur; 'from the western end of the Peninsula de Hicacos from Matanzas Bay eastwards, 23 dive sites have been marked along the coast. Underwater scenery includes submarine caves and channels running out towards the drop-off; this area has become the island's main scuba training centre.' (IUCN, 1988). There are nine marked dive-sites along the Blue Circuit beaches (Playa del Este). Other listed dive sites include: Barlovento Marina; Guardalavaca; Carbonera; Golfo de Ana Maria; Casilda in Sancti Spiritus Province, and the Jardines de la Reina archipelago. For the aficionados of cave-diving several interesting sites exist, including those at Cepero Cave in Varadero and at Playa Giron. For something completely different, keen divers and underwater photographers should consider diving on the unusual muddy substrate coral and sponge reefs in Golfo Guananayabo, in the shrimp fishing area.

Special Interest: Caribbean manatee is found along both coastlines (e.g. Golfo Guananayabo and the Rio Cauto estuary). The iguanid lizard (*Cyclura nubila*), sadly hunted and greatly reduced in numbers, is still found on some isolated islands and rocky shores of the mainland. Cayo Largo is an important seabird nesting site.

Other Wildlife: Caribbean manatee and American crocodile are still found in Cuban waters. Loggerhead, green and hawksbill turtles nest on various Cuban beaches.

Conservation Issues: On an island with a population of almost ten million people it is hardly surprising that coastal marinelife has come under pressure. Havana Bay suffers from a degree of urban pollution as well as oil pollution. Sadly spearfishing has, until recently, been left uncontrolled (although according to tourist brochures it is actually prohibited throughout Cuba) resulting in serious depletion of reef stocks.

Legal Aspects: A legal framework for marinelife protection is provided by the Ley de Proteccion del Medio Ambiente y del Uso Racional de los Recursos Naturales (1980). Wildlife on all cays is presently protected and other legal instruments are in the process of being formulated.

3.11 : CURAÇAO

Location: 12°N, 69°W. Situated 66km north of the coast of Venezuela, Curaçao forms part of the Netherlands Antilles, and lies between Aruba and Bonaire in the Windward Islands of the Lesser Antilles. As with Bonaire, the issue is confused by the fact that it is also part of the Leeward group of the Netherlands Antilles!

Physical Description: Curaçao, 60km long by 3-2km wide, with a land area of 440sq. km, is the largest island of the Netherland Antilles. Its development by Dutch colonists, has led to a remarkable similarity with parts of Holland. Beaches, many of which are suitable for beach diving, are much less developed here than at nearby Aruba. Undulating hills are covered by pine trees and cacti.

Climate: High summer temperatures are tempered to some extent by steady sea breezes, predominantly from the north-east (average daily temperature 28°C). Rainfall is low (average 500mm), with maximum precipitation in November and December and the driest period in August.

Electricity Supply: 110 volts at 50 cycles.

Visitor Accommodation: See also diving centres below. Listed major hotels include the following: Avila Beach Hotel (PO Box 791, Willemstad, Curaçao, Netherland Antilles; 599-9614377); Coral Cliff Resort and Beach Club (PO Box 3782, Santa Martha Bay, Curaçao, Netherland Antilles; 599-9641610: telex:1 008); Curaçao Caribbean Hotel and Casino (PO Box 2133, Willemstad, Curaçao, Netherland Antilles; 599-962500); Curaçao Plaza Hotel & Casino (PO Box 229, Willemstad, Curaçao, Netherland Antilles; 599-9612500); Holiday Beach Hotel and Casino (599-9625400); Hotel Holland (599-988014; telex:1 405); Las Palmas Hotel and Vacation Village (PO Box 2179, Piscadera Bay, Curaçao, Netherland Antilles; 599-9625200); Lions

Dive Hotel and Marina (599-9618100); Park Hotel (599-9625240); Princess Beach Hotel and Casino (599-9614944); Trupial Inn Hotel (599-978200).

Diving Centres: Curaçao Seascape at Curaçao. Caribbean Hotel and Casino (PO Box 2133, Willemstaad, Curaçao, Netherland Antilles; 599-9625000; fax: 599-9625905; telex:1146 COCUR NA; manager: Bart Schasfoort) offers a range of PADI courses including open-water certification and operates a 12m Delta, a 5m Delta jet boat, beach diving and complete watersports; Coral Cliff Diving at the Coral Cliff Hotel (599-9641610; fax: 599-9641781; telex: 1008 CLIFF NA; manager: Mike Feyts) is the only diving base on the western side of the island and is a PADI centre offering five day resort courses and access to 28 favourite diving sites; Underwater Curaçao at Lions Dive Hotel and Marina (599-9611644; fax: 599-9618200; telex:1226 LDIVE NA) and Curaçao Seaquarium (PO Box 3102, Bapor Kibra, Curaçao, Netherland Antilles; 599-9616666, fax: 599-9613671; manager E Bolle) offers boat (12m and 11m vessels) and shore diving with PADI instructors, including certification courses. The Lions Diving Hotel, with 72 airconditioned ocean-view rooms, together with many other guest facilities, claims to have the largest air station in the Caribbean and has a very well equipped dive shop, Masterdive, on site. Curaçao Diving (599-9614944; fax: 599-9614131; telex: 1268 ISLES NA) at Princess Beach Hotel and Casino is a complete resort with diving facilities close to some excellent dive sites. Curaçao Exotic Dive at Las Palmas Hotel (599-9625200; fax: 599-9625864; telex: 1080 ARFRO NA) also offers shore dives including PADI certification courses.

In addition to the above shore based facilities divers should consider using one of the live-aboard dive boats based in the vicinity. The *Antilles Aggressor* (contact: See and Sea Travel Service, Inc., 50 Francisco Street, San Francisco, California 94133, USA) is a floating diving resort with facilities to take divers to all the best diving sites in the area.

Marine Environment, General: Sea temperatures are steady, between 26°C in February and 28°C in September. Waves and strong currents off the north coast generally mitigate against diving there. The south coast is however sheltered from the trade winds and is much calmer with a north-west current of around one knot. The waters around Curaçao are generally very clear, a reflection of the low level of nutrients in the sea. The island is surrounded by fringing reefs, 50 to 100m wide, sloping down to a sandy bottom at 50 to 60m deep.

Recommended Dive-Sites: Most diving in Curaçao occurs along the west coast. Some of the popular dive sites are listed below. In addition to these Seascape Curaçao have recently added thirty more sites, distributed along the west coast. These are indicated on the dive-site map.

Coral Cliff: 5m-30m. Extensive reef-dive at Boca St Martha. Varied marine-life. Good night diving. Access from shore. Blauw Bay: 2m-30m+. Dive close to shore. Steep wall with impressive views into very deep water. Superior Producer: 30m. Wreck of 60m long coaster, sunk in 1978 due to cargo shifting and taking water. Access from boat or shore but strong currents at times so take care. Site is buoyed but not in Park. Prolific growths of *Tubastrea* corals. Penetration dives possible. Seaquarium: 5-30m. In the Underwater Park. Can be accessed from shore. Rich fauna. Dive buoy No. 2. Jan Thiel: 15-18m. Dive buoy No.4. Extensive coral terrace with numerous reef fish. Caracas Bay/Tow Boat: 5m-30m. Dive buoy No.8. Wreck of small tug on shallow terrace. Also deep reef wall to 30m. Then promontory followed by deep canyon. Many fish. Spanish Water: 10m. Hans Hass's first encounter with a coral reef took place here. Punt Kanon (East Point). Generally too exposed here for diving. Only for the very experienced. Dangerous but rich!
Other Buoyed sites in Marine Park:
Buoy 1. Wandering Buoy. In front of Princess Beach Hotel. Buoy 2. Bapor Kibra. Near partly exposed wreck. Lush shallow coral garden around mooring.Buoy 3. Boka di Sorsaka. Shallow. Off lagoon Jan Thiel. Very colourful undercut ledge at 5m. Buoy 4. Jan Thiel: 15-18m. Rich coral terrace. Buoy 5. Piedra di Sombre: 10-39m.

CURAÇAO

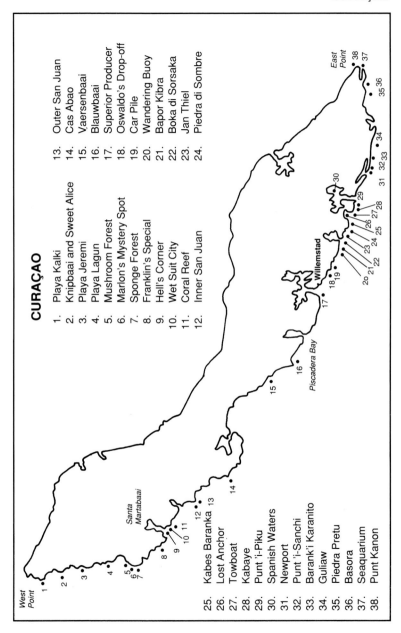

1. Playa Kalki
2. Knipbaai and Sweet Alice
3. Playa Jeremi
4. Playa Lagun
5. Mushroom Forest
6. Marlon's Mystery Spot
7. Sponge Forest
8. Franklin's Special
9. Hell's Corner
10. Wet Suit City
11. Coral Reef
12. Inner San Juan
13. Outer San Juan
14. Cas Abao
15. Vaersenbaai
16. Blauwbaai
17. Superior Producer
18. Oswaldo's Drop-off
19. Car Pile
20. Wandering Buoy
21. Bapor Kibra
22. Boka di Sorsaka
23. Jan Thiel
24. Piedra di Sombre
25. Kabes Baranka
26. Lost Anchor
27. Towboat
28. Kabaye
29. Punt 'i-Piku
30. Spanish Waters
31. Newport
32. Punt 'i-Sanchi
33. Barank'i Karanito
34. Guliaw
35. Piedra Pretu
36. Basora
37. Seaquarium
38. Punt Kanon

Shallow rich reef and a spectacular wall. Superb scenery. Buoy 6. Kabes Baranka: 3-33m. Shallow terrace to vertical wall. Buoy 7. Lost Anchor: 3-30m+! Mooring connected to an old heavy chain.traced to 85m and still going down! The bay was itself created by a massive landslide. Buoy 8. Towboat: 5-30m. Described above. Buoy 9. Kabaye: 10-30m. Vertical wall covered in black coral, sponges etc. Buoy 10. Punti Piku: 15-20m. Two dives from this buoy: (a) across terrace to wall; (b) reef slope. Choose according to current direction. Buoy 11. New Port: 5-10m. Shallow terrace with diverse marinelife. Buoy 12. Punti Sanchi: 5-20m. Exposed cape with frequent strong currents. Experienced divers only. Buoy 13. Barank'i Karanito: 20m. Swim along right of drop-off (when facing sea) for gorgonian rich wall and some dramatic scenery plus good fish sites. Buoy 14. Guliaw: 18m. Exposed site and choppy seas. Dense coral cover. Small wall. Old anchor on terrace. Buoy 15. Piedra Pretu: 25-30m. Spectacular vertical wall. Lush shallow terrace. Wall goes straight down from 9m to 33m. Rich black coral and colourful soft-corals. Numerous groupers. Buoy 16. Basora: 15m. Roughish boat ride to get here but site somewhat protected by tip of island. Dramatic site with plentiful marinelife.

Special Interest: The Caribbean Marine Biological Association (CARMABI) is located on Curaçao, at Piscaderabaai. It has been a pioneer of coral-reef research in the Caribbean and many studies have taken place around Curaçao itself.

Conservation Issues: Curaçao Underwater Park (12°06'N, 68°42' – 68°54'W) (postal address: Curaçao Underwater Park, Netherlands Antilles National Parks Foundation (STINAPA), c/o CARMABI, PO Box 2090, Piscaderabaai, Curaçao, Netherland Antilles; 599-9624242) on the leeward coast of Curaçao, from the eastern tip of the island extending 20km westwards, comprises 600ha of reefs and 436ha of bays, from the highwater mark to 60m. Diving sites within the park are buoyed (see above) and conservation rules are in force. These are as follows:
(1) Do not remove anything, either dead or alive, from the Park.

You may fish, and keep your catch, but only fishing in the traditional manner with hook and line is allowed. Collection of coral of any kind is a criminal offence, and may result in a fine of up to 5,000 guilders or two months imprisonment. Equipment used in committing a criminal act, including boats, may be confiscated.

(2) Do not step on the coral, they are living animals! Prevent unintentional contact with coral through good buoyancy control when diving.

(3) Do not anchor in coral. Either use the mooring buoys or select a sandy area for anchoring.

(4) Do not spearfish. This can result in fines of up to 2,500 guilders or one month imprisonment.

(5) Help keep the Park clean in order to preserve it for future generations. Notify Park staff of any wrong-doings.

Legal Aspects: Reef Management Ordinance (1976) provided the legal basis for establishment of protected marine areas and for the creation of the Curaçao Underwater Park in 1983.

3.12 : DOMINICA

Location: The island of Dominica (15°20'N, 61°22'W), approximately equidistant from Martinique to the south and Guadaloupe to the north, is the most northerly of the Windward Islands.

Physical Description: This small (790sq. km) volcanic island is steep and rugged with dramatic mountains clothed in verdant tropical rain-forest and with a coastline primarily comprised of cliffs and rocky promontories, with few beaches. There are over 300 rivers and countless magnificent waterfalls carrying the island's abundant rainfall to the sea.

Climate: Relatively high annual rainfall (at the coast: 1,700-1,800mm) with the wet season between June and October. Air temperatures average 24.2°C in January and 27.2°C in July. The dry season is February to mid-June. Moderate trade winds have a pleasant cooling effect. Hurricanes, such as Hurricane David in 1979, occasionally cause havoc during the rainy season.

Electricity Supply: 220-240 volts at 50 cycles.

Visitor Accommodation: Castle Comfort Guesthouse specialises in handling divers (445-2188). Other listed accommodation is as follows: Anchorage Hotel (445-2638); Castaways Hotel (445-6244); Coconut Beach (445-5393); Continental Inn (445-215); Emerald Pool Hotel (448-8095); Evergreen (448-3288); Fort Young Hotel(448-5000); Layou River Hotel (449-6281); Layou Valley Inn (449-6203); Papillotte Wilderness Retreat (448-2287); Portsmouth Beach Hotel (445-2638); Reigate Hall Hotel (448-4031); Sans Souci Apartments; Sisserou Hotel (448-3111); Springfield Plantation (445-1401); Vena's Hotel (448-3286).

Diving Centres: Overlooked by many Caribbean divers, Dominica offers some interesting underwater adventures. There are a few wrecks in the vicinity and these tend to be uncovered by hurricanes. Underwater scenery can be extremely impressive and unusual, offering underwater photographers a host of new opportunities. Dive Dominica, based at Castle Comfort Diving Lodge where Derek Perryman is located (448-2188; fax 448-6088; PO Box, 63, Roseau, Dominica), is a good source of up-to-date diving information. Dive Dominica Ltd, founded in 1984, is affiliated to NAUI, SSI and NASE. It operates two dive-boats and can serve 24 divers, offering full facilities including equipment hire. Special courses include Open Water I & II as well as resort courses. This is a NAUI Dream Resort, situated on the water, offering professional and personal service to visiting divers. The centre specialises in dive-packages and all divers can be assured of a warm welcome from its proprietor Derek Perryman. There is also a diving centre based at the Anchorage Hotel.

Marine Environment, General: True coral-reefs do not occur around the shores of Dominica, whose shallows are considerably affected by freshwater run-off from the mountains, but reef-building corals do occur in patches, attached to hard substrata. What corals do flourish here are primarily on the west coast and on north-facing promontories with the richest coral development reported from Petite Baie and Toucari. The shallow ledges surrounding the precipitous island terminate in exquisite vertical walls with, along the leeward coast, gin-clear water and unspoilt marinelife. The dramatic above-water scenery of Dominica is mirrored by its equally impressive underwater environment, with submarine cliffs and pinnacles, arches, caves and even subsurface hot springs offering divers some of the most interesting diving in the Caribbean. Most sites are close to shore since the seabed does tend to drop-off into the depths quite rapidly, with soundings of over 180m within a kilometre of the shoreline the rule rather than the exception.

Recommended Dive-Sites: Dive-sites are primarily on the west or leeward coast and the diving and holiday industry is now picking up its feet after suffering a severe set-back in the form of Hurricane David. Along the sheltered coast visibility is often in excess of 30m with a groundswell from the west, picking up black volcanic sediment, being the key factor in reducing water clarity. Fortunately the sand is heavy and settles quickly once the swell abates. While visibility may be relatively poor around river mouths, the major dive-sites are south of the village of Loubiere, on the south-west coast, in an area without rivers entering the sea.

Sites recommended by NAUI diving instructor Derek Perryman include Scotts Head and sites within the Soufriere Bay area. The list of sites located on the accompanying map and described below, has been kindly prepared by Derek to whom we are grateful for permission to reproduce it here.

Key to sites shown on diver's map:

• Site 1: Des Fous. Large rock off sheer cliff interwoven by crevices and valleys. This massive 'condominium' rests on a sandy bottom. Depth Profile: 6-43m. Exposure Scale: 4. Best Season: July-October. Main Biological Features: Schools of margate, Bermuda chub and snapper. A few southern stingrays and the odd nurse shark. Abundance of gorgonians and black coral on wall. Main Physical Feature: Main rock area joins an incredible wall which drops down to 60m. A few overhangs and some small caves in the area. Safety Comments: Heavy currents and surge dictates careful choice of day for this dive which is only for experienced divers.

• Site 2: The Suburbs. Rock formations on shelf running off south coast falling away on drop-off and walls. Depth Profile: 6-55m. Exposure Scale: 3. Best Season: July-October. Main Biological Features: Schools of margate, chub, and snapper. The odd stingray. Soft corals on drop-offs and walls. Main Physical Features: In some areas the shelf runs out at around 15m with large rock outcrops rising from it, to a height of 6-9m. Where the terrace terminates, it drops steeply into the deep blue water of the Dominica-Martinique Channel. Safety Comments: Heavy currents and surge make this a dive for experienced divers.

• Site 3: The Village. Rocky shelf falling off to s steep drop-off and wall. Depth Profile: 12-55m. Exposure Scale: 3. Best Season: June-

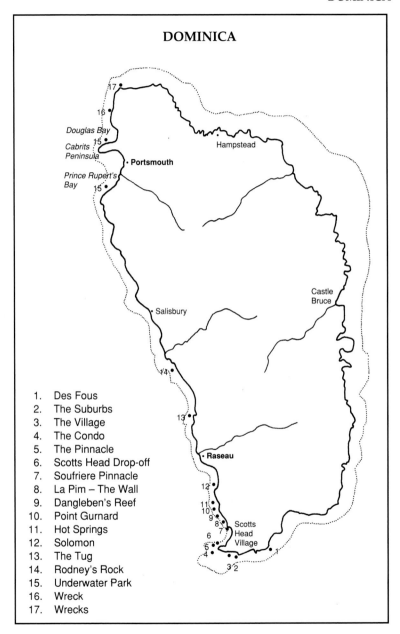

DOMINICA

17
16
Douglas Bay
15
Cabrits
Peninsula
Hampstead
• **Portsmouth**
Prince Rupert's
Bay
15

Castle
Bruce

• Salisbury

14

13

• **Raseau**

12
11
10
9
8
7
6
5
4
3 2
1

Scotts
Head
Village

1. Des Fous
2. The Suburbs
3. The Village
4. The Condo
5. The Pinnacle
6. Scotts Head Drop-off
7. Soufriere Pinnacle
8. La Pim – The Wall
9. Dangleben's Reef
10. Point Gurnard
11. Hot Springs
12. Solomon
13. The Tug
14. Rodney's Rock
15. Underwater Park
16. Wreck
17. Wrecks

November. Main Biological Features: Schools of margate, chub, and ocean trigger-fish. A few big snappers and small stingrays. Main Physical Features: Scattered rocks on a sandy bottom building up to more dense and solid formations as one moves south on the shelf, towards the abrupt drop-off. Safety Comments: Moderate to heavy currents and sometimes heavy surge. This site is for experienced divers but does have its good days.

• Site 4: The Condo. Massive rock sitting on a sandy bottom, interwoven with crevices and small caves. Depth Profile: 4.5-21m. Exposure Scale: 3/2. Best Season: Year-round. Main Biological Features: Schools of soldier-fish; grunts; small snappers; shrimp; soft corals; wire coral and tube sponges. Main Physical Features: Northern face of the rock (which runs east-west) drops to 9-12m. This is the side with the crevices and caves. The southern face drops to 21m and is partially overhung. Safety Comments: Light to heavy current and sea depending on the day makes this site suitable for both experienced and less experienced divers.

• Site 5: The Pinnacle. A pinnacle just west of Scotts Head. Depth Profile: 12-46m. Exposure Scale: 3/2. Best Season: Year-round. Main Biological Features: Abundance of black-bar soldier-fish; schools of grunts; baby barracuda, and bait-fish. Yellow-tail jacks, bar jacks, and other pelagic fish come in to feed on the bait fish along the north wall. Huge sting rays and midnight blue parrot-fish are sometimes observed here. Soft corals and a range of interesting sponges occur. Main Physical Features: Top of the pinnacle reaches to within 3m of the surface. At about 9m there is a fantastic arch, running through the pinnacle, which is perfect for both standard 35mm lens and wide-angle photography. Safety: Light to heavy current and moderate to light sea conditions are the norm at this site.

• Site 6: Scotts Head Drop-Off. Shallow ledge along the Scotts Head point, on the northern arm of the bay there is a dramatic drop-off. Depth Profile: 6-37m. Exposure Scale: 1. Best Season: Year-round. Main Biological Features: Range of tropical reef-fish, scorpionfish, the odd flying gurnard, sponges and nudibranchs. Main Physical Features: Very protected extensive area of good diving which can be dived several times without diving the same place twice. It is suitable for all grades of divers from snorkellers to experienced divers. Safety Comments: This is a safe diving site.

• Site 7: Soufriere Pinnacle. Pinnacle rising out of the Soufriere Bay with a wall to the west. Depth Profile: 6-46m. Exposure Scale: 1. Best Season: Year-round. Main Biological Features: Soft corals, sponges, black-corals, tropical reef-fish. Main Physical Features: Main pinnacle rises to within 1.5m of the surface. Safety Comments: Very calm seas and only slight currents.

• Site 8: La Bim – The Wall. Extensive wall running from the shore to the north-west for 2.5km, forming a ledge from shore to the west. Depth Profile: 6-37m. Exposure Scale: 1. Best Season: Year-round. Main Biological Features: Soft corals, sponges and an abundance of black-coral cloak the wall. Schools of small tropical reef-fish and large schools of blue chromis occur here. A good site also for nudibranchs. Main Physical Features: Average depth of the ledge at the top of the wall is 6m. It drops away to as deep as 245m in some places. Safety Comments: A safe dive for all levels of divers providing care is taken in depth control on the dive. It is all too easy to go too deep for too long here!

• Site 9: Dangleben's Reef. A reef running from the shore to the west. Depth Profile: 9-37m. Exposure Scale: 1 to 2. Best Season: Year-round. Main Biological Features: Extensive coral-growth, both hard and soft. Large barrel sponges, tube-sponges, iridescent vase sponges, black coral. Schools of tropical fish including parrot-fish, snapper, chromis, jacks and the odd barracuda. Main Physical Features: This reef starts off shallower near the shore and gets deeper as it runs out to the west. The northern side slopes but the southern side sheers off into a deep wall. The main ridge is interwoven with pinnacles and valleys. Safety Comments: Suitable for diving by snorkellers and a range of scuba graded divers. The inner portions, near the shore, offer interest to snorkellers and novices, while the outer slopes are reserved for experienced scuba divers since the current here can be quite strong.

• Site 10: Point Gurnard. This point drops off to a sandy bottom quite abruptly. Exposure Scale: 1-2. Best Season: Year-round. Main Biological Features: Soft corals, sponges, and a few hard corals adorn this drop-off. File-fish, spotted drums, spotted morays, schools of soldier-fish and chromis are seen here. Bloodstars, crabs, rock lobsters and shrimps inhabit the caves. Trumpet-fish sleep in one of the caves at night. Main Physical Features: There are a few small caves at this point. One of these, with an entrance at 14m, can be penetrated and goes in about 30m. Safety Comments: Generally a very safe dive but sometimes the current can be quite strong. It is a good night-dive.

• Site 11: Hot Springs. Submarine hot freshwater spring in shallow water, close to shore. The reef is nearby, slightly further offshore. Depth Profile: 1.5-30m. Exposure Scale: 1. Best Season: Year-round. Main Biological Features: Many sponges, soft corals, puffer fish, porcupine-fish, lobster (at night) and nudibranchs can be seen at this site. Also schools of soldier-fish, squirrel-fish and squid around the hot-water, together with the occasional elusive octopus. Main Physical Features: There is a main hot-water vent near shore at 1.5m, and in this area are many other small vents out of which streams of tiny bubbles rise to the surface, like drops of liquid crystal. The reef stretches offshore from this area with part of its westernmost face dropping off sharply. It is an excellent night dive. Safety Comments: This is a safe dive-site.

• Site 12: Solomon. Narrow bands of reef above a sandy seabed, running parallel to the shore, at various depths. Depth Profile: 6-18m. Exposure Scale: 1. Best Season: Year-round. Main Biological Features: Sponges, soft corals, schools of squirrel-fish, sometimes huge spider crabs. Main Physical Features: Bands of granite with coral covering form the reefs which run at different depths, parallel to shore. Safety Comments: Safe site and a good place for night-diving.

• Site 13: The Tug. A wreck at 27m on a sandy bottom. Depth Profile: 17-27m. Exposure Scale: 3. Best Season: Year-round. Main Biological Features: Schools of snapper, margate, and tropical reef-fish in and around tug. Barracuda, jacks and mackerel patrol. Plenty of wire coral. Main Physical Features: An intact tug, 17m long, lying on a sandy bottom. Safety Comments: Some current, limited visibility near the surface. Need for care against entanglement in fishing

lines, ropes etc. Experienced divers only.
• Site 14: Rodney's Rock. Depth Profile: 3-18m. Exposure Scale: 1. Best Season: Year-round. Main Biological Features: Schools of tropical fish, morays, soft corals and sponges. Main Physical Features: Rocky point to the west dropping off to a sandy bottom. There is a fissure running through the rock which gives one the impression of diving in a cave. Safety Comments: A safe dive.

Special Interest: Forest life on Dominica is very special and worth visiting at, for example, the Northern Forest Reserve. The Cabrits National Park is a historic area.

Other Wildlife: In all 166 birds have been recorded from Dominica, of which 59 breed there. There are two endemic birds, the red necked parrot (*Amazona arausiaca*) and the imperial parrot (*A. imperialis*). Recent estimates put the population of the latter on Dominica at around 60 birds. Over 1,000 species of flowering plant have been recorded in Dominica, including six endemics.

Conservation Issues: There has been a degree of over-fishing for lobsters, conch, turtles and other marinelife.

Legal Aspects: Cabrits National Park has legal status. The Forestry and Wildlife Act (No.12, 1976) provides for protection of turtles but there have been difficulties with enforcement.

Medical Facilities: Princess Margaret Hospital at Goodwill offers local medical facilities. The nearest recompression facilities are at Barbados, Martinique and Guadaloupe.

3.13 : DOMINICAN REPUBLIC

Location: The Dominican Republic forms the easterly portion of the large island whose historic name of Hispaniola is still used to describe the geographic rather than the political entity.

Physical Description: This country, occupying the eastern two-thirds of Hispaniola, is 48,433 sq. km in area. Much of the island's centre is mountainous while the coastline varies from rugged rock to some attractive sandy beaches and several quite large river estuaries.

Climate: Rainfall is high with maximum precipitation from May to November. The average temperature is 25°C with August being warmest month and January the coolest.

Electricity Supply: 110-120 volts at 60 cycles.

Visitor Accommodation: Numerous hotels of all standards are available in the Dominican Republic. Puerto Plata Beach Resort (586-4243; fax: 586-4377) is close to one of the main diving areas.

Diving Centres: Puerto Plata Diving Club (982-8303) offers chalet accommodation and interesting diving, including archaeological visits to the submerged town of Matanzas.

Also contact Mundo Submarino (99 Gustavo Mejia Ricart, Dominican Republic, 566-0344) and Buceo Dominicano (960 Abraham Lincoln Ave, Dominican Republic, 567-0346).

Marine Environment, General: The Dominican Republic's lush mountains, impressive river systems and extensive agriculture, together with its large coastal mangrove swamps and shallow lagoons, have a combined effect upon coastal marinelife, rendering large tracts of the intertidal zone and shallows highly productive in terms of small clams and shrimps, but not necessarily clear enough

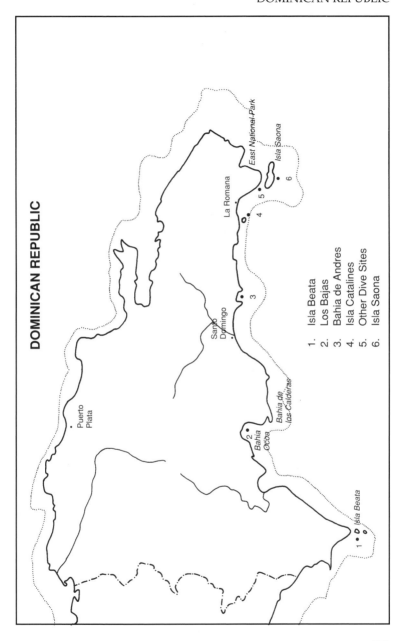

DOMINICAN REPUBLIC

Puerto Plata

Santo Domingo

La Romana

East National Park

Isla Saona

Bahia de los Calderas

Bahia Ocoa

Isla Beata

1. Isla Beata
2. Los Bajas
3. Bahia de Andres
4. Isla Catalines
5. Other Dive Sites
6. Isla Saona

to offer many good diving sites. Of the island's estimated 1,576km of coastline only about one-tenth is bordered by coral-reefs.

Fringing coral-reefs occur between Cabo Isabela and Puerto Plata and to the east of Rio San Juan. In addition there are small barrier reefs in Bahia de la Jina and a larger similar reef running parallel with the shore, between Nisibon and Charca de Bavaro.

Tides are semidiurnal with a mean spring range of 90cm on the north coast and 30cm on the south coast.

Recommended Dive-Sites: Los Bajos in Bahia Ocoa has a deep reef of *Acropora cervicornis* from 21 to 30m, which is renowned for its rich resources of fish, crayfish and crab populations.

Isla Catalina and Bahia de Andres on the south coast have dive sites. Punta Cauceda on the south coast has been recommended as a marine park.

Off the south coast of Isla Saona is a popular place for diving. A good stretch of reef, suitable for scuba diving, runs for about 12km off the west coast of the peninsula to the south-east of La Romana and Isla Saona. 'Some of the most attractive marine scenery in the Dominican Republic is found off Punta Lanza on the west coast of Isla Beata.' (IUCN, 1988).

Special Interest: Manatee occur off the coast, especially in the bay of Las Calderas. Leatherback turtles nest on beaches while greens, hawksbills and loggerheads are also in the vicinity.

Conservation Issues: Spearfishing has been virtually uncontrolled (despite legislation) and has caused considerable damage to some reef-fish populations.

Mangroves are locally exploited whilst marinelife in general has suffered through over-fishing, particularly of lobsters, conches, turtles, and even corals which are collected and sold as ornaments, a practice either banned or strongly discouraged in most other parts of the Caribbean.

Legal Aspects: Although coral-collecting requires a licence, most takes place without permission being granted. Other laws refer to the use of spearguns for fishing lobsters and to the exploitation of turtles.

3.14 : GRENADA

Location: (12°N 61°W). A tiny island at the southerly end of the Lesser Antilles chain, with St Vincent to the north, Tobago to the south-east and Venezuela due south. The dependencies of Grenada include around twenty smaller low lying islands in the Grenadines, a group which it shares with St Vincent.

Physical Description: The total land area of these volcanic islands is only 344sq. kms. Grenada itself is quite mountainous with the highest point, on the summit of Mount St Catherine, at 840m. North of Grenada, the 34sq km island of Carriacou has a quiet charm all of its own.

Climate: Tropical with dry season from January to May. Relatively heavy rainfall, at 1,300mm per year on the coast to 5,000mm per year in the mountains. In the hurricane belt.

Electricity Supply: 220 volts at 50 cycles.

Visitor Accommodation: Spice Island Inn (PO Box 6, Belmont, St George's, Grenada; 444-4258/4423, telex: 3425), particularly well situated on Grande Anse Beach, has 20 beach cottages and ten private pool suites. Secret Harbour Hotel (PO Box 11, St George's, Grenada; 444-4439/4548, telex 3425) at Mount Hartman Bay on the south coast combines considerable character with comfort. Other hotels are: Blue Horizons Cottage Hotel (4316); Calabash (PO Box 342, Grenada; 444-4334); Coral Cove (PO Box 187, Grenada; 444-4217/4422); Gem Apartments Hotel (Morne Rouge, Grenada; 444-4224/5536); Horseshoe Beach Hotel (PO Box 174, Grenada; 444.4410/4244); Hotel Coyaba (PO Box 336, St George's, Grenada; 444-4129, telex 3428); La Sagesse Nature Centre (PO Box 44, St David's, Grenada; 444-6458) and Ramada Rennaissance Hotel (PO Box 441, St George's, Grenada; 444-4371, telex 3468). On Carriacou accommodation is available at Cassada Bay Resort (PO Box 440, Grenada; 443-7494, telex:3425); Prospect Lodge (443-7380) and Silver Beach Resort (443-7337). A central reservations clearing house operates in New York, telephone (212) 840 6636 and Canada, (800) 468 0023.

Diving Centres: The HMC diving centre operates from the Ramada Renaissance and Coyaba Hotels. Further information is obtainable from Mosden Cumberbatch, HMC Dive Centre, c/o Ramada Renaissance, PO Box 441, St. George's, Grenada (444-4371; telex: 3468 GA). In Carriacou, the Carriacou Dive Centre, managed by Mario Bullen (443-7337; telex: 3425 GA) provides scuba facilities.

Marine Environment, General: Grenada and the Grenadines are on a submarine shelf known as the Grenadine Platform. Most of this is between 36 and 40m deep. Coral reefs are somewhat limited because of the depth, but are scattered around the coastline of the main islands, primarily along the sheltered areas where wave action and turbulence do not inhibit coral growth. Studies on corals occurring here indicate that *Acropora palmata*, *Porites porites*, *Montastraea annularis*, *Agaricia agaricia*, *P. astreoides* and *Siderastrea siderea* account for over 90 per cent of the coral cover.

Recommended Dive-Sites: Dive-sites are scattered along the north and east coast with a few also off the south coast. Carriacou also has extensive reefs off its east coast and offers some interesting diving, as do the other small islands of Petit Martinique and London Bridge (south of Ronde). A favourite diving site, just off Grenada's Grand Anse Beach, is the wreck of *Bianca C*, a luxury cruise liner of the Italian Costa line which caught fire and sank here in 1961. The wreck lies in relatively deep water, with the stern at 30m and the bows at 60m. Mosden Cumberbatch of the HMC Diving Centre on Grande Anse Beach is an experienced diver on this wreck and is available to guide divers.

Other Wildlife: Loggerhead, leatherback, hawksbill and green turtles nest on many beaches around Grenada and the Grenadines.

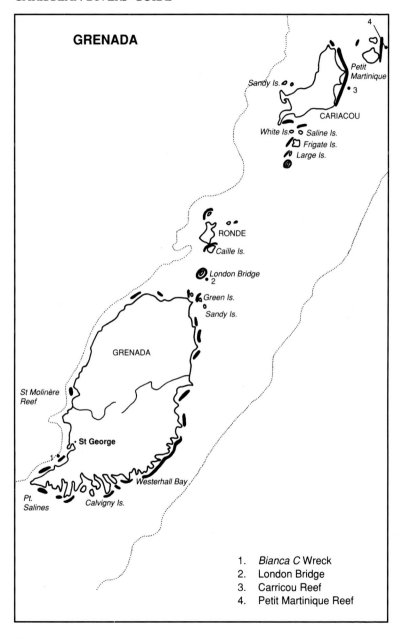

GRENADA

4

Petit
Martinique

Sandy Is.

• 3

CARIACOU

White Is. Saline Is.
Frigate Is.
Large Is.

RONDE

Caille Is.

London Bridge
2

Green Is.

Sandy Is.

GRENADA

St Molinère
Reef

St George

1 •

Westerhall Bay

Pt.
Salines   Calvigny Is.

1. *Bianca C* Wreck
2. London Bridge
3. Carricou Reef
4. Petit Martinique Reef

There is one endemic bird, the Grenada dove (*Leptotila wellsi*), related to, but distinct from, the grey-fronted dove. Birds endemic to the region of the Lesser Antilles are the Grenada flycatcher, scaly-breasted thrasher, Lesser Antillean bullfinch and several others.

Conservation Issues: Damage to reefs has been caused by visitors walking on corals and by the old practice of fishing with explosives. Recently however certain reef areas have been designated as protected areas. These are indicated on the map and include: 1. On Grenada: (a) Molinere Reef to St George's North; (b) Canoe Bay to Point Salines, St George's; (c) Calivigny Island to St George's; (d) Westerhall Bay to Southern Seascape; (e) La Sagesse to St. David's; (f) Conference Bay, Pearls to Northern Seascape, St Andrew's; and (g) Sugar loaf, Levera, Green Island and Sandy Island (St.Patrick's). 2. On Carriacou: (a) White Island, Saline Island and Frigate Island; (b) Sabayan; (c) Linlair Theboud; (d) Sandy Island and Mabouya; and (e) Tyrell Bay.

Legal Aspects: Beach Protection Ordinance (1955) establishes a framework for the legal protection of coastal sites.

3.15 : GUADELOUPE

Location: The twin islands of Grande Terre and Basse Terre, which together form the main landmass of Guadeloupe, lie almost due south of Antigua and north of Dominica (16°N, 62°W).

Physical Description: The archipelago of islands forming part of Guadeloupe are all administered as an overseas department of France. Despite their close proximity to each other Basse Terre (943 sq km) and Grande Terre (585sq.km), connected by a road bridge, differ markedly in their basic character, with the former comprising a volcanic, mountainous, rain-forested landmass, while the latter is a much lower limestone island where vegetation is more characteristic of semi-arid conditions with dry woodland and cactus scrub. There are a number of attractive beaches around the coast, especially along the south shores of Grande Terre. Mt Soufriere (1,484m) on Basse Terre is an active volcano whose occasional discharges of larva flow towards the south-west and south coasts of the island, affecting land and marinelife. In addition to the two larger islands the Guadeloupe group also includes the islands of Marie Galante, La Desirade and the Saintes Archipelago.

Climate: Rainfall on Basse-Terre (over 7,500mm) is considerably higher than that on Grande-Terre (800-1,500mm). Humidity is relatively high in summer and temperatures are average for this part of the Caribbean (around 28°C). Prevailing winds are from the east. On the periphery of the hurricane belt.

Electricity Supply: 220 volts at 50 cycles.

Visitor Accommodation: (See also Diving Centres). The major hotels offering diving facilities to their guests are as follows: Arawak Hotel (BP 396, Guadeloupe, French West Indies; 590-842424); Auberge de la Distillerie (590-942591); Auberge de la Plongee-Chez Guy (BP

4, Guadeloupe, French West Indies; 590-988172, telex: 919436 GL); Bois Joli Hotel (590-995038, fax: 590-902187); Ecotel-Guadeloupe (590-842020, fax: 590-90218); Golf Marine Club (BP 26, Guadeloupe, French West Indies; La Marina, (590-886060, fax: 590-842626); Hotel Meridien St Francois (BP37, Guadeloupe, French West Indies; 590-884071, fax: 590-885100); L'Esperance (BP 1, Guadeloupe, French West Indies; 590-988663); L'Ilet de la Plage (590-842073, tlx:919174GL); La Creole Beach Hotel (BP 19, Guadeloupe, French West Indies; 590-842626, fax:590-902187); Le Coucou des Bois (590-954225); Novotel Fleur d'Epee (590-908149, ext 396); PLM Azur Marissol (590-908444); Relais Bleus de la Soufriere (590-902187, telex:919522); Relais du Moulin (590-882396); Salako Hotel (BP 8, Guadeloupe, French West Indies; 590-842222); Toubana (BP 63, Guadeloupe, French West Indies; 590-882578).

Diving Centres: Approximately 15 hotels on Guadeloupe offer scuba diving along with other watersports (see visitor accommodation list). In practice this probably means that one of the island's CMAS qualified diving instructors has a contract with the hotel to look after the diving interests of their guests. Aqua-Fari and International Club (590-842626, fax: 590-843804, telex: 919836) is headquartered at the Creole Beach Hotel, Pointe de la Verdure. This is convenient for access to the Cousteau Reserve and the Fajou Reef, and is run by CMAS, NAUI and PADI instructors. The diving organisation (equipped for around 30 divers) is actually co-owned by French diver Alain Verdonck and American diving enthusiast John Lehew. Apart from their main base at the Creole Beach Hotel they have a dive base on the beach at Pigeon Island, adjacent to an excellent diving area, and they run diving desks at several hotels including Hotel Arawak and Salako Hotel.

Two diving clubs or centres are situated on the beach at Malendure, opposite Pigeon Island. These are Chez Guy (590-988172, fax: 590-820296) and the Nautilus Club. While the former is probably the largest diving centre on the islands, catering for up to 50 divers, the latter is actually a private, non-commercial club. These two clubs are the main source of diving boats and facilities for the hotels. Les

Heures Saines (BP 1, Guadeloupe, French West Indies; 590-987017, fax: 590-902187) is a well equipped diving centre, catering for 25 divers, based at the old Club Med site at Deshaies. Centre Nautique on the small archipelago of Les Saintes, 15 minutes away by air from the main island, organises dives to several excellent sites around these tiny islands. Meridien Diving (BP 37, Guadeloupe, French West Indies; 590-885100, fax: 590-884071, telex: 919733), based at Hotel Meridien St Francois has facilities for up to 14 divers.

Marine Environment, General: Coral-reef development around Guadeloupe is somewhat limited, due to the destruction of shallow reefs by storms combined with terrestrial influences such as rainwater run-off and volcanic impact. Replacing coral on many shallow reefs are rich algal beds of Sargassum weed. The best-developed reefs around Basse Terre are in the sheltered bays formed by the adjacent main islands, the Grand and Petit Cul de Sac Marin, as well as off Goyave and Petit Bourg on the east coast of Basse Terre. Along the east coast of Grande Terre there are extensive calcareous algal reefs forming barriers whilst narrow fringing reefs occur along the south coast, between Pointe des Chateaux and Gosier. Whilst drop-offs do not occur around Grande Terre, there is a sharp increase in colourful marinelife at around 40m depth where one moves from an almost coral-free zone to a deeper more densely overgrown seabed where gorgonians add much colour to the seascape.

Recommended Dive Sites: Two popular dive-sites are inside the Grand Cul de Sac Marin which is considered to contain some of the best coral-reefs in the entire Lesser Antilles. The Cousteau Reserve is on L'Ilet Pigeon (Pigeon Island) one kilometre off the west coast of Basse Terre, opposite Malendure. Waters around these twin volcanic rocks are probably the most popular diving area in Guadeloupe. The windward side of the island is generally considered too rough for diving. If one wishes to visit an offshore location, somewhat off the usual bubble route, contact Aqua Fari at the Creole Beach Hotel which offers two-day diving excursions to the minute northerly islet of Fajou, tucked inside the Grand Cul de Sac Marin – the huge bay

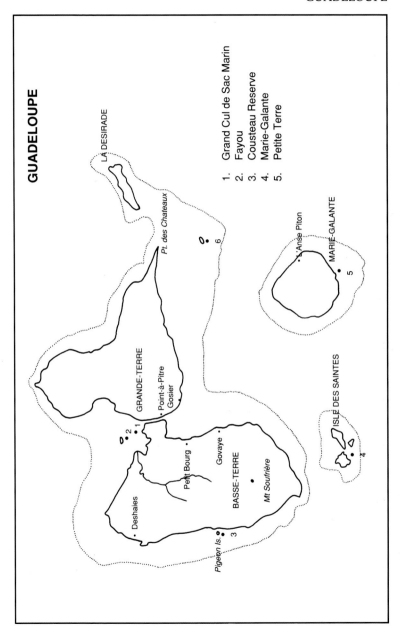

GUADELOUPE

1. Grand Cul de Sac Marin
2. Fayou
3. Cousteau Reserve
4. Marie-Galante
5. Petite Terre

LA DÉSIRADE

Pt. des Chateaux

GRANDE-TERRE

Point-à-Pître
Gosier

Anse Piton

MARIE-GALANTE

Deshaies

Petit Bourg

Govaye

BASSE-TERRE

Mt Soufrière

Pigeon Is.

ISLE DES SAINTES

separating Grande Terre and Basse Terre. Other island dive sites are off the south side of the two main islands, at the almost round Marie-Galante (reached by boat from Pointe-a-Pitre) and at the tiny Petite Terre. Diving around Les Saintes, due south of Basse Terre, organised by Club Nautique, based there, is very rewarding.

Special Interest: Many iguanas on the smaller islands.

Other Wildlife: Mangroves and sea-grasses form important coastal habitats around Guadeloupe. Small islets within the lagoon of the Grand Cul de Sac Marin provide nesting sites for the magnificent frigate-bird, the white-tailed tropic-bird and the cattle egret. Guadeloupe woodpecker is endemic to the island. The island and its surrounding waters are important for breeding seabirds, including Audubon's shearwater, the red-billed tropic-bird, the white-tailed tropic-bird, the brown booby, the laughing gull, the roseate tern, the bridled tern, the sooty tern and the brown noddy.

Conservation Issues: Dredging, sand-mining, coastal development, fishing and various other activities threaten the delicate reefs of Guadeloupe which appear unable to withstand much pressure. Turtles and their eggs have traditionally been harvested locally.

Legal Aspects: Guadeloupe, as an overseas department of France, shares its legislation. Legislation to protect leatherback turtles, turtle eggs, berried lobsters and crayfish (spiny lobsters) under 14cms, together with live corals, is already enacted (No. 79-6, AD/3/3, of April 1979).

Medical Facilities: Recompression facilities are available in Guadeloupe.

3.16 : HAITI

Location: Primarily occupying the western third of the big island of Hispaniola (shared with the Dominican Republic), Haiti also includes a number of offshore islands.

Physical Description: Haiti's exceptionally rugged terrain, with mountains reaching 2,674m, make much of its territory virtually inaccessible. While there undoubtedly remains much to be discovered about its terrestrial wildlife, its marine ecology is also poorly investigated. Sadly, much of the original rain-forest has been destroyed by indiscriminate harvesting for firewood, causing depletion of topsoil. The country's 1,500km coastline has some spectacular views and several beautiful beaches, but many of these are quite difficult to reach.

Climate: Weather in Haiti depends upon altitude with relatively low rainfall (less than 300mm) in the north-west, and high precipitation (over 4,000mm) in the mountainous south-west. The driest months, December to March, coincide with the tourist season.

Electricity Supply: 110-120 volts at 60 cycles.

Visitor Accommodation: The status of Haitian hotels is in a state of flux at present. One of the best places (when it is operating) is Club Mediterranée's Magic Isle (12-5131) situated at Montrouis, on one of the most attractive beaches in Haiti.

Diving Centres: Ibo Beach (17-1200), on Caique Island, runs a dive-boat and rents equipment to guests, but it is recommended to check the status of diving facilities before arriving. Kaliko Beach Resort (12-5773) is at La Gonave Bay, approximately one hour's drive from Port-au-Prince, and adjacent to a beach where diving facilities are available. Ouanga Bay Hotel (12-5774) is popular with some scuba diving groups and has recently been used as a base by an Italian dive tour operator.

Marine Environment, General: Very little information is available on the marinelife of Haiti. We do know that the destruction of mountain forests there has led to increased run-off from the land which, in turn, has greatly increased the turbidity of some inshore waters, damaging coral-reefs. Additionally, Haiti has long engaged in the collection and export of live corals and shells, causing severe damage to some reefs in the Bay of Gonave. Hawksbill turtles are also collected for their shells. In short, marinelife has a relatively poor chance of flourishing in those areas which are accessible to local people. There are however some encouraging signs of change with local people themselves showing an interest in conservation and pressure mounting to create some marine reserves at suitable locations such as the small islands of Les Arcadines.

Recommended Dive-Sites: Although little information is available, the main diving locations are as follows: along the north coast of Ile-a-Vache; around Les Isles Cayemites and the Baie des Baraderes; at the south-east tip of La Gonave; off Sand Key and Les Irois in Port au Prince Bay; at Pointe Pathron, off Les Arcadines; a short distance north-west of Gonaives; and, in calm weather, along the exposed north coast, on either side of Cap-Haitien. A recent survey carried out by USAID, recommended that marineparks be created at Morne Rouge and Ile-a-Vache.

Special Interest: There have been a number of diving expeditions to Haiti in search of Columbus's flagship, the *Santa Maria*, which sank in these waters.

Other Wildlife: This is an important area for breeding seabirds, with twelve species nesting within the region. Green, loggerhead and hawksbill turtles all nest on mainland beaches and at small offshore islands.

Conservation Issues: The protection of marinelife in Haitian waters has received little serious attention and several areas of reef have suffered considerable damage.

Legal Aspects: A decree dated 1978 and a subsequent law passed in 1979 deal with marinelife and fishery resources. The administrative body responsible for overseeing the protection of land and marine wildlife is the Service Protection Environnement et Faune of the Direction des Ressources Naturelles.

Medical Facilities: No recompression chamber is available on Haiti. There is a relatively high incidence of Aids.

1. Morne Rouge
2. Ile-a-Vache
3. Les Isles Cayemites
4. Bay des Baraderes
5. La Gonave
6. Pointe Pathron
7. Les Irois
8. Gonaives
9. Cap Haitien

HAITI

ILE DE LA TORTUE

Cap-Haitien

• Gonaives

LA GONAVE

HAITI

• Port-au-Prince

Jacmel

Les Cayes

3.17 : HONDURAS

Location: Occupying that bulge in the neck of land separating North and South America, Honduras possesses an extensive coastline bordering the Caribbean (together with a short stretch of Pacific shoreline), and a number of offshore islands: Cayos Cochinos; Isle de Utila; Roatan; Barbareta; Guanaja and Islas del Cisne (Swan Island). Since virtually all diving tourism to Honduras focuses on the Bay Islands, especially Roatan and the nearby reefs, this account also refers primarily to this location.

Physical Description: Roatan and the other Bay Islands, Utila and Guanaja, are on the edge of a deep ocean trench, along the Bonacca ridge. The undulating island of Roatan (area 12,740ha) lies approximately 96km offshore. Surrounding waters, peppered with small sand cays and islets, are deep, clear and rich in marinelife.

Climate: Average rainfall is around 2,000mm per year, with most precipitation occuring in the autumn. East or south-easterly trade winds blow fairly consistently, moderating air temperatures within the range 25°C to 30°C.

Electricity Supply: 110 volts at 60 cycles.

Visitor Accommodation and Diving Centres: For current information contact Honduras Tourist Board, c/o Honduras Embassy, 115 Gloucester Place, London W1H 3BJ (UK: 01 486 4880). During recent years there have been some major tourism developments on Roatan, catering for growing numbers of divers. One of the most recent of these is on Fantasy Island (504-45-1222), a private 15 acre island linked to the south shore of Roatan by a bridge. It is an entirely self contained resort with 39 luxury rooms and additional standard rooms under construction at the time of writing. The resort offers a high standard of comfort and all facilities which visiting divers may require, including two 12m dive-boats.

The Reef House Resort, Roatan (PO Box 40331, Roatan, Honduras; 512 681 2888, telex: 78229) is a 16-room traditional base for divers visiting Roatan and is the longest established of the present ten diving centres on the Bay Islands, being constructed in 1965. It offers both shore and boat dives and is well managed. In order of size, starting with the largest, Bay Island resorts are: Anthony's Key Resort, Roatan (US callers: (800) 227-DIVE; 305-858-DIVE, fax: 305-858-5020) built in 1969, 50 rooms and four 13m boats; Fantasy Island Resort, Roatan (US callers: (800) 451-4398, 404-953-2944, fax: 404-859-0250) mentioned above, opened in 1989, presently 39 rooms and three 9m boats; Posada del Sol, on Guanaja (US callers: (800) 642-DIVE, 407-624-DIVE, fax: 407-627-0225) built in 1979, 24 rooms and three boats in the 13m range; Coco View Resort, Roatan (US callers: (800) 451-4398, 404-953-2944, fax: 904-588-4158), built in 1983, with 20 rooms and three dive boats from 13m to 15m; Romeo's Resort (Brick Bay, Roatan, Bay Islands, Honduras; 504-45-11-27, fax: 504-45-15-94) built in 1987, also with 20 rooms and three 13m boats; Baymans Bay Club on Guanaja (US callers: (800) 524-1823, 305-525-8413, fax: 407-627-0225), built in 1974, with 16 rooms and two 9m boats; the Reef House resort mentioned above, built in 1965, also with 16 rooms and a single 11m dive boat; the Buccaneer Inn (504-45-1032), built in 1974, with 15 rooms, and two dive boats, 6m and 9m long; Sunrise Hotel, Roatan (US callers: (800) 635-7049, in Honduras: 504-451-265), built in 1985, with 12 rooms and a 9m dive boat; and finally the Plantation Beach Resort on Cayos Cochinos (US callers: (800) 628-3723, fax: 904-641-5285) built in 1977, with 9 rooms and two quite large dive-boats, around 12 to 14m in length.

Live-aboards include the Amethyst (US callers: 409-835-3400); Bay Islands Aggressor (US callers: (800) 348-2628); Isla Mia (US callers: (800) 334-4088) and the Ocean Spirit (US callers: (800) 338-3483). The MV Isla Mia is based at French Harbour Yacht Club, (Roatan, Bay Islands, Honduras, 504-45-1478).

Marine Environment, General: The combination of deep, clear water, good water exchange, high light penetration and hard substrata, have resulted in flourishing coral-reefs around Roatan and the adjacent islands. An extensive barrier and fringing reef system, reminiscent of Belizean reefs, provides endless possibilities for diving and underwater exploration.

Recommended Dive-Sites: Roatan's excellent diving has earned it an impressive reputation among well travelled divers. Its reefs, forming well developed spur and groove systems, are fascinating to swim among, creating numerous caves, and tunnels, all of which harbour rich invertebrate and fish life. There are numerous dive sites, each basically comprising a shallow coral-garden followed, at around 20-25m, by a steep drop-off or sloping coral wall. Along the south coast of Roatan there are several sheltered bays and lagoons where conditions are excellent. Regularly visited sites include Mary's Place named after local diver Tino Monterosso's wife. It lies just east of Fantasy Island and is marked by a permanent mooring. The reef is split into a long narrow channel with several side fissures, all of which are great to swim through, taking care not to damage reeflife. Other sites in Tino Monterosso's itinerary include Insidious Reef and its associated Enchanted Forest, Calvin's Crack, Parrot Point Drop-Off and Carib Bight.

Special Interest: Ancient Mayan ruins at Copan on mainland. Parrots on some islands.

Medical Facilities: Take protection from insects, especially biting sand flies. Nearest recompression chamber is at Roatan, Anthony's Key Resort.

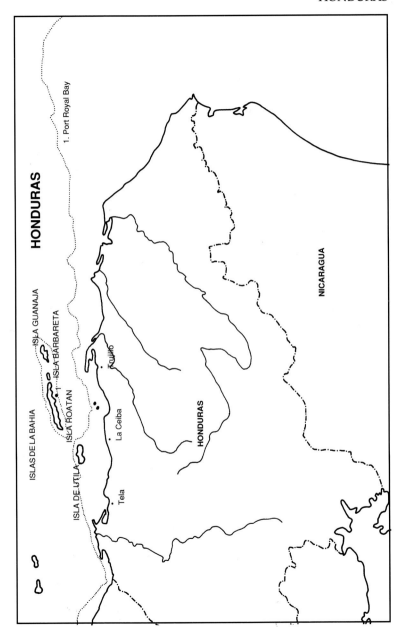

HONDURAS

1. Port Royal Bay

ISLAS DE LA BAHIA

ISLA GUANAJA

ISLA BÁRBARETA

ISLA ROATAN

ISLA DE UTILA

Trujillo

La Ceiba

Tela

HONDURAS

NICARAGUA

3.18 : JAMAICA

Location: 18°N 77°W. Jamaica lies 150km south of Cuba, south-east of the Caymans and south-west of Haiti. It is closer to the geographic centre of the Caribbean than are any of the other islands forming this unique, semi-enclosed sea.

Physical Description: Jamaica is a large (10,962sq km) mountainous (maximum height over 2,000m) island bordered, on its northern side, by a very narrow shelf followed by precipitous drop-offs into the Cayman Trench, reaching over 7km in depth. The southern shores are more gently inclined, across a broad, relatively shallow platform. The eastern portion of the island is dominated by the Blue Mountains whilst the western area is lower.

Climate: Cool in the mountains and warm at the coast, Jamaica offers a variety of climates, depending upon location. The rainy months are May and October. Winds are predominantly north-easterly, with occasional hurricanes from July to October. The coldest months are January and February, the warmest July and August. In the winter season (15 December to 30 April) there is a chance of 'Northerns', northerly winds and rough seas which put a temporary halt to diving activities for one or two days.

Electricity Supply: The electricity supply in Jamaica varies between 110 volts and 220 volts, depending upon location. In most tourist locations it will be 110 volts and will have American type plugs.

Visitor Accommodation:
Ochos Rios area: Club Caribbean, (PO Box 65, Runaway Bay, Jamaica; 973-3509), serviced by: Sundivers Jamaica (PO Box 212, Runaway Bay Jamaica; 973-2346), Shaw Park Beach Hotel, (974-2522/4), serviced by Sea and Dive Jamaica (74 Main Street, Ochos Rios, Jamaica; 974-5762); Sea Palms (US contact: (212).953-7910), serviced by

Fantasea Divers (PO Box 103, Ochos Rios, Jamaica; 974-2353); Marine View Club (974-2822), serviced by Garfield Diving Station (PO Box 394, Ochos Rios, Jamaica; 974-2822).

Montego Bay area: Chalet Caribe Hotel (PO Box 365, Montego Bay, Jamaica; 952-1364/5) is well situated next to some of the best diving in Montego Bay and is a popular venue for divers. It is serviced by Poseidon Nemrod Divers (PO Box 152, Reading, St James, Jamaica; 952-3624). These operators have another facility at the hotel strip in Montego Bay and can offer divers a selection of hotels and villas including: Chalet Caribe Hotel, Round Hill, Unity Hall Resorts, Gloucester House, Fantasea Resort, Seawind, Caribic House.

Cariblue Hotel, (PO Box 610, Montego Bay, Jamaica; 953-2022); Wyndham Rosehall Beach Hotel and Country Club (PO Box 999, Montego Bay, Jamaica; USA contact: (800) 822-4200), and Jack Tar Montego Beach Hotel, an all inclusive resort, are all serviced by Sea World (PO Box 610, Montego Bay, Jamaica; 953-2180).

Sandals, located in Montego Bay, Ochos Rios and Negril is an all inclusive resort where one dive a day or an introductory scuba course is included in the package. Half Moon Resort and Golf Club in Montego Bay (953-2211) is a self contained resort with its own diving centre.

Negril area: Hedonism II, (PO Box 25, Negril; 957-4200), an all inclusive resort with one dive per day or an introductory scuba lesson is included in the package; Negril Beach Club (957-4323) serviced by Negril Scuba Centre, (957-4425); Negril Tree House (PO Box 29, Negril, Jamaica; (809. 957-4287), serviced by Blue Whale Divers (957-4438); Rock Cliff Resort (957-4331), with spacious comfortable villas with air conditioning and all rooms overlooking the sea, serviced by Sundivers Jamaica (957-4331).

Diving Centres: Most of the diving centres in Jamaica are along the north or west coasts. In Jamaica all dives from diving centres are guided and visitors may not hire gear from them unless it is to partake in a guided dive supervised by the centre. Similarly, scuba tanks cannot be filled by centres unless it is for a dive guided by that particular centre. This is a safety regulation which is adhered to by all members of the Jamaica Association of Dive Operators (JADO). Most visiting divers are not familiar with the water conditions and in order to ensure the safety of divers this regulation has been in effect for several years and is endorsed by the Jamaica Tourist Board. This organisation has played an important role in organising the industry and has instituted a licencing system based on international standards.

Poseidon Nemrod Divers, run by Theo and Hannie Smit, is situated at Reading, St James (PO Box 152, Reading, St James, Jamaica; 952-3624). This is a PADI affiliated diving school established in 1980 and operating with a staff of six plus a 9m dive boat which carries a maximum of six divers. Courses run from introductory level to assistant instructor and include several specialities. The centre operates from two locations, Chalet Caribe Hotel (10km from Montego Bay) and Marguerite's (on the hotel strip in Montego Bay), offering the best sites on the north coast, including some shore-based wall-dives. The centre has a strict rule against divers taking any form of marinelife while diving.

Negril Scuba Centre (957-4425), situated at Negril Beach Club, is run by Karen McCarthy and operates under PADI. It specialises in a personalised service for small diving groups (up to 20 divers) and offers beginners courses, open water and advanced certification. Night diving with the Negril Scuba Centre is an especially rewarding experience.

Sundivers Jamaica (973-2346), also at Negril, and based at the Rock Cliff, claims to be Jamaica's only PADI 5-star instructor development centre. It offers resort courses, certification for beginners and instructors, and specialities including deep diver, night diver, photographer, underwater research, navigation and search and recovery. Guided boat dives are run daily with 20 pre-selected dive sites close to the shore.

Marine Environment, General: Sea surface temperatures range from 24°C in January to 29.8°C in July. Tides are somewhat irregular with an amplitude varying between 20cm and 36cm. The main drift is to the west. Reefs along the north coast are rich in invertebrates, varied in form and quite dramatic in appearance. The existence of Discovery Bay Marine Laboratory on the north coast has helped to promote many investigations of marinelife along these shores and I recall with great pleasure a visit to the laboratory and a dive off its shores, soon after the discovery there by the late Professor Tom Goreau of a new class of sponge. Goreau's infectious enthusiasm for Jamaica's fascinating marinelife contributed greatly to the growth of diving tourism in these waters, not to mention the tremendous contributions he made to marine science.

Discovery Bay itself remains one of the most interesting diving areas along the north coast of Jamaica (although it is not directly served by a commercial diving centre). There are within its boundaries a number of different marine communities, from shallow and rich marine grass beds to deep and fascinating sponge communities. Indeed, not far off Columbus Park, there is a sponge bed, at around 20m, in which some of the specimens are as large as a bath-tub! Sadly, Hurricane Allan, which struck this region in 1980, did extensive damage to large sections of Jamaica's reefs, particularly in the Columbus Park area. Beyond the reef which runs across the entrance of the bay, underwater visibility is exceptionally clear and the reef-face is rich in corals and sponges. The unusual sclerosponges occur in shaded crevices in shallow depths, or out on the rock face in deeper water.

Recommended Dive-Sites: Diving conditions along the north coast of Jamaica are some of the best in the Caribbean. The Montego Bay Marine Park is a major centre for divers with guided snorkelling parties plus at least three scuba-diving centres using the area. 'The buttress zone of the reef, with its combination of walls, canyons and tunnels, together with a rich fauna of corals and fish, provides particularly exciting snorkelling and shallow scuba-diving. The fore-reef escarpment with its precipitous drop-offs forms an ideal dive site for experienced divers'. (Wells, S.: IUCN, 1988). A series of shoredives, accessible from the jetty at Chalet Caribe Hotel include the following: Hannie's Fish-feeding Station which has been established since 1981 as a local reserve where hand-feeding of reef-fish is encouraged; Canyon 1 which is a cave with its entrance at 9m and its exit at 21m – on the cave walls one can see the rare sclerosponge first discovered by the late Professor Tom Goreau; Canyon 2, alongside Canyon 1, with a narrow tunnel where crayfish are often seen and where a nurse shark sometimes rests; Black Coral Rock, a relatively deep promontory of coral rock rising from around 30m to about 20m, and covered with black corals, sponges, gorgonians and surrounded by fish; The Window and Duppy's Hole, consisting of a short tunnel, entered at 18m, ending in a small cave – one exits up to the shallow reef through a vertical chimney; The Arena, so named because the configuration of reef around the sandy patch is reminiscent of a Roman arena; Pillar Coral Reef, dominated by large upright stands of pillar-coral; The Classroom, a shallow dive, 6 to 9m, often used for examining divers. Boat dive sites from the same base include Wintergarden which is an 24 to 27m wall dive featuring large pale gorgonians. Nearby is Sponge Plunge, another deep wall-dive featuring many large sponges.

Poseidon Divers run the following series of boat dives from Marguerite's in Montego Bay: Widowmakers Cave, with an entrance on the wall at 24m and an exit via chimney to the shallow reef; Basket Reef where the wall drops sheer from 15 to 45m and where many basket sponges occur; Old Airport Reef, which is a shallow pretty dive; The Point, where the wall drops away from 18 to 61m and where a current sweeps along at 2 knots, carrying experienced divers on a magnificent drift dive; Doctor's Cave Reef, which is essentially a beginners' dive on a shallow sheltered reef; and finally No name Reef, which offers an interesting dive at around 12m.

Other sites include the coast at Negril, by boat from Negril Scuba Centre and in Discovery Bay and off fringing reef outside the bay.

Special Interest: The supposed site of Columbus's landing on Jamaica is at Columbus Park, on the west side of Discovery Bay. Jamaica, unlike many dive locations in the Caribbean, has an interesting variety of post dive activities including river-rafting, climbing the waterfalls, visits to 'Great Houses' and other historic sites. There are caves to explore together with plenty of wild countryside

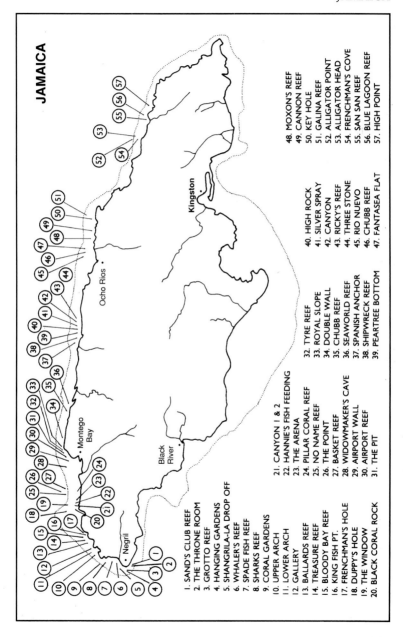

JAMAICA

Kingston

Ocho Rios

Montego Bay

Black River

Negril

1. SAND'S CLUB REEF
2. THE THRONE ROOM
3. GROTTO REEF
4. HANGING GARDENS
5. SHANGRILA-LA DROP OFF
6. WHALER'S REEF
7. SPADE FISH REEF
8. SHARKS REEF
9. CORAL GARDENS
10. UPPER ARCH
11. LOWER ARCH
12. GALLERY
13. BALLARDS REEF
14. TREASURE REEF
15. BLOODY BAY REEF
16. KING FISH PT.
17. FRENCHMAN'S HOLE
18. DUPPY'S HOLE
19. THE WINDOW
20. BLACK CORAL ROCK

21. CANYON I & 2
22. HANNIE'S FISH FEEDING
23. THE ARENA
24. PILLAR CORAL REEF
25. NO NAME REEF
26. THE POINT
27. BASKET REEF
28. WIDOWMAKER'S CAVE
29. AIRPORT WALL
30. AIRPORT REEF
31. THE PIT

32. TYRE REEF
33. ROYAL SLOPE
34. DOUBLE WALL
35. CHUBB REEF
36. SEAWORLD REEF
37. SPANISH ANCHOR
38. SHIPWRECK REEF
39. PEARTREE BOTTOM

40. HIGH ROCK
41. SILVER SPRAY
42. CANYON
43. RICKY'S REEF
44. THREE STONE
45. RIO NUEVO
46. CHUBB REEF
47. FANTASEA FLAT

48. MOXON'S REEF
49. CANNON REEF
50. KEY HOLE
51. GALINA REEF
52. ALLIGATOR POINT
53. ALLIGATOR HEAD
54. FRENCHMAN'S COVE
55. SAN SAN REEF
56. BLUE LAGOON REEF
57. HIGH POINT

(the Cockpit Country), trips to a rum manufacturing plant, visits to working plantations, tours to the south coast – all in all, too much for a single holiday!

Other Wildlife: Caribbean manatee (*Trichechus manatus*) and turtles (mostly green and hawksbill) are found around the coast. Jamaica has 25 endemic bird species. Seabird breeding colonies on Jamaica and associated islands are important. Among the locally breeding species are the white-tailed tropic-bird; the magnificent frigate-bird; the brown pelican; the laughing gull; the royal tern; the roseate tern; the bridled tern; the least tern and the brown noddy. Hawksbill, loggerhead and green turtles nest on Jamaica. The American crocodile occurs along the south coast, especially in the Black River Morass area.

Conservation Issues: Interest and activities in the conservation field in Jamaica are focussed and co-ordinated by the Jamaica Conservation and Development Trust (PO Box 1225, Kingston 8, Jamaica; 92-66878). Unfortunately the poor management of protected marine areas in Jamaica has led to the serious depletion of marinelife in those places where it should have been safe from Man's interference. The fact that a change for the better has occurred can be largely attributed to divers themselves – people such as Theo and Hannie Smit, keen divers and conservationists who arrived in Jamaica in 1980. One of their first actions was to protect the area in front of Chalet Caribe Hotel, thus creating an informal marine park. This, combined with other actions, resulted in the Marine Parks Action Committee being established. The development of interest led to a study sponsored by the Organisation of American States (OAS), on the feasibility of a Marine Park in Montego Bay. At the same time a Jamaica Conservation and Development Trust was the established leading to the establishment of a USAID study and the signing of an agreement between the USAID and the Jamaica Government for the establishment of two pilot projects for a national parks system of wildlife management. One of these is the John Crow National Park, located in the Blue Mountains, while the other is the expanded

Montego Bay Marine Park.

Since August 1989, the Montego Bay Marine Park has been reinstated and expanded as part of a national parks plan and at the time of writing a visitors' centre is planned and recruitment of a park manager and wardens was under discussion. Private initiative has led to a mooring programme in Montego Bay, reducing reef damage by diving boats.

Legal Aspects: The legal protection of marinelife around Jamaica has been in force since 1945 when the Wildlife Protection Law was passed, placing effective bans on harming or collecting black coral, marine turtles, iguanas, crocodiles and the Caribbean manatee. More recently, spiny lobsters have received partial protection. Montego Bay Marine Park enjoys its protection as a result of legislation passed in 1974 when the Beach Control (Protected Area) (Montego Bay) Order was passed under the Beach Control Law of 1955, and through its reinstatement which took place in August 1989. Ochos Rios Marine Park was legally instated by a similar local order passed in 1966, under the Beach Control Law. At the time of writing moves are afoot to ensure more effective enforcement of Jamaica's protective legislation. No amount of legislation will make much difference, however, if divers themselves do not take care, on every dive, to prevent any form of damage to the country's fragile reefs and wildlife.

Medical Facilities: There are hospitals in the major tourist areas and most of the larger hotels have a resident nurse. A recompression chamber for the diving community is situated at Discovery Bay Marine Laboratory.

3.19 : MARTINIQUE

Location: 14°45'N 60°55'W. The French island of Martinique forms part of the Windward Islands, and is situated roughly equidistant from Dominica to the north and St Lucia to the south.

Physical Description: Martinique is a volcanic island, 1,079sq.km in area, with the highest point formed by Mont Pelée (1,397m), an active volcano which towers over much of the island, providing a constant reminder of its dramatic eruption in 1902 when 40,000 people were killed. Columbus described the island, which he discovered in 1495, as 'the best, most fertile, most delightful and most charming land in the world'. Many of the beaches, forest reserves and protected marine habitats retain that unique allure which so captivated the early explorer.

Climate: Rain-forest still survives on Martinique where annual precipitation can reach 7,000mm in the mountains whereas it can be as low as 1,016mm in coastal regions. Most rain falls from May to November when humidity can be quite high. The prevailing winds are easterly trades and a stormy season affects the east coast in the first half of the year, while hurricanes may occur during the hurricane season in the latter half of the year. Summer temperatures, reaching 32°C at times, are generally moderated by easterly trade winds, and the mean annual temperature is 26°C.

Electricity Supply: 220 volts at 50 cycles.

Visitor Accommodation: There are a host of hotels and smaller guest houses on Martinique. Some recommended venues are: Bakoua Beach Hotel (596-660202, fax: 596-762287); La Bateliere Hotel (596-614949, fax: 596-616229); Novotel Diamant (596-764242, fax: 596-762287); Meridien Trois Islets (596-660000, fax: 596-660074, telex: 912641) and PLM Azur Carayou (596-660404). In addition, there are many other excellent hotels providing access to watersports including: Calalou Hotel (596-683178); Diamant-Les-Bains (596-764014) which faces Diamond Rock; the newly opened Imperatrice Village on the beach at Anse Mitan (phone 596-630682 for up-to-date information); La Dunette Hotel Sainte Anne (596-767390, fax: 596-606668) which is right on the beach; and Manoir de Beauregard (596-767340, fax: 596-736693).

Diving Centres: The following list of diving centres was submitted to this publication by the Department of Tourism of Martinique. Oxigene Bleue (contact Eric Bourgeois, BP 96, 97229 Trois-Ilets, Martinique, French West Indies, 596-577256); Planete Bleue (contact Pascale Pivette, Marina-Pointe du Bout, 97229 Trois-Ilets, Martinique, French West Indies, 596-660879); Sub Diamond Rock (contact Andre Aldea or his wife, Hotel Novotel Diamant, Pointe La Cherry, 97223 Diamant, Martinique, French West Indies, 596-764242; fax: 596-762287; telex: 912392); Tropica Sub, Hotel La Bateliere (contact Guy Lize, 97233 Schoelcher, Martinique, French West Indies; 596-614949; fax: 596-616229); Restaurant la Guinguette (97250 Saint-Pierre, Martinique, French West Indies, 596-771502); Histoires D'Eau (contact Madame Delourmel; BP 1, 97227 Sainte-Anne, Martinique, French West Indies); Bathy's Club (contact Christine Formisano, Hotel Meridien, Pointe du Bout, 97229 Trois-Ilets, Martinique, French West Indies, 596-660000; fax: 596-660074; telex: 912641); Evasion Caraibe (contact Joel Espinasse, 97228 Sainte-Luce, Martinique, French West Indies); UCPA, (contact Michel Metery, Piscine du Carbet, 97221 Carbet, Martinique, French West Indies).

A diving centre is under development at Presqu'ile de la Caravelle. Meridien Trois Ilets has one of the first Martinique diving centres on its premises, and their lead has been followed by most of the large hotels. A former hotel, Latitude, has been converted into a major diving centre, the Carib Scuba Club (596-780227, fax: 596-660074) which caters for around 20 divers. Bathy's Club (see above) provides scuba diving facilities for up to 30 divers at the Bakoua Beach Club, PLM Azur Carayou and Meridien Trois Ilets Hotel. Sub Diamond Rock (see above) at the Novotel Diamant has facilities for 22 divers. Tropica Sub Diving Centre (see previous) at the Hotel La Bateliere has facilities for 30 divers.

Marine Environment, General: Martinique experiences relatively high turbidity at inshore locations, often reducing visibility underwater. Tidal range is 70cm. Away from the shallows, however, visibility is frequently around 30m and there are several very interesting diving areas. Along the geologically younger northern and western coasts of the island there are few coral reefs and the seabed features almost vertical drop-offs together with considerable volcanic sedimentation. Prior to recent hurricanes the south and east coasts had quite well-developed shallow coral-reefs.

Recommended Dive-Sites: Rocher de la Perle off the north-west point is a volcanic pinnacle of rock which has an impressive covering of sponges, black corals and fan corals below 15m. It can be reached by driving to the end of the coast road of Precheur. Take care however for there is sometimes rough water with a strong current flowing between the shore and the rock. Along the north-west coast, corals in shallow water have been virtually eliminated by repeated hurricanes. Further down the west coast Cap Enragé and Baie de St Pierre are popular diving sites. Cap Enragé, or Angry Point, has large underwater caves, penetrating at least 18m into a submarine cliff. Within these shaded habitats are large schools of soldier-fish and numerous spiny lobsters. To the north of Cap Enragé, at St Pierre, divers can explore the wrecks of at least twelve ships caught off guard by the terrible volcanic eruption of Mont Pelée in 1902. Among them are an Italian yacht, a 50m sailing ship, several cargo ships, barges and a tug. An additional wreck, the *Dalia*, which sank in 1930, can be reached by a short swim from the town pier. For rich coral-growth one needs to dive off the south coast, particularly near Ste Luce. Rocher du Diamante, Diamond Rock, south of the small settlement of Le Diamante; Anse Arlets, just south of Cap Salomon, and La Grande Savane off Ste Anne are popular sites towards the south-west of Martinique. Sea-grass beds in sheltered bays along the easterly coast, south of Pte du Diable,

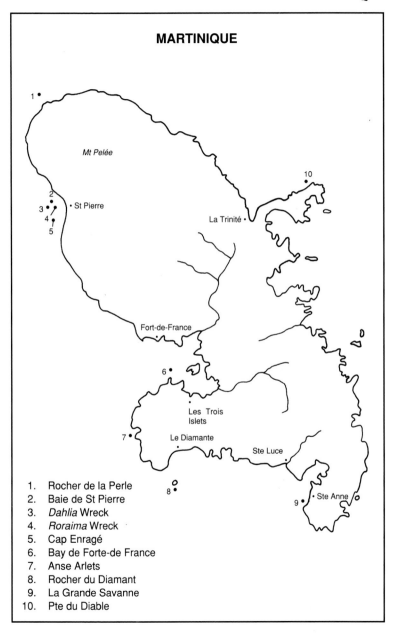

MARTINIQUE

1. Rocher de la Perle
2. Baie de St Pierre
3. *Dahlia* Wreck
4. *Roraima* Wreck
5. Cap Enragé
6. Bay de Forte-de France
7. Anse Arlets
8. Rocher du Diamant
9. La Grande Savanne
10. Pte du Diable

reported to cover 10,000ha, are also worth a dive since they are largely undisturbed. The southern portion of Baie de Fort-de-France, where visibility is not great but where marinelife is quite prolific, is also worth a look. There are a number of wreck dives, such as the Roraima, off St Pierre.

Other Wildlife: Among Martinique's birdlife is an island endemic, the Martinique oriole which lives in forests up to 550m above sealevel.

Conservation Issues: Over-fishing has caused an almost total collapse of the queen conch population and edible fish have also been greatly reduced in numbers. Marine turtles are heavily exploited, for their eggs, their meat and their shells. The loss of fringing mangroves has been largely responsible for the increased coastal turbidity with its subsequent effect on shallow-water corals and other marinelife.

Legal Aspects: A closed season for lobster fishing extends from October to March.

Medical Facilities: There is a recompression chamber on Martinique.

3.20 : MEXICO – YUCATAN PENINSULA

Location: While Mexico itself is a large country, taking the giant's share of the land bridge between North and South America, and occupying huge tracts of the Pacific (6,760km) and Atlantic/Caribbean/Gulf of Mexico (2,900km) shorelines, from the viewpoint of Caribbean divers, all the interest focuses on one small portion, forming the western boundary of the Caribbean proper: the eastern coastline and islands of the Yucatan Peninsula. This account restricts itself to dealing with this area. The island of Cozumel , 48km by 16km (20°N, 87°W) lies 13km east of the Yucatan coast.

Physical Description: Cozumel is a low-lying coral island, surrounded by what have been described as some of the best diving areas in the world.

Climate: Annual rainfall averages around 1,100-2,000mm in the south, with much less, around 700mm, in the north. Most precipitation occurs from June to October. Hurricanes may hit the area between August and October. Cozumel has a warm, semihumid climate

Electricity Supply: 110 volts at 60 cycles.

Visitor Accommodation: A major centre is at Cancun, where all tourist hotels offer diving facilities. Club Méditerranée is at Punta Nizuc. Scuba Cancun (PO Box 517, Cancun, Q.Roo, Mexico 77500, 988-3-10-11 and in evenings: 4-23-36) is described as the only PADI 5-star training facility in Cancun. It is a NAUI Dream Resort with recompression chamber on premises. The Club Caribe Hotel at Akumal, approximately 100km south of Cancun, also has a PADI diving centre (c/o Kaapalua Dive Shop, PO Box 13326, El Paso, Texas 79913). On Cozumel the Galapagos Inn Dive Resort (529-872-0663) is a beachfront hotel close to town and caters for diving groups or individual divers. This is not a complete listing and the regular diving press carries numerous classified advertisements for villas or apartments available for divers to rent.

Diving Centres: There are many professionally operated diving centres on Cozumel which is the focal point for divers. Agua Tours SA Cancun (30227; US contact: (011) 529 883 0403) caters for diving groups. Ramon Zapata Novelo arranges the hire of diving equipment at the Park Nacional Chankanaab on Cozumel. Sun Tours operate the triple-decker *B/M Carnaval Cancun* which takes visitors to Isla Mujere from Playa Linda pier The Akumal Dive Shop (contact Dick Blanchard, PO Box 1, Playa Del Carmen, QR, Mexico 77710) has 4 diving instructors and is affiliated to PADI, NAUI and SSI. In Cabo San Lucas the longest established diving centre is Amigos del Mar-Baja (PO Box 43, Cabo San Lucas, BCS, Mexico; 213-546-1447) which is affiliated to PADI, NAUI, CMAS, and FMAS. This centre offers diving tours to Gordo Banks and Cabo Pulmo. Also on Cabo are Cabo Divers (PO Box 61,Cabo San Lucas, BCS, Mexico, 706-843-0747) where a PADI certified instructor and other diving facilities are available.

Marine Environment, General: This eastern seaboard of Yucatan also forms a key segment of the western limits of the Caribbean proper. Circulatory currents within the tropical sea result in some upwelling currents along the shoreline, replenishing nutrients and bringing colder water to the surface. Semidiurnal tides occur. A major fringing/barrier coral-reef system borders the northern segment of the east coast of Yucatan, stretching for approximately 350km, from the north-easterly cape to Tulum.

The main area which divers head for is around the island of Cozumel. This is something of a conservation success story since although the island has been popular for several decades, the reefs began to deteriorate quite seriously in the 1970s, primarily as a result of uncontrolled spearfishing together with commercial coral collecting. The declaration of Cozumel's reefs as a marine reserve in 1980 has brought about a marked revival in their condition, supporting a flourishing diving tourism industry.

Recommended Dive-Sites: Four major diving areas exist off the Caribbean coast of Mexico:

• *Akumal*: A large barrier reef skirts this 16km long palm-fringed beach west of Cozumel and south of Cancun. The best diving locations are at the Hotel Villa Maya Bungalows; off Club Akumal; near the Akumal Caribe Hotel; and close to Hotel Capitan Lafitte. The waters have 60m visibility and are warm throughout the year. At Xel-Ha Lagoon, a wildlife refuge just south of Akumal, there is a deep rock-surrounded inlet of exceptionally clear water – a favourite location for snorkellers.

• *Cancun*: Along the north-east portion of Yucatan peninsula there are some important diving areas, with the centre of activity at Cancun which has considerable accommodation for visiting divers. It is perfectly situated for swimming and diving among coral-reefs abounding with life. All the larger hotels maintain boat centres with equipment for hire and organised diving trips available. The Xcaret inlet, surrounded by jungle, and the site of various caves and ruins of Mayan civilisation, is an outstanding setting for scuba diving. Sites around nearby Isla Mujeres (see below), such as Los Manchones, Cuevons, Bandera and El Garrafon are favourite venues for divers based in Cancun.

• *Cozumel*: The real 'jewel in the crown' of Mexican diving is the island of Cozumel and its surrounding reefs. Here one may find dramatic drop-offs, exhilarating walls and vertigo-inducing water clarity! The best known and most popular dive site is Palancar Reef, which lies about 1.5km off the island and extends in a line parallel with the shore for about 4.5km. Both here and at the more southerly reef of Colombia, the drop-offs are superb but are for experienced divers only, since they involve fairly deep diving in the 30-45m range. Maracaibo Reef and its drop-off lies off the southern tip of Cozumel, starting at 36m the seabed plunges vertically, far beyond the limits of compressed-air scuba diving. Other sites around Cozumel include Paraiso reef and the airliner wreck which lies at its northern extremity, La Ceiba, Chankanaab, Tormentos, Yocab, Tunich, San Francisco, Cardona, La Francesca, Herradura, Barracuda and Ladrillas reefs. The prime diving season is May-Septem-

MEXICO (YUCATAN PENINSULA AND ISLANDS)

1. Chinchorro and Los Manchones
2. Akumel:
   a) Hotel Villa Maya Bungalows
   b) Club Akumal
   c) Hotel Capitan Lafitte
   d) Xel-Ha Lagoon
3. Cozumal:
   a) Palancar Reef
   b) Columbia
   c) Maracaibo Reef
   d) Paraco Reef
   e) Airliner Wreck
   f) La Ceiba
   g) Chankanaab
   h) Tormentos
   i) Yocab
   j) Tunich

k) San Francisco
l) Cardona
m) La Francesca
n) Herradura
o) Barracuda
p) Ladrillas Reefs
q) Chancanab Lagoon

4. Cancun
5. Xcaret
6. Isla Mukeres:
   a) Los Manchones
   b) Cuevons
   c) Bandera
   d) El Garrafon Underwater Park

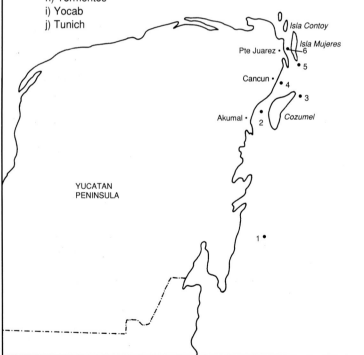

ber and daily trips to Palancar are arranged from Aqua Safari. Another favourite dive site is Chancanab Lagoon, a sheltered body of water which has a very abundant fish population. Currents can be quite strong and it is recommended to use dive guides. Virtually all the larger hotels cater for divers or will provide the necessary information on local facilities.

• *Isla Mujares*: The clear waters of the coral-reefs and lagoons around these islands are renowned among scuba-divers worldwide. Divers may visit El Garrafon Underwater Park. Ferries leave for the island from Puerto Juarez eight times daily, and from Punta Sam four times daily. The local dive base, Gustavo's Mexico Divers, rents boats and equipment. Garrafon Beach has very clear water and some attractive shallow-water coral-gardens.

• *Chinchorro and Los Manchones*: Four- to six-day diving trips depart from Cancun to Banco Chinchorro which lies about 24km off the coast of eastern Yucatan, between Xcalak and El Ubero. Garden eels are locally abundant in the lagoons, as well as queen conches, and fish are plentiful. This is also an area with abundant shipwrecks. Los Manchones Reef is popular with scuba divers whilst Isla Contoy has some well-developed shallow reefs accessible to snorkel divers.

Special Interest: The gorgonian (*Plexaura homomalla*) is being harvested off the coast of Qintana Roo for use in medical research, as it has been found to be an important source of prostaglandins. There is a major black-coral industry on Cozumel, with over 500 black coral carvers employed to make jewellery and ornaments from the polished skeletal remains of the deep-water black coral. There are numerous old and not so old shipwrecks in Mexico's Caribbean waters, particularly around Xel-Ha and Akumal. Underwater exploration of the latter area has produced many finds from Mexico's early colonial period.

Other Wildlife: On Cozumel there are three small mammals endemic to it: the pygmy raccoon (*Procyon pygmaeus*) which is relatively common among mangroves, the coati (*Nasua nelsoni*) and the jabali (*Reithrodontomys spectabilis*). The Caribbean manatee (*Trichechus* *manatus*) may also be present on Cozumel and is certainly found along the east coast of Yucatan. Among birds, there are two endemic species, the Cozumel thrasher (*Toxostoma guttatum*) and the Cozumel vireo (*Vireo bairdi*). Among seabirds, one may see magnificent frigate-birds, brown boobies, brown pelicans, laughing gulls, brown noddies, sandwich terns, sooty terns, little terns and the olivaceous cormorants. Loggerhead, hawksbill, green and leatherback turtles nest on Cozumel.

Conservation Issues: Diving tourism and the attendant development of land-based tourism facilities is placing coastal marinelife under increased pressure. Dependence upon black corals to supply the carvers on Cozumel has inevitably led to a depletion of black coral in moderate depths.

Legal Aspects: The value of Cozumel's magnificent marinelife as a tourism attraction was recognised some years ago and a large protected area was designated in 1980. 'This extends from the International Pier south to Punta Celerain at the southern tip of the island, between high tide mark and the 50m isobath'. (IUCN, Wells,S., 1988). Diving tourism is so important to the area that moves are afoot to create one large protected area out of the whole island of Cozumel and its surrounding reefs.

3.21 : MONTSERRAT

Location: 16°45'N, 62°10'W. A small (approx. 100sq. km) volcanic island, forming part of the Leeward Islands, roughly halfway between Nevis and St Kitts to the north-west, and Guadeloupe to the south-east. Antigua is its nearest neighbour to the north-east, 43kms away. The coastline consists of steep promontory cliffs interspersed with sheltered coves and a few, fairly inaccessible white sand beaches, together with others of grey-brown volcanic sand. The island is surrounded by deep water, with depths of 90m within a few hundred metres of the shore at the southern end of the island.

Physical Description: An emerald green island sitting in azure-blue water, Montserrat is one of the most attractive islands of the Caribbean. Although hurricanes have removed most of the primary rain-forest, regeneration has produced secondary rain-forest.

Climate: Tropical, with relatively low humidity. Temperatures rarely fluctuate much more than 5°C from the means, which range from 24°C in January to 28°C in September, with an annual mean of 26°C. There is an average of eight hours of sunshine each day. It is on the hurricane belt, which may affect the island from June to November. Rainfall varies, with a mean on the west coast of 1070mm and in the mountains of 2050mm. The wettest months are between June and January.

Electricity Supply: 220-240 volts at 60 cycles.

Visitor Accommodation: The Vue Point Hotel has scuba facilities and is a popular family-run hotel about ten minutes' drive north of the main settlement of Plymouth. At the time of writing, following the devastations of Hurricane Hugo, it is the only functioning hotel on the island. Prior to Hugo, other listed accommodation was at Coconut Hill Hotel (491-2144), Flora Fountain Hotel (491-3444),

Hideaway, Lime Court Apartments (491-3656), Montserrat Springs Hotel and Villas (491-2481), Shamrock Villas (491-2434) and Wade Inn (491-2881). It would be wise to check on current availability before going.

Diving Centres: Scuba diving is a relatively new introduction to the tourist facilities on Montserrat and at the time of writing the only location with special facilities was the Vue Point Hotel (491-5210; fax: 4813), where Chris Mason runs a PADI-affiliated diving base. The centre, established in 1988, operates with a staff of two and rents diving gear as well as operating a 6m, five diver boat. Among the PADI courses on offer are open water, divemaster, advanced rescue and, of course, resort.

Marine Environment, General: Surrounded by deep water, scattered with numerous patch reefs in the shallows (except along the windward east coast), heavily fished for local consumption, Montserrat's marine environment offers some very pleasant diving conditions to those who choose to visit the island for a vacation incorporating a range of activities.

Recommended Dive-Sites: Scuba diving and snorkelling sites are mainly along the west and south coasts. The Pinnacle: is an offshore dive-site which provides one of the most exciting dives around the island. Large schooling barracuda swim close to divers, offering excellent photographic opportunities. Massive coral-heads with their associated parrot-fish and angel-fish offer impressive photo-settings. Shoaling crevalle are common in midwater. It is an open-water dive site suitable for advanced divers. The depth is 21m and visibility is excellent. Noon Tang is famous as a fish-feeding station where divers may hand feed grouper, sand-tile fish and morays. Queen conches are frequently seen here, as are their predators, sting-rays and nurse-sharks. The depth is 21m and visibility is clear. It is suitable for beginners. O'Garro's Wall is not a true wall-dive, but a very dramatic drop-off to 400m. As one might expect, visibility is excellent and there are some big fish, including large barracudas. It

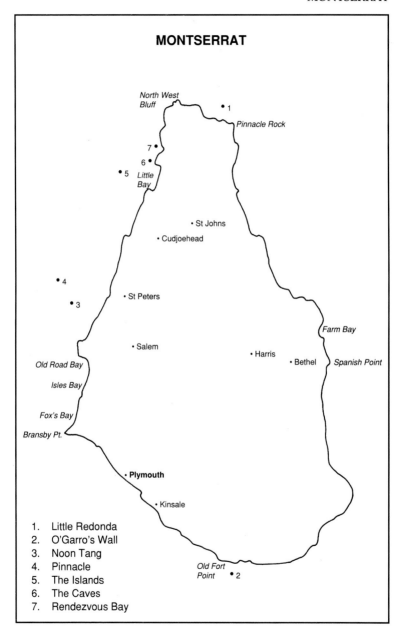

MONTSERRAT

North West Bluff

• 1

Pinnacle Rock

7 •

6 •

• 5 *Little Bay*

• St Johns

• Cudjoehead

• 4

• St Peters

• 3

Farm Bay

• Salem

• Harris
• Bethel *Spanish Point*

Old Road Bay

Isles Bay

Fox's Bay

Bransby Pt.

• **Plymouth**

• Kinsale

1. Little Redonda
2. O'Garro's Wall
3. Noon Tang
4. Pinnacle
5. The Islands
6. The Caves
7. Rendezvous Bay

Old Fort Point • 2

is an awe-inspiring dive, not for the faint-hearted, and is a good place for seeing sharks. The depth is 18-40m and the rating advanced. Little Redonda is on the windward side of the island and consists of a mound, rising above the level seabed, and breaking surface to form a rock, 60cm above sea-level, in an area where the sea is usually quite rough. When the weather is calm it offers some interesting diving with many large pelagic fish as well as turtles. The area is renowned also for its lobsters. The visibility is average; the dive depth is 15m or so, and it is a dive for advanced level divers. The Caves, under a sheer cliff, is often chosen as the second dive of a day's outing. It features shallow caves with big fish. Barracudas and jacks are always in evidence and one may also observe octopus. The dive depth is 9m, visibility is good, and its rating is suitable for beginners. A diving light adds greatly to the enjoyment of the dive and a camera is essential! The Islands are large patch reefs on a sandy bottom, resembling islands. Yellow-tail snapper and other snapper characterise the site. The depth is 18m, visibility is good and the rating is suitable for beginners.

Special Interest: An attempt to boost lobster populations has been made by the construction of artificial reefs in the shallows. Montserrat retains a special relationship with Ireland since many of its early settlers were Irish and they have named various buildings and settlements after Irish places.

Other Wildlife: The Montserrat oriole is endemic to the island, especially in wet forest above 800m. Small numbers of green, hawksbill and leatherback turtles nest on the island's beaches.

Conservation Issues: Reefs are threatened by sand-mining at Fox's Bay and Farm Bay. Spearfishing is unfortunately still carried out and has had a devastating effect on accessible reef-life.

Legal Aspects: Turtles are partially protected. At the time of writing, no designated marine park exists.

3.22 : NEVIS AND ST KITTS

Location: The adjacent small islands of Nevis and St Kitts, lying due west of Antigua, are here considered together since they are quite similar in their marine features.

Physical Description: Both of these attractive islands are volcanic in origin, with Nevis comprising a volcanic cone, 36 sq. km in area, compared to the somewhat larger St Kitts, which is 65sq. km.

Climate: The average temperature is 26°C. Rainfall is around 1,750mm with Nevis slightly drier than St Kitts.

Electricity Supply: 220 to 240 volts at 50cycles, with some hotels also providing 110 volts.

Visitor Accommodation: Hotels on St Kitts and Nevis are among the best in the Caribbean. St Kitts has the Fairview Inn (465-2472), the Fort Thomas Hotel (465-2695), the Frigate Bay Beach (465-8935), the Golden Lemon (465-7260), the Jack Tar Village Royal St Kitts (465-2651), the Ocean Terrace Inn (465-2754), the Rawlins Plantation (465-6221), the Island Paradise Beach Village (465-8004), the Leeward Cove (465-2654), the St Christopher Beach condominium complex, the Sun 'n Sand Beach Village (465-8037), the Blakeney Hotel (465-2222), Canne-a-Sucre, Conareef Cottages, and Tradewinds (465-2681) as well as some small guesthouses. Nevis has the Golden Rock Hotel (465-5346), the Hermitage, the Montpelier Plantation Inn (465-5462), Pinney's Beach Hotel (465-5207), the Nisbet Plantation (465-5325), and the Old Manor Estate, as well as rentable accommodation at the Rest Haven Inn (465-5208). The Nevis Four Seasons is due for opening in 1991.

Diving Centres: The Ocean Terrace Inn (465-2754) is home for Pro Divers, owned and managed by Auston Macleod, which offers a full range of diver services including training for resort and PADI certification courses (open-water to assistant instructor). It is the only such instruction facility on St Kitts. Nevis has a NAUI diving facility, Safari Divers, with instruction by Ellis Chaderton. Caribbean Watersports is a general watersport shop at the Jack Tar Royal Hotel.

Marine Environment, General: Recent studies around St Kitts have revealed considerable coral reef development along the east coast and off Frigate Island.

Recommended Dive-Sites: In the words of resident diver Auston Macleod, 'the sites we dive are all first class as the waters are totally unspoilt by tourism, leaving fish and invertebrate life plentiful. Wreck, wall, drift, night, canyon, reef and mini-wall sites are numerous and varied.' Popular sites on the Caribbean sides of St Kitts and Nevis include: Brimstone Shallows, a wall dive ranging from 15 to 42m; Nevis Caverns, a fascinating cavern dive from 9 to 12m; The Monkeys which consists of reef and canyons from 12 to 21m; Nags Head, a mini-wall dive from 9 to 18m; and Sandy Point, a mini-wall and canyon dive from 12 to 36m. On the Atlantic side of the islands, where water tends to be even clearer than on the Caribbean side, but where access to sites generally involves more uncomfortable boat-rides (more suitable for experienced divers than novices), sites include Grid Iron, consisting of well-developed elkhorn coral-reefs extending from 6 to 18m; Redonda Bank, which is inundated with canyons, caves and deep crevices (15-36m); and White Holes, comprising clear sandy hollows surrounded by coral (6-15m). Divers seeking additional information on St Kitts and Nevis may wish to contact Auston Macleod (465-2754 or 465-3223; fax: 465-1057).

Medical Facilities: The most readily available recompression facility is at Puerto Rico, approximately one hour away by air.

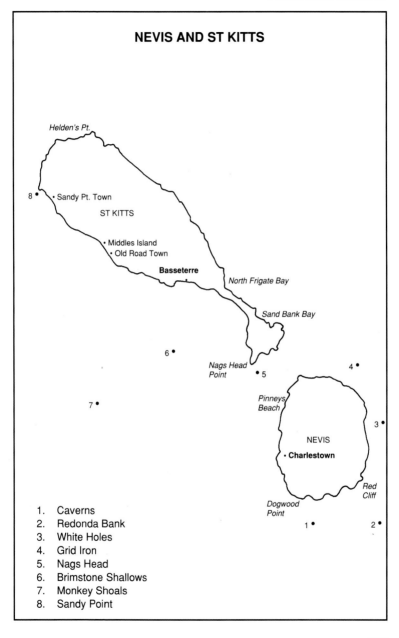

NEVIS AND ST KITTS

Helden's Pt.

8 •

• Sandy Pt. Town

ST KITTS

• Middles Island
• Old Road Town

Basseterre

North Frigate Bay

Sand Bank Bay

6 •

Nags Head
Point

• 5

4 •

Pinneys
Beach

3 •

NEVIS

• **Charlestown**

7 •

Red
Cliff

Dogwood
Point

1 •

2 •

1. Caverns
2. Redonda Bank
3. White Holes
4. Grid Iron
5. Nags Head
6. Brimstone Shallows
7. Monkey Shoals
8. Sandy Point

3.23 : PUERTO RICO

Location: 18°30'N 67°W. The easternmost island of the Greater Antilles, Puerto Rico lies due east of the Dominican Republic and due west of the Virgin Islands.

Physical Description: The large island of Puerto Rico (8,897sq. km) is dominated by a central mountain range, the Cordillero Central with a maximum altitude of 1,338m. One result of the island's extremely rugged terrain is that almost all the major settlements are situated around the coast.

Climate: The south coast is in something of a rain-shadow area, created by the high plateau of the Cordillero Central. To the north of this, average annual rainfall can be over 5,000mm whilst to the south it seldom exceeds 1,000mm. The month of May and the hurricane season (August-October) account for most of the rainfall. Temperatures range between 28.1°C average summer temperature (in September) and 25.5°C in February.

Electricity Supply: 110-120 volts at 60 cycles.

Visitor Accommodation: The major hotels offering accommodation to divers in the San Juan area are the Radisson Normandie Hotel, the Caribe Hilton Hotel (721-0303), the Sands Hotel, the El San Juan Hotel (US contact: (800) 468-2818), the Condado Beach Hotel, La Concha Hotel (US contact: (800) 468-2822) and the Condado Plaza Hotel (US contact (800) 468-8588) and are serviced by Caribe Aquatic Adventures (724-1882 and 765-7444) run by Karen and Tony Vega. The Hyatt Dorado Beach Hotel and the Hyatt Cerromar Hotel located outside San Juan in Dorado are also serviced by Karen and Tony Vega, who have their office in the San Juan Bay Marina (PO Box 2470, San Juan, Puerto Rico; 00902-2470). There are also numerous smaller hotels and guesthouses available in the same area and also scattered all around the island.

Diving Centres: The following diving centres are currently operating in Puerto Rico: Coral Head Divers, Humacao (850-7208); Caribbean School of Aquatics, Santurce (723-4740, 728-6606); Caribe Aquatic Adventures, San Juan (724-1882, 765-7444); Castillo Deep Sea-Fishing, Carolina (791-6195, 726-5752); Benitez Deep-Sea Fishing Charters, Miramar (723-2292); La Cueva Submarina (872-3903, 872-1094); El Mundo Submarino (791-5764); San Juan Scuba Shoppe at Villa Marine Shopping Center, Fajardo (863-8465); Caribbean Marine Services at Culebra (742-3555) and Aquatic Underwater Adventure (890-6071).

Among the above, Caribe Aquatic Adventures is a NAUI pro facility, and is affiliated with PADI. It operates a 5m Boston whaler for local dives, an 8m sloop for deserted island sailing and diving picnics and the 18m *MV San Antonio* for sunset cruises and private charters. Resort courses are offered, through to assistant instructor level. It was the first diving operation in Puerto Rico to receive the NAUI Pro Facility Award for Excellence. A 17-year veteran in the business, the centre (located at San Juan Bay Marina close to all the major hotels) also offers deep-sea fishing, jet-skiing and other watersports. This centre is also a good information source for divers visiting Puerto Rico. The Caribbean School of Aquatics Inc. (1 Taft Street, Suite 10F, San Juan, Puerto Rico 00911; Sales Office: La Concha Hotel, Ashford Avenue, Codado, San Juan) runs an 11m dive charter boat, *Innovation*. Further information is available by calling Captain Greg Korwek (728-6606), preferably in the evenings.

Marine Environment, General: There is a predominantly westerly flow of water along the northern and southern coasts of the island. The tidal range is about 30cm with a semidiurnal pattern. Most coral-reef development is along the south coast.

Recommended Dive-Sites: Most scuba diving sites are along the north-east coast, around the small islands and cays which together comprise La Cordillera. This is in fact a narrow submarine ridge, about 29km long, upon which various islands emerge. The best known of these islands are Icacos and Palominitos Islands, situated 1.9km off the main island. Surrounded by shallow and submerged reefs, these offer a range of interesting dive-sites. It is not necessary to dive deep around Puerto Rico in order to see abundant coral-formations or exotic marinelife, and because of the generally shallow depths most dives last from 45 mins to an hour per single tank.

Off the south-east coast are more submerged reefs, some of which lie as deep as 34m. All of these sites are accessible by short boat rides lasting 15-30 minutes. Most dive-sites off the Caribbean sides of the island (the east, south and west coasts) have good visibility of 12-30m for most of the year.

Sea-grass beds around Bahia de Jobos provide interesting diving. Some of the most dramatic diving is to be had away from the main island. Set out in the open sea, 80 km west of Puerto Rico, between it and the Dominican Republic, lies the important Islas Mona. Difficult to reach and exposed to the elements, these two small rocky islands nevertheless offer some unique biological experiences, both above and below water. On land they are a refuge for over 50 endemic species such as the Mona ground iguana, as well as various other reptiles, snails, birds and even a fresh-water caveshrimp. Nine seabird species breed on narrow ledges set among high sea-cliffs which surround the island and continue in a vertical, soft coral encrusted, wall for about 30m below the surface. Weather permitting, diving conditions are superb with 60m visibility and the chance to meet humpback whales, pilot whales and many big fish, including tuna and blue marlin. The uninhabited islands are exposed to high waves. The boat anchorage at Playa de Pajaros is only suitable in fine weather.

Culebra is a small residential island located approximately 15.5km east of the main island. It is surrounded by beautiful virgin reef gardens and plentiful marinelife. Culebra is also a wildlife refuge for the endangered sea-turtle and offers divers good opportunities to see them, particularly off nesting beaches.

Off the south-west end of Puerto Rico is La Parguera and the Phosphorescent Bay, which makes a unique night diving environ-

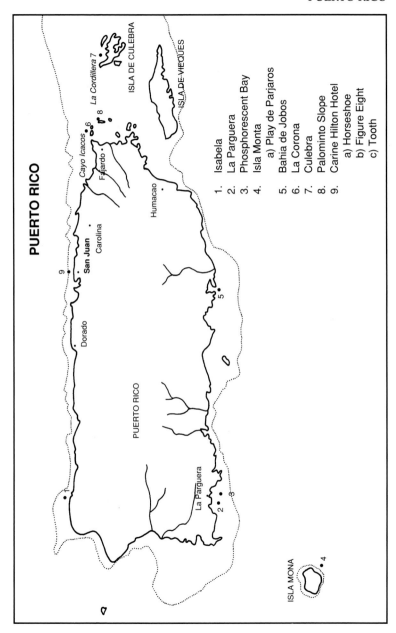

PUERTO RICO

1. Isabela
2. La Parguera
3. Phosphorescent Bay
4. Isla Monta
    a) Play de Parjaros
5. Bahia de Jobos
6. La Corona
7. Culebra
8. Palominto Slope
9. Carine Hilton Hotel
    a) Horseshoe
    b) Figure Eight
    c) Tooth

ment. Besides the numerous submerged reefs around the area, there is a good wall dive 45 minutes by boat away from this site. The edge of the wall is in about 18m and drops off into the ocean's depths, offering superb water clarity.

Off the north-west end of Puerto Rico is Isabela, an area well known for its numerous caves – flooded by both seawater and freshwater. Although special training is required for most of these dives there are a few open boulder-like sea-tunnels and chutes more suitable for the novice diver.

Dive sites regularly visited by Caribe Aquatic Adventures include the reef adjacent to the Caribe Hilton Hotel where sheltered water of only 4.5 to 6m depth, offers safe training and some interesting marinelife including sea-horses and octopus. The Horseshoe, Figure Eight and Tooth dive-sites, close to the outer reef, attract experienced divers. There is a series of large tunnels and chutes winding in and around the reef, together with a large variety of shoaling fish. The La Corona dive-site on Icacos Island, is a relatively shallow dive, around 10m or so: a good site for macrophotography, where the coral is particularly well formed and where fish can be hand-fed. The Palominito Slope off the island of the same name is a submerged reef with a gradual slope to a depth of 21m. It is inhabited by numerous tropical fish, occasional stingrays, lobsters and large moray eels.

Special Interest: There are endemic species on Islas Mona and humpback whales off the coast, particularly around the Islas Mona during the months of January and February, due to their winter migration.

Other Wildlife: Caribbean manatee occur on sea-grass beds in less disturbed areas such as La Cordillero, Bahia de Jobos, Isabella and San Juan. Puerto Rico has no less than twelve endemic species of birdlife. The Puerto Rican parrot (*Amazona vittata*) now survives in the rain-forest within the Luquillo Forest in eastern Puerto Rico. Although there is no shortage of suitable nesting beaches, turtles seem to prefer those on Culebra Island.

Conservation Issues: Various factors have led to somewhat of a decline in Puerto Rico's coastal marinelife. Corals in particular have suffered as a result of increased run-off and subsequent siltation caused by land clearance for agriculture and housing. Spearfishing has been left uncontrolled (although it is frowned upon by dive operators) and fishing with explosives was, until recently, a favourite method of fish capture. Shell- and coral-collecting (also at the time of writing not controlled by government regulations) have also been quite widespread and it has been left to diving operators to mount their own control measures. Manatees and turtles are protected by Puerto Rican law. A release programme for blue marlins of 90kg or less was initiated in 1987 and is especially influential during the many sport fishing tournaments held on the island. Urban and oil pollution have also had their effects on shallow reefs.

Legal Aspects: The islands fall under US protective legislation.

Medical Facilities: The most easily accessible recompression chamber is at St Thomas in the US Virgin Islands.

3.24 : SABA

Location: Situated 45km south of St Maarten/St Martin and 240km east of Puerto Rico. It is the smallest island of the Netherlands Antilles.

Physical Description: Saba is a small (13sq km), circular, uniquely attractive and unspoilt island, with a resident population of just over 1,000. It is dominated by a volcanic peak, reaching 915m at its centre. Steep sided mountains fall sheer into the sea and continue underwater. In winter there are no beaches but during summer there are two small dark volcanic sand beaches, one of which can be reached by a very steep road starting from the tiny capital which bears the unusual title of The Bottom.

Climate: Tropical. Because of Saba's high altitude the climate is somewhat cooler compared to some other islands in the Caribbean. Daytime temperatures range from 25°C to 32°C. At night, in Windwardside, temperatures may fall to as low as 20°C so a light sweater or jacket can be necessary. The mean rainfall is 1,067mm per year.

Electricity Supply: 110 volts at 60 cycles.

Visitor Accommodation: Saba can be reached via St Maarten. Windward Airlines make the journey four or five times a day, and a ferry called *Style* departs from St Maarten daily at 9.00am daily, except Mondays. The island has five hotels: Captain's Quarters (599-46-2201); Juliana's Apartments, Windwardside (599-46-2269); Scouts Place (599-46-2205); Sharon's Ocean View (599-46-2238); and Cranston's Antique Inn (599-46-3218). The Tourism Office (599-46-2231) has a list of available cottages for weekly rent.

Diving Centres: In 1988 2,500 scuba divers and 600 snorkellers visited Saba Marine Park. During the year the visitors made 12,000 scuba dives! There are presently three live-aboard dive-boats which regularly visit Saba: *The Caribbean Explorer* (run by Explorer Ventures Ltd), the *Coral Star* (Aquanaut Cruises) and the *Sea Dancer* (Divi Hotels). There are, at the time of writing, three operating dive shops on the island: Sea Saba, Saba Deep and Wilson's Dive Shop. All three dive shops have excellent teams of instructors and dive-masters who can offer full certification and resort courses. Saba Deep, Saba's original dive shop operated by Mike Meyers, has two 8m boats. Sea Saba (PO Box 530, Windwardside, Saba, Netherlands Antilles; 599-42-3777), operated by Joan and Lou Bourque, who have been diving around Saba since 1981, has 11 and 12m boats and runs dive packages in conjunction with Captain's Quarters and Juliana's Apartments. Wilson's Dive Shop, run by Wilson McQueen, established in 1988, has two 6m boats.

Each dive shop runs two scheduled dive trips per day. Extra dives, night-dives or snorkelling trips are available on request.

Marine Environment, General: Formed by a volcano, Saba does not lie on a shallow bank so the surrounding waters are deep and clear. Its shoreline does not benefit from the protection of a fringing reef system and is relatively exposed. A deeper-water coral-reef does exist off the south coast of Saba, on the edge of a narrow platform. This comes to within 24m of the surface and has 90 per cent coral cover. The sea-mounts which form favourite dive sites also have coral cover on their tops, and have a truly spectacular fish fauna.

Recommended Dive-Sites: Because Saba does not have an extensive coral ring around it, shore dives are not the highlight of diving here. However, dive shops have a selection of 15 different shallow dive sites and 17 deep sites from which to choose. Shallow sites include Torrens Point and Ladder Labyrinth. The latter is a maze of corals and sponges among sandy alleyways, primarily *Montastrea annularis*, *Colpophyllia natans* and *Porites astreoides*, *Xetospongia* and various gorgonians. The site is a favourite of cleaner fish which have established many cleaning stations in the vicinity, attracting a wide range of client fish.

Third Encounter, Outer Limits, Twighlight Zone and Shark Shoal are the names of undersea pinnacles of unsurpassed beauty, inhabited by large tame groupers, jacks, turtles, sharks and rays. The pinnacles come to within about 27m of the surface and then plunge down to well over 300m! Once down on the current swept peaks of these great submarine mountains, one is garlanded by deepwater gorgonians and some quite cheeky fish. Sharks are seen frequently around Saba, especially at these pinnacles, and one should also keep an eye out for the large tiger and Nassau groupers.

The Outer Limits dive site is the apex of a submarine volcano, consisting of a pinnacle rising sheer from 600m to within 24m of the surface. The 360° drop-off is surrounded by many large fish, making for spectacular and dramatic scenery and a very rewarding dive for experienced divers (dive time 20 mins at 30m).

Diamond Rock is a great dive in moderately protected waters, more suitable for intermediate divers than Outer Limits. The dive lasts for about 35 minutes at 24m and consists of a visit to another volcanic pinnacle surrounded by literally tons of fish. The numerous walls, crevices and other structures make for a cathedral effect. Tent Reef is a long, shallow ledge above a sandy alleyway, with undercuts and overhangs, gradually changing into a steep wall. An abundance of friendly fish and various invertebrates make this a very enjoyable dive. The wall itself drops to around 45m or so and has a large resident barracuda, affectionately known as Budah, and two big French angel-fish, Bonnie and Clyde. Custom's House Reef, a deep patch reef inhabited by several dozen barracuda; Hole in the Corner, a shallow elkhorn coral forest; Greer Gut; and Giles Quarter Deep, a long offshore reef, all offer exciting and interesting dives.

Special Interest: Saba is not only famous for its diving sites, but also for the hiking trails. Before the construction of The Road, the only access to villages and agricultural areas on the island was a network of paths and stairwells. Many of these were overgrown or simply disappeared through lack of use after the road opened. Recently some of these paths and stairwells have been restored by the Saba

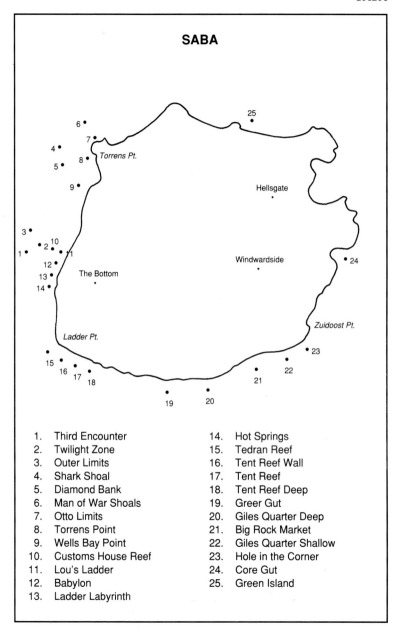

SABA

1. Third Encounter
2. Twilight Zone
3. Outer Limits
4. Shark Shoal
5. Diamond Bank
6. Man of War Shoals
7. Otto Limits
8. Torrens Point
9. Wells Bay Point
10. Customs House Reef
11. Lou's Ladder
12. Babylon
13. Ladder Labyrinth
14. Hot Springs
15. Tedran Reef
16. Tent Reef Wall
17. Tent Reef
18. Tent Reef Deep
19. Greer Gut
20. Giles Quarter Deep
21. Big Rock Market
22. Giles Quarter Shallow
23. Hole in the Corner
24. Core Gut
25. Green Island

Conservation Foundation. An interpretive trail system of seven paths has been developed. This system provides access to a variety of scenic areas, including secondary rain-forest, coastal bluffs, tidepools and the remains of a short-lived sulphur mining operation. Signboards, constructed by local artists, are installed at strategic points along the trails, elucidating aspects of Saba's fascinating natural history.

Taxi drivers on the island provide interesting guided tours and will happily regale the interested visitor with details of Saban folklore.

In Windwardside, the Harry L. Johnson Memorial Museum houses the antiques and memorabilia of this famous Dutch sea-captain's former home.

Other Wildlife: Frequently seen at all dive sites are hawksbill and green turtles, in addition to bull, blacktip and whitetip sharks. Sleeping nurse sharks are another common sight, usually observed while resting under shallow ledges.

On land several birds can be seen, such as tremblers, hummingbirds, red-tailed hawks and American kestrels. One dive-site, called Green Island, is just as fascinating above water as below, for here, during May, is the nesting site of the brown noddy and natural habitat for a host of other fauna including a non-poisonous snake, an iguana, tree frogs and Saban lizards. Among the trees, one can observe magnificent wild orchids.

Conservation Issues: The Saba Marine Park was established in 1987 by the Marine Environment Ordinance. The objective of the park is to preserve and manage the islands marine resources for the benefit and enjoyment of the people. The park stretches around the entire island, from the highwater mark down to 60m, as well as at the two offshore sea-mounts. In order to obtain the most satisfactory compromise between different uses of the environment, a zoning system has been applied. This comprises: (1) a multiple use zone, where both fishing (only for residents) and diving are permitted; (2) five recreational diving zones where no fishing or anchoring is allowed;

(3) an all-purpose recreational zone for swimming, boating, anchoring and snorkelling; (4) an anchoring zone.

For more information about the Saba Marine Park contact the park manager, Susan Walker (PO Box 18, Fort Bay, Saba, Netherlands Antilles; 599-46-3295).

The Marine Park is administered by the Saba Conservation Foundation, a body active also in other fields, and dedicated to preserve the natural beauty of Saba, above and below water.

Legal Aspects: The Marine Environment Ordinance Saba, 1987, (A B Saba, 1987, Nos 10 and 11) established the legal framework by which marine waters surrounding Saba were incorporated into a marine park. Within the park it is prohibited to take any coral or other bottom-dwelling organisms. Divers are especially requested to use good buoyancy control to avoid damage to corals. Turtle- and conch-catching are prohibited, as is fishing. Visiting yachts must only anchor in areas outside the designated diving zones, while diving boats from 15m to 30m which visit dive sites must tie-up to the orange mooring buoys provided for this purpose.

Medical Facilities: A decompression chamber is planned on the island and should be on site prior to publication of this book. The chamber has been donated by the Royal Netherlands Navy following an initiative by Dr J. Buchanan, chief of Saba's hospital. It is a four person recompression facility and is to be administered through the Saba Marine Park, operated by a team of volunteers from the diving community.

3.25 : ST BARTHELEMY

Location: The island of St Barthélemy or St Barts, is situated on the St Martin Plateau, 25km southeast of St Martin.

Physical Description: This small (25sq. km) rocky island (population around 2,200), known as the Normandy of the Tropics, has a single town and freeport: Gustavia. The island was named after Columbus' brother. The coast is indented by wave-cut cliffs, it has 14 gleaming white beaches and there are several uninhabited offshore cays including Ile Fourche, Ile Bonhommie, Ile Fregate, Ile Toc Vers and La Tortue.

Climate: The average annual temperature is 27°C. Rainfall is relatively light.

Electricity Supply: 220 volts at 50 cycles.

Visitor Accommodation: There is a reasonable selection of hotels from the luxurious to more modest establishments. La Bulle Diving Club is highly recommended. The owners run a small, personalised, friendly diving club located on a calm beach, in a tropical garden, with attractive cabins. Non-divers are also welcome there. The Hotel Manapany comprises 32 seaside cottages with a full range of guest facilities (590-276655; telex: 919215 GL MAPY). St Barts Beach Hotel (BP 81, 97133 St Barthélemy, French West Indies; 590-276273; telex: 919885 TURBE) is a 36-room hotel overlooking a beautiful white sand beach. The Hotel Filao Beach (BP 167, 97133 St Barthélemy, French West Indies; 276224; telex: 919973 FILAO) has 30 luxurious rooms arranged in an arc around the pool/restaurant, overlooking St Jean's Bay, El Sereno Beach Hotel (590-276480, fax: 590-277547; telex: 919039) has 20 bungalows and a private beach. The Tropical Hotel (BP 147, 97133 St Barthélemy, French West Indies; 590-276487, fax: 590-278174, telex: 919336 GL) also has 20 bungalows around a patio close to a beach. The Village St Jean Hotel (BP 23, 97133 St Barthélemy, French West Indies; 590-276139, telex: 919057 GL) has 20 single or double cottages and is family-owned and operated; the Hotel Emeraude Plage (BP 41, 97133 St Barthélemy, French West Indies; 590-276478, telex: 919167 GL) is directly on the beach of St Jean bay and consists of 25 spacious bungalows adjacent to a scuba base. Tom-Beach Hotel (590-277096, telex: 919153), served by Marine Service Diving Club, has 12 rooms and is also on the beach. Les Ilets Fleuris (590-276422) has seven apartments, each with a seaview. Grand Cul De Sac Beach Hotel (BP 81, 97133 St Barthélemy, French West Indies; 590-276070, fax: 590-902187) has 52 units right on the beach. The Hotel Guanahani (a member of the 'Leading Hotels of the World') is magnificently situated on the coast and has 80 de luxe rooms together with a full range of facilities (BP 109, 97133 St Barthélemy, French West Indies; 590-276660, fax: 590-277070, telex: 919575).

Diving Centres: There are several diving centres on St Barts. Marine Service at the Yacht Club quay in Gustavia has a diving department, established since 1984, managed by Guy Blatteau (590-277034; telex: 919 897 GL; fax: 590-277036). The centre has PADI and French diving instructors, operates an air-refilling station and runs two dive shops including equipment rental. It is also associated with the Hotel Guanahani at Grand Cul de Sac, Marigot. Dive with Dan is a PADI facility at the Emeraude Plage Hotel (590-276478). Club La Bulle (590-276893), founded in 1986 also on St Jean beach, handles visiting divers and offers a very friendly service under the watchful eye of proprietors Jean Luc Delagree and Angela McDonald. La Bulle is affiliated to the French Federation of divers FFESM and provides training and certification facilities. They operate a 7m diving boat, powered by two 55 hp engines, which generally carries up to six divers.

Marine Environment, General: Situated on a relatively shallow bank, averaging around 27m, coral reefs around the island have a broad base from which to develop. An 8km wide shallow reef more or less encircles the island and extensive reefs formed by the stinging hydroid/coral *Millepora* occur between St Barts and La Tortue.

Recommended Dive Sites: There are at least 15 regular dive sites along the leeward side of the island, with dive depths of 3-18m. Many of these are ideal for novice divers since there is virtually no current to contend with and visibility is good, from 15 to 45m. The Sugar Loaf is a particularly attractive location taking divers from 3 to 27m and is considered the best dive on St Barts. The site is in open water, at the reef-edge, and comprises a submarine cave inhabited by grouper, barracuda and lobsters. Les Petites Saintes, near the entrance of Gustavia harbour, is a dive full of fish, turtles, rays and even nurse sharks. Three dive-sites near Gros Ilet are on a 12m wall. A towering sea-mount, known as La Baleine, is also a popular dive site while Les Deux Baleines is in more open water and can have a current flowing over it. Pointe a Columbier is the place where Caribbean and Atlantic waters meet. Underwater there are two dramatic 18m walls and many small caves inhabited by a range of fishlife. Currents occur primarily along the windward reefs.

Other Wildlife: Loggerhead and leatherback turtles occur around the island and its nearby cays.

Conservation Issues: Like elsewhere in the area, sand-mining has created some problems in the past. At the time of writing there are no specially preserved or protected sites around St Barts.

Medical Facilities: The nearest recompression chamber is at St Thomas, US Virgin Islands.

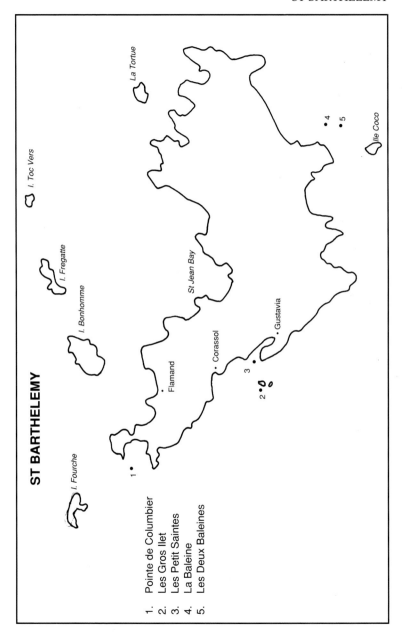

ST BARTHELEMY

La Tortue

I. Toc Vers

I. Fregatte

I. Bonhomme

St Jean Bay

Ile Coco

• 4
• 5

• Gustavia

Corassol •

3
•

2
• 🌙

Flamand
•

I. Fourche

1
•

1. Pointe de Columbier
2. Les Gros Ilet
3. Les Petit Saintes
4. La Baleine
5. Les Deux Baleines

3.26 : ST. EUSTATIUS

Location: St Eustatius, also known as Statia, is 285km east of Puerto Rico, 170km east of St Croix, 56km due south of St Maarten (fifteen minutes by air), and 27km south-east of Saba. Its capital is Oranjestad.

Physical Description: Described as the 'historic gem of the Caribbean', St Eusatius is one of the few remaining Caribbean islands that has not been given over to high rise condominiums, time-shares, casinos, traffic jams, and crowded shopping streets (not to mention crime). It is an unspoilt, quiet small island (8km by 3km), offering an ideal escape for unwinding and resting, if that is your goal. Once the centre of trade in the new world, with more than 8,000 people living there, today it is a quiet backwater with only 1,800 permanent residents. Apart from some attractive coastal waters, and a long stretch of white sand beach, the southern part of the island has a beautiful extinct volcano, the Quill, inside the crater of which rainforest vegetation flourishes. The northern end is hilly and uninhabited. The central part of the island, surrounding the airport, is given over to agriculture.

Climate: Warm and pleasant throughout the year (mean monthly temperatures 27°C), described in the tourist brochures as a 'permanent June'. Sea temperatures are around 24°C to 28°C. Light to brisk easterly trade winds moderate temperatures and provide good sailing conditions. The annual rainfall is 1,070mm and November is the wettest month. Hurricane damage is rare – Hugo in 1989 was the first direct hit in 60 years.

Electricity Supply: 110 volts at 60 cycles.

Visitor Accommodation: There are three main hotels: the Golden Era Hotel with ten rooms (599-3-2345/2445); La Maison Sur La Plage also with ten rooms (599-3-2256); and the Old Gin House with 20 rooms (599-3-2319). All of these are well situated on the beach and of a good standard. The Talk of the Town Bar and Restaurant was, at the time of writing, in the process of opening eight new guest rooms. Other smaller accommodation includes: Alvin Courtar Apartments (599-3-2218/2340); Harry's Efficiency (PO Box 82, St Eustatius, Netherlands Antilles); Henriquez Apartments (599-3-2299); Lens Apartments (Box 58, Cherry Tree, St Eustatius, Netherlands Antilles; 599-3-2226); Richardson Guesthouse (599-3-2378); Sugar Hill Apartments (599-3-2305); Cherry Tree Villa; and Juria Villa (599-3-2291). If you are in need of assistance contact the local tourist board (599-3-2433).

Diving Centres: There are two dive shops, Dive Statia, owned by Mike and Judy Brown, at Orange Baai (599-3-2435) and Golden Rock Dive Centre (St Eustatius Enterprises) (599-3-2319). Dive Statia is located in an old building right on the Caribbean beach. The centre, affiliated to Scuba Schools International (SSI), offers visiting divers equipment rental and guided dives, including the facilities of their dive-boat. Mike Brown is a Divecon Instructor, able to certify to dive-master level.

Marine Environment, General: St Eustatius belongs to the Windward group of the Netherland Antilles. It has primarily a rocky shoreline, with shallow sandy areas, some with extensive sea-grass beds, sloping into deep water. The area has a variety of corals, gorgonian sea-fans and colourful sponges as well as some impressive fishlife.

Recommended Dive Sites: Most diving is in the 12 to 24m depth range, although there are a couple of good sites for snorkelling and shallow training dives. Diving is on the reefs and on the ballast stone remains of the old trading ships. These no longer resemble ships since their wood has rotted away, leaving only the vague shape of a hull with the ballast and possibly an anchor to indicate the former presence of a shipwrecked vessel lying on the seabed. Old pottery shards, clay pipe stems and an occasional blue trade bead can be found on the sites and may be kept by divers. However, if an intact artifact is discovered it must immediately be handed over to the Historical Foundation Museum.

Please note that St Eustatius is an archaeological marine park and it is prohibited to spear fish or collect any marine artifacts. Underwater metal detectors are not permitted. All diving takes place on the Caribbean side of the island.

Special Interest: The waters around this island are littered with the remains of seventeenth and eighteenth century sailing vessels. Unfortunately most of the remains charted by archaeological studies are still buried in sand and would require expensive excavation efforts to expose them. However, after each storm there is the possibility that something new will be found.

Other Wildlife: There is tropical rain-forest inside the crater of the Quill. There are at least 17 orchid species growing on the island.

Conservation Issues: Marine conservation laws are in force. There are presently discussions regarding the creation of a marine national park. All divers must be accompanied by a land-based instructor who has responsibility for ensuring that visitors do not damage local sealife.

Medical Facilities: The nearest recompression chamber is on St Thomas, US Virgin Islands, approximately 45 minutes away by light aircraft, however, a new chamber is presently being installed on Saba, a 5 to 10 minute flight away.

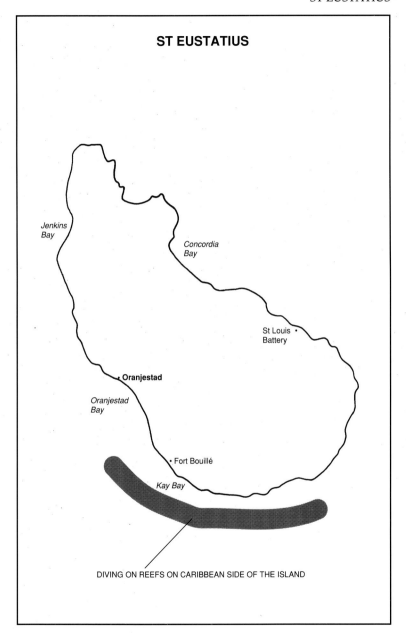

ST EUSTATIUS

Jenkins
Bay

Concordia
Bay

St Louis •
Battery

• **Oranjestad**

Oranjestad
Bay

• Fort Bouillé

Kay Bay

DIVING ON REEFS ON CARIBBEAN SIDE OF THE ISLAND

3.27 : ST LUCIA

Location: 13°55'N 60°59'W. St Lucia lies towards the northern end of the Windward Islands, flanked by Martinique to the north, St Vincent to the south and Barbados 176km ESE.

Physical Description: Seen from the air, St Lucia (43km long by 22.5km wide) is a verdant green, lushly vegetated, convoluted, craggy, volcanic island surrounded by clear blue sea, and indented by numerous small bays and harbours. Several small islets lie offshore, inviting exploration both above and below water. It has been described as the most beautiful island in the Caribbean. There are two extinct volcanic cones, the Pitons, and a dormant volcano, Soufrière, which may easily be visited, and where one may watch sulphur springs bubbling and steam rising. The highest point is Mount Gimie (959m) but the most striking features are the twin volcanic spikes of Gros Piton (798m) and Petit Piton (750m).

Climate: The annual rainfall averages between 1,500mm and 3,500mm, depending upon location, with most falling between June and November. Easterly and north-easterly trade-winds, averaging 11-21 knots, blow for most of the year. The temperature range is 21°C to 32°C.

Electricity Supply: 220-240 volts at 50 cycles.

Visitor Accommodation: The bulk of St Lucia's tourism is based on package holidays. Anse Chastanet (PO Box 809, St Lucia; 454-7354; telex: 6370 ANCHASTA LC), situated on the southern part of St Lucia's Caribbean coastline, near Soufrière, caters especially for scuba divers and other watersport enthusiasts. Other hotels are: Bois d'Orange Holiday Villas (452-8213), Caribees Apartment Hotel (452-4767), Le Sport (452-8551), Club Méditerranée St Lucia (455-6001), Club St Lucia (452-0551), Couples II (452-4211), Cunard La Toc Hotel and Suites (452-3081), East Winds Inn (452-8212), Green Parrot Inn (452-3399), Halcyon Beach Club (452-5331), Harmony Apartel (452-8756), Islander Hotel (452-8757), Marigot Bay Resort (453-4357), Morne Fortune Apartments (452-3603), St Lucian Hotel (452-8351), New Vigie Beach Hotel (452-5211), Villa Apartments (452-2691), and Windjammer Landing Villa Resort (452-1311).

Diving Centres: Most of the hotels can arrange diving facilities through one of the diving centres. Scuba St Lucia at Anse Chastanet (proprietor: Nick Troobitscoff), managed by Joyce and Chris Huxley, takes a special interest in accommodating divers and includes a film-processing laboratory. It offers all-found diving holidays. It is a PADI 5-star training facility, and is a subsidiary of Anse Chastanet Hotel. Employing seven full time PADI instructors, six dive-masters and other supporting staff, the centre provides resort and introductory, courses, open water certification, and assistant instructor courses, including several speciality courses (e.g. deep-diver, wreck-diver, night-diver, underwater photographer, search and salvage, marinelife identification certification, drift-diver and equipment specialist). The dive centre itself is situated below Anse Chastanet Hotel, at the water's edge, next to a good beach dive site, incorporating a spectacular drop-off from 6 to 43m. The centre, which has been operating since 1981, is equipped with five 6-11m dive boats (*Norma*, 11m, 20-pax; *Flattop*, 10m,20-pax; *Midushi*, 10m, 12-pax; *Jancey*, 8m, 10-pax; and *Duskey*, 6.5m, 8-pax). It has an E6 film laboratory and numerous other facilities. Apart from diving, guests at Anse Chastanet can enjoy windsurfing, mini-sailing and tennis at no extra charge. Buddies Dive Centre (25288) is operated by Phil and Lynda Warrall and situated at Castries. Dive St Lucia, located at Vigie Beach Cove, is owned by Junior Alcee, whilst The Moorings Scuba Centre is at Marigot Bay (34357) and also offers diving facilities. Couples Resort, Le Sport and Club Med have diving facilities for guests only. Windjammer Diving caters for guests at Windjammer Landing in Labrelotte Bay.

Marine Environment, General: The tidal range is about 35cm. Coral growth and marinelife in general are rich around the coast of St Lucia. In places strong currents stimulate flourishing stands of sponges (such as *Xetospongia muta*), soft corals and gorgonians (e.g. *Iciligorgia schrammi*). The mass mortality of the black spiny sea-urchin, *Diadema antillarum*, has led in places to a reduction in algal grazing and a subsequent spreading of algae over shallow reefs. However, this was a temporary phenomenon and has not done any permanent damage to the reefs.

Recommended Dive-Sites: Anse Chastanet is one of the main diving areas around St Lucia although the area can sometimes be dangerous, due to strong currents. The steep slopes of the volcanic mountain Petit Piton continue underwater, forming dramatic diving territory. Marine caves exist at several sites, including Grand Caille Point, where an upwelling current can occur. Forty species of coral and 149 fish have been recorded within the Anse Chastanet area. Right in front of Anse Chastanet and the Scuba St Lucia diving centre is an impressive shore-dive which is used to orientate divers. Boats visit even more impressive sites such as Superman's Flight, a drift dive along the magnificent Piton wall, Coral Gardens, Jalousie, Malgretout, the Blue Hole, the wreck of the *Lesleen M*, Anse La Raye and Anse Cochon. Nearby boat dives include Fairyland, Turtle Reef, Grand Caille, Trou Diable, The Pinnacles, Hummingbird Drop-off, and others too numerous to mention.

Other diving areas are Anse Galet reef, Anse Galette, Anse l'Ivrogne and the Maria Islands.

The following are dive-sites recommended by Scuba St Lucia, Anse Chastenet.

Anse Chastanet Reef: 18m. Coral wall from 6-40m. Sheltered. Tame fish for hand feeding. Large cavern. Currents at west point. Turtle Reef: 12-15m. Compact reef in Anse Chastanet Bay, 12-40m. Includes Porsche 911 at 14m! Unpredictable currents. Wreck of *Lesleen M*: 20m. 50m Freighter sunk Oct.1986. Attractive encrusting growth. Garden eels in sand near wreck. Special care – currents. Use anchor line for descent and ascent. Easy access to engine room. Anse La Raye: 9-12 m. Shallow wall with large boulders at base. Large schools of Bermuda chub, southern sennet and French grunt. Can have strong currents. Anse Cochon: 6-15m. Sheltered bay, sandy bottom with rock/coral outcrops. Many soft corals and sponges. Check for boat traffic. Fairyland: 6-40m. Shelf from 6 to 18m, followed by wall from 21 to 40m. Strong currents give abundant clean, large coral formations making for a pretty dive site and lots of fishlife. Unusual currents call for experienced divers. Grand Caille (Patois for 'Big House'): 12-18m. Wall from 6 to 46m. Deep-water gorgonia, barrel sponges and schooling fish. Check current. Trou Diable ('Devil's Hole'): 6-11m. Very colourful shallow dive with large rock formations creating canyons and overhangs. Corals go down to 37m and there is a nice dive from 15 to 21m. Morays, snake eels, spotted drum, crabs and lobsters. Check for currents and boats. Pinnacles: 15m. Very spectacular site with four pinnacles or under-water mountains rising to within diveable depths from the surface. Large expanses of red and black soft corals, seahorses, schooling fish. Despite the fact that this is one of finest dive sites in Caribbean it is near a local rubbish-dump, resulting in reduced visibility after rain. At the time of writing plans are afoot to change this. Hum-mingbird: 0-24m. Wall descends to 24m. An interesting dive but with poor visability.after rain. Sea whips, large barracuda; hot sul-phurous emissions from a small fissure. Malgré Tout ('Despite Everything'): 18m. Steep slope with lots of coral, yellow tube-sponges and large barrel-sponges. 6-40m. Occasional currents. Superman's Flight: 18m. Very steep slope at base of Petit Piton mountain. 6-40m. Deepwater gorgonian on wall, large sponges, many fish. One particular section of wall is especially colourful. Often strong cur-rents. Piton Wall: 18m. Wall at base of Petit Piton. 6-40m. Sheltered. Good soft coral and sponge formations. Underwater landslides. Check for currents and boats. Jalousie: 18m. At base of Gros Piton Mountain. Steep slope with very large barrel sponges. 6-30m. The unusual sargassum trigger-fish is often seen at this site, at around 18m. Barracuda, good coral growth. Coral Gardens: 18m. Steep slope from 6-37m. Well developed corals, tube-sponges, soft corals, schooling fish, sargassum trigger-fish. Currents. Fishing canoes in area. Do not interfere with fish-traps. Gros Piton Terrace: 24m. At

ST LUCIA

1. *Volga* Wreck
2. *Lesleen M* Wreck
3. Anse Chastenet
    a) Malgré Tout
    b) Anse la Raye
    c) Fairyland
    d) Turtle Reef
    e) Grand Caille
    f) Trou Diable
    g) Pinnacles
    h) Hummingbird Drop-off
4. Grand Caille Point
5. Blue Hole
6. Superman's Flight
7. Petit Piton
8. Piton Wall
9. Gross Piton Terrace
10. Jalousie
11. Anse Gallette Reef
12. *Waiwinette* Wreck
13. Maria Island

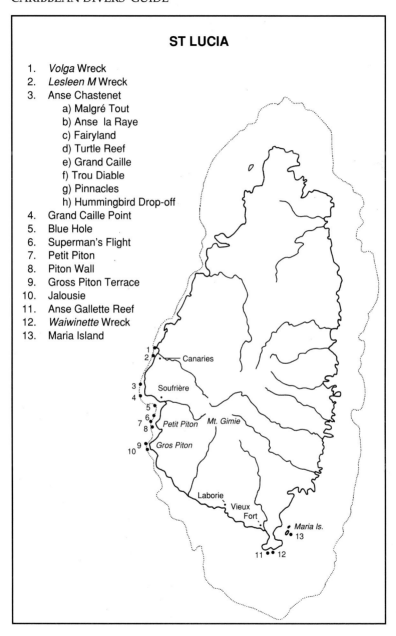

base of Gros Piton; a terraced slope with many sponges. 6-30m but best dived at 24m. Moderately exposed. Many fish, an interesting step-formation of the slope. Strong currents. Blue Hole: 30m. Sand-shute from surface down to 40m with a rocky cliff face on south side. This interesting geological feature is covered by coral-whips and sponges and has large queen angels and queen triggers. Proximity to river-mouth results in poor visibility after rain. Wreck of Wouwinet: 28-34m. 84m freighter in exposed situation with strong currents, big swells, and frequently unsuitable diving conditions. Good fish-life with many large species.

Special Interest: Green and hawksbill turtles nest on isolated beaches on the Atlantic and south coasts of the island. Wreck dives around St Lucia include: the *Volga*, just outside Castries, in 6m of water; the *Waiwinette*, which is a large freighter lying in 27m off the south end of St Lucia; and the *Lesleen M*, which was sunk by the Fisheries Department, in 18m, near Anse Cochon. This is a good dive for underwater photographers.

Other Wildlife: There are four endemic birds on St Lucia with the St Lucian Parrot (*Amazona versicolor*) probably the most famous, if not the most numerous. The population has been severely hit in recent years by hurricanes. The 1980 hurricane left about 100 birds, but the population had reached 250 or so by 1986. There has been no survey since the 1989 hurricane. An endemic ground lizard, *Liophus ornatus*, is found on Maria Major. Several other endemic lizards occur.

Conservation Issues: Land-based development, both for buildings and for agriculture, poses a major threat to shallow reefs since increased run-off carries sediments into the sea, increasing turbidity and killing some corals. Dredging has a similar effect, in addition to causing coastal erosion. Considerable research has taken place in St Lucia, aimed at accommodating the various local uses of the marine environment. Efforts are being made to educate divers and fishermen about how not to damage the reefs around St Lucia. A recent brochure on the subject quoted seven 'never statements' – worth repeating here, and equally applicable for all coral reef diving areas: 1. Never touch or remove any plant or animal found within a coral-reef; 2. Never stand on or touch any coral; 3. Never harass or intimidate any coral reef inhabitant; 4. Never use a spear-gun within, above or around a coral-reef; 5. Never set pots on or near to a coral-reef; 6. Never place a boat's anchor on or too close to a coral-reef; 7. Never buy corals, coral souvenirs or coral jewellery!

Legal Aspects: Maria Islands and surrounding waters are a protected area (Wildlife Protection Ordinance, 1980, Section 7). Fisheries legislation provides protection for turtles, corals and aquarium fish.

Medical Facilities: Nearest recompression chambers are at Martinique (739797; Hopital de la Maynard); and at Barbados (436-6185; Barbados Defence Force). Scuba St Lucia has established an emergency route to ensure a quick transfer of divers from water to chamber in case of diving accidents.

3.28 : ST MAARTEN/ST MARTIN

Location: The island of St Martin is administratively divided into a northern, French part (St Martin) and a southern Dutch part (St Maarten). Political boundaries are of little relevance to either the fish or divers however. The island is situated between Anguilla to the north and St Barthélemy to the south, and forms part of the Leeward Islands.

Physical Description: The development of hotels and condominiums has taken up much of the land of the island, leaving as its most redeeming feature the coastal waters which surround the island and offer interesting diving at moderate depths. There are some fine white sand beaches.

Climate: The wettest period is September to November. Temperatures average around 27°C. Wet-suit weather is December to April.

Electricity Supply: On the Dutch side it is 110 volts at 60 cycles, whilst on the French side it is 220 volts at 50 cycles.

Visitor Accommodation: On the Dutch side of the island, St Maarten, there are numerous hotels, villas and condominiums available. Rather than list them here it is suggested that divers should contact Le Roy French of the Ocean Explorers Dive Centre (Simpson Bay, St Maarten, Netherland Antilles; 599-5-45252) for advice or assistance if required. On the French side, St Martin, Grand Case Beach Club, (BP 339, St Martin, French West Indies; 590-875187, ext.25) is a 75-unit beach hotel served by Under The Waves (see Diving Centres below). L'Habitation de Lonvilliers has 253 units and is served by a diving centre of the same name. Other hotels on St Martin include: Club Le Grand Beach Resort (BP 99, St Martin, French West Indies; 590-875792); Club Orient (590-873385); Coralita Beach Hotel (BP 175, St Martin, French West Indies;590-873181), La Belle Creole A Conrad International Hilton (590-875866); La Belle Grand Case (590-878346); Laguna Beach Hotel (590-878997); Le Galion Beach Hotel (BP 1, St Martin, French West Indies590-873177); Le Pirate Hotel (590-877837) and Le Royale Louisiana (590-878651).

Diving Centres: Ocean Explorers Dive Centre (599-5-45252), situated at Simpson Bay, is owned by Le Roy French who is an old hand at Caribbean diving. Using an 8m, twin 150hp, Robalo dive boat, *Ocean Explorer*, Le Roy takes groups of up to seven divers to carefully selected dive sites. Operating as a NAUI 'dream resort', the centre offers training and certification for divers.

Marine Environment, General: Surrounded by relatively shallow waters (18-27m), the island nevertheless offers some interesting diving with extensive sea-grass beds, some small coral reefs dominated by elkhorn coral, and a more or less continuous band of reef running around the north and east coast of the island, for a distance of 25km. Sea temperatures range from 22°C to 27°C.

Recommended Dive-Sites: Although the dive-sites around St Martin are not considered deep (they average around 14m), marinelife is abundant and, given calm weather, visibility can reach 38m. Le Roy French of Ocean Explorers, lists the following regularly visited dive sites (see map): French Reef (4-8m); Cay Bay Reef (4.5-9m); Explorers Reef (9-14m); The Maze (8-14m); Proselyte Reef (4.5-14m); The Alleys and Cable Reef (8-20m); Hens and Chicks (6-21m); Molly B'Day islet (4.5-18m); Flat Island (12m); Spanish Rock (3-9m); Creole Rock (3-8m) and Long Bay Reef (6-8m). In addition he keeps one site up his sleeve, of which he writes: 'Not located on our dive map for security reasons, this is the best dive in the area (14-27m). Large rambling coral reef. Tame fish in large quantities. This is a "blue water" dive. Barracudas, morays, turtles, lobster, everything imagineable. Fantastic site.'

Other Wildlife: Eleven seabird species nest on islets off the southeast coast.
Conservation Issues: No collecting or spearfishing is permitted on dives.

Legal Aspects: A marine reserve exists on the south coast of the small island of Tintamarre, off the north-east coast of St Martin.

Medical Facilities: The most conveniently situated recompression chamber is at St Thomas, US Virgin Islands.

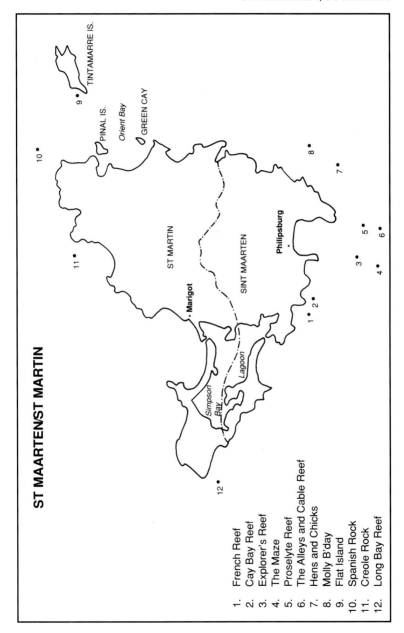

ST MAARTEN/ST MARTIN

TINTAMARRE IS.

PINAL IS.

Orient Bay

GREEN CAY

ST MARTIN

SINT MAARTEN

Philipsburg

Marigot

Simpson Bay

Lagoon

1. French Reef
2. Cay Bay Reef
3. Explorer's Reef
4. The Maze
5. Proselyte Reef
6. The Alleys and Cable Reef
7. Hens and Chicks
8. Molly B'day
9. Flat Island
10. Spanish Rock
11. Creole Rock
12. Long Bay Reef

3.29 : ST VINCENT

Location: 13°15'N 60°56'W. Forming part of the Windward Islands, this volcanic island, with the northern Grenadines, is flanked by Grenada to the south and St Lucia to the north. Barbados lies approximately 160km to the east.

Physical Description: A recently active volcano, Soufrière (1,219m), dominates the northern end of the island while the south is formed by the eroded remains of several extinct volcanoes. This heavily cultivated and attractive island is approximately 29km long and 18km wide, with a land area of 522sq. km. While the eastern side offers views of a dramatic rugged surf-washed coastline, the sheltered western side has more gentle but none the less spectacular scenery, including many beaches. In addition to the main island, St Vincent's territory includes 28 small rocky islands – real hideaway locations such as Bequia, Mustique, Palm, Canouan, Petit St Vincent, Mayreau and Union. Many of the smaller islets and cays are uninhabited and all have magnificent white sand beaches and clear water.

Climate: Tropical marine climate, primarily influenced by northeast trade winds. Temperatures, moderated by the trade winds, range between 19° and 35°C. The rainy season is June to December and rainfall varies with altitude (1,500mm on the south-east coast to 3,500mm on the higher ground). Hurricanes occur occasionally, between July and early October.

Electricity Supply: 220 volts at 50 cycles.

Visitor Accommodation: The following is a list of hotels, apartments and guesthouses in St Vincent and the Grenadines.
• *St Vincent Hotels*:
Cobblestone Inn, Kingstown (456-1937); CSY Hotel, Blue Lagoon

(Box 491, St Vincent; 458-4308); Emerald Valley Hotel and Casino (458-7421); Grand View Beach Hotel, Umbrella Beach Hotel (PO Box 530, St Vincent; 458-4651); Villa Point (458-4811); Haddon Hotel, Kingstown (456-1897); Heron Hotel, Kingstown (457-1631); Mariners Inn, Villa Beach (458-4287); Sunset Shores Hotel, Villa Beach (PO Box 849, St Vincent; 458-4411); The Last Resort Hotel, Indian Bay Beach (458-4231); Villa Lodge Hotel (458-4641); Young Island Resort (PO Box 211, St Vincent; 458-4826) with a resident scuba pro and a dive shop nearby.

• *St Vincent Apartments*:

Bambi's Beach Apartments, Indian Bay (458-4934); Belleville Apartments (458-4776); Breezeville Apartments, Villa Point (458-4004); Indian Bay Beach Hotel Apartments (458-4001); Macedonia Rock Hotel (458-4076); Ratho Mill Apartments, Ratho Mill (458-4849); Ricks Apartments, Cane Hall (458-4409); Ridge View Terrace Apartments (456-1615); The Umbrella Beach Apartments, Villa (458-4651); Tropic Breeze Hotel (458-4631); Yvonette Apartments, Indian Bay Beach (458-4021).

• *St Vincent Guest Houses*:

Bella Vista Inn, Kingstown Park (457-2757); Kingstown Park Guesthouse (456-1532); Mermaid Inn (457-4628); Olives (456-1821); Sea Breeze Guesthouse, Amos Vale (458-4969); The Moon, Amos Vale (458-4656); Foot Steps (458-6433).

• *Bequia Hotels and Guesthouses*:

Bequia Beach Club (458-3248); Frangipani, Port Elizabeth (458-3255); Friendship Bay Hotel (458-3222); Julie's Guesthouse, Port Elizabeth (458-3304); Keegan's Guesthouse (458-3254); Lower Bay Guesthouse (458-3675); Plantation House Hotel (458-3425); Spring on Bequia (458-3414); Old Fort (458-3440).

• *Southern Grenadines Hotels and Guesthouses*:

Anchorage Yacht Club, Union Island (458-8244); Clifton Beach Hotel, Union Island (458-8235); Seaview Development, Union Island (456-1833); Sunny Grenadines, Union Island (458-8327); Charlie's Guest House, Mustique (458-4621); Cotton House, Mustique (456-4777); Firefly House, Mustique (458-4621); Canouan Beach Hotel (458-8888); Crystal Sands, Canouan (456-4099); Villa La Bijou,

Canouan (456-4099); Palm Island Beach Club, Prune Island (458-4804); Petit St Vincent Resort (458-4801); Salt Whistle Bay, Mayreau (VHF channel 16).

Diving Centres: Dive St Vincent (PO Box 864, St Vincent; 457-4714 or 457-4948) is a fully equipped dive-base on Young Island Dock, run by Bill Tewes who offers divers the facilities of his 8m and 7m boats, and includes night-dives and some interesting excursions, such as a trip to Bequia, in his itinerary. Courses include NAUI, PADI, and CMAS from the resort course to assistant instructor level. Bill Tewes also offers equipment repair and sales or rental of dive gear. Another St Vincent-based dive centre is that of Earl and Susan Halbich at Mariners Watersports and Yacht Charters (458-4228). Divers may wish to combine a little sailing in their plans, perhaps discovering the beauty of islands such as Bequia and Mustique.

Dive Bequia (458-3504 or 458-3425; fax: 458-3612; telex: 7500 CWAGENCY VQ) is a somewhat exclusive operation (not for the budget traveller) based at the private beach of the Plantation House Hotel on Bequia. They operate a 7m Mako boat and specialise in small groups with no more than four divers for each NAUI instructor. The base is owned and managed by Bob Sachs. Apart from the diving itself, Bequia is a unique location and Bob Sachs helps his visitors to gain the true flavour of the place by taking them to uninhabited islands where they can relax between dives.

Clubhouse Sunsports (458-3577 or VHF channel 68; telex: 7587 FRANGI VQ) at Hotel Frangipani on Bequia runs a dive base with NAUI instructors. Nancy Boake is in charge there and she organises resort and certification scuba courses, with the aid of her 7.5m Sun Diver boat.

Marine Environment, General: The coral reefs around St Vincent are in a relatively early stage of development following considerable volcanic activity during the late-Pleistocene and recent periods. Relatively small reefs exist along the south coast, at Johnson Point, Indian Bay and on the east side of Young Island. On the southern portion of the east coast discontinuous reefs stretch along the ex-

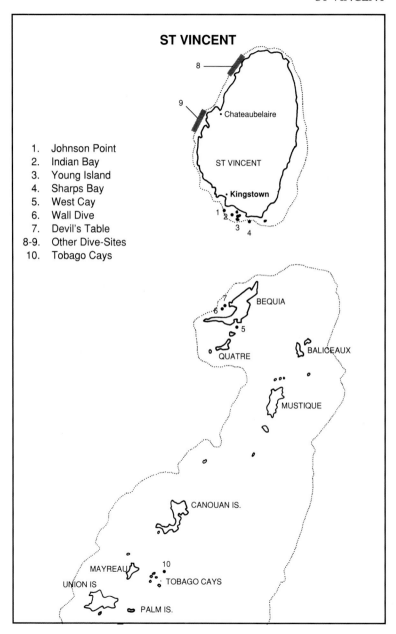

ST VINCENT

1. Johnson Point
2. Indian Bay
3. Young Island
4. Sharps Bay
5. West Cay
6. Wall Dive
7. Devil's Table
8-9. Other Dive-Sites
10. Tobago Cays

Chateaubelaire

ST VINCENT

Kingstown

BEQUIA

QUATRE

BALICEAUX

MUSTIQUE

CANOUAN IS.

MAYREAU

UNION IS

TOBAGO CAYS

PALM IS.

posed shoreline but most scuba diving takes place along the more sheltered west coast where some reefs also exist, to the north and south of Chateaubelair.

The Grenadines have some dramatic marine scenery, with extensive bank barrier reefs off some islands.

Recommended Dive-Sites: Tobago Cays offer some good snorkelling sites. New Guinea Reef is particularly rich in black coral, gorgonians and sponges. Bottle Reef, beneath the old English Fort, is so named after the old bottles, antique collectors' pieces, which litter the site. The Forest is, predictably enough, full of giant, tree-like gorgonians. The Garden, equally predicatably is both pretty and full of small fish, reminiscent of birds feeding at a garden bird table. The Wall is precisely what it claims to be; starting from 6m and plunging vertically into the depths, covered with invertebrates including some sizeable black coral trees. The Drift is not for the faint hearted since a three-knot current sweeps divers over the reef, past huge groupers effortlessly holding position in the water column. The Coral Castle consists of some large colonies of brain coral and other species. If one is looking for a practice dive, Turtle Bay is as good a place as any to check out gear. Local wrecks include the hurricane sunk *Seimstrand*, a coastal freighter of 37m, lying in 26m of water, which is rapidly gaining a coating of hard and soft corals together with other invertebrates and a host of resident fish.

Diving at Bequia is well organised and offers some superb dive sites. A recent article in *Harpers and Queens* drew comparisons with those two other favourite locations: the Red Sea and the Maldives. Certainly the water can be very clear and fishlife perfectly tame. Large pelagics may be seen here, together with good populations of reef fish. On its sheltered side Bequia has a wall dive, designated as a marine park, where spearfishing is prohibited and where traps, nets and anchoring are also not permitted. On the Atlantic side of West Cay, at the southernmost end of Bequia, one may see some large aggregations of pelagic jacks and other predators, whilst the sheltered side of the same reef has an easier atmosphere, full of reef fish. Devil's Table at Bequia now has a wrecked yacht, lying in 27m.

Other Wildlife: Green, hawksbill and leatherback turtles all occur in these waters, nesting on St Vincent's beaches. There are two island endemic birds, the St Vincent parrot (*Amazona guildingii*) and the whistling warbler.

Conservation Issues: There is a closed season for turtles. Most tourist diving operations have their own rules aimed at protecting the marine environment. Coastal pollution is a potential threat to inshore marinelife. The St Vincent National Trust has recently activated an Environmental Committee which is studying the feasibility of establishing marine national parks.

3.30 : TRINIDAD AND TOBAGO

Location: The two islands of Trindad and Tobago are closer to Venezuela and the mainland of South America than they are to any of the other Caribbean islands. Indeed, they are actually situated on the Venezuelan continental shelf.

Physical Description: The two islands cover a combined land area of 5,128sq. km. Trinidad has large expanses of fairly flat country, dissected by three mountain ranges, a feature which led to the island's name. Although the island's economy has largely been based upon oil and industry, much of its wildlife has been protected and important wetlands exist at Caroni Swamp and the Nariva. A dramatic natural feature is the huge pitch lake, first reported by Sir Walter Raleigh in 1595, in the south of Trinidad, formed by asphaltic oil seeping into a mud volcano. Tobago, 29km to the north-east of Trinidad, is a smaller and prettier island, more popular for holidaymakers and more reminiscent of other Caribbean islands to the north and west.

Climate: Somewhat cooler in the highlands that at the coast, temperatures nevertheless average 23°C at night and 29°C in daytime.

Electricity Supply: Supply is not standardised. Both 100 and 230 volts at 60 cycles are used.

Visitor Accommodation: At the time of writing, none of the hotels on Trinidad itself offered in-house scuba diving facilities. Virtually all the action in this regard is on Tobago which is such a small island that one could stay at any of the listed venues and still be within easy reach of the beach-based diving centres. Tobago accommodation includes: Arnos Vale Hotel (at time of writing leased out to an Italian tour company); Cocorico Guest House (639-2961); Coral Reef Guest House (639-2536); Crown Point Condominiums (639-8781);

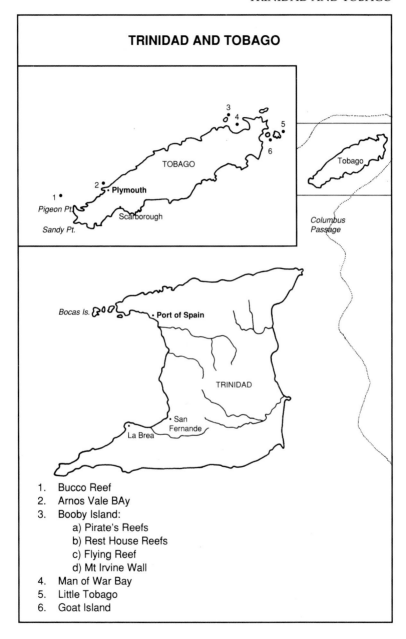

TRINIDAD AND TOBAGO

TOBAGO

Plymouth

1

Pigeon Pt.

Sandy Pt.

Scarborough

Tobago

Columbus
Passage

Bocas Is.

Port of Spain

TRINIDAD

San
Fernande

La Brea

1. Bucco Reef
2. Arnos Vale BAy
3. Booby Island:
    a) Pirate's Reefs
    b) Rest House Reefs
    c) Flying Reef
    d) Mt Irvine Wall
4. Man of War Bay
5. Little Tobago
6. Goat Island

Della Mira Guest House (639-2531); Horizons at Mt Irvine Estates; Kariwak Village (639-8545); Man-O-War Cottages (639-4327); Mount Irvine Bay Resort (639-8871); Sandy Point Beach Club (639-8533); Tropikist Beach Hotel (639-8512); Turtle Beach (639-2851).

Diving Centres: Dive Tobago Ltd (Pigeon Point, PO Box 53, Scarborough, Tobago, 639-2266, 639-2385, 639-3695), owned and managed by James Young, was established in 1979 and has been successfully organising diving around Tobago for over ten years. The centre is affiliated to ACUC; PADI and NAUI and employs eight staff. Resort and certification courses are offered by the centre, which has three 9m dive-boats and one 5m boat. Dive Tobago offers one-and-a-half hour snorkelling trips to the coral gardens, during which snorkellers are assisted by a dive-master.

Marine Environment, General: A vital difference exists between Trindad and Tobago in that whilst Trinidad's marine environment is heavily influenced by the muddy estuarine waters of the Gulf of Paria, Tobago is much less affected by the Orinoco outflow and has some clear water with good coral growths, particularly at Buccoo Reef. Off the north-west tip of Trinidad, the Bocas Islands are separated by deep current-scoured channels, forming a bottle-neck through which the Guyana Current streams north into the Caribbean. Turbulence and cool water upwellings frequently accompany this relatively fast flow (up to three knots).

Recommended Dive-Sites: Buccoo Reef for snorkelling; Sandy Point; Arnos Vale Bay, Tobago; North-eastern tip of Tobago including Man-O-War Bay, Goat Island and Little Tobago; north side of Booby Island; Pirate's Reef and Rest House Reef. Dive Tobago Ltd lists Flying Reef, an Atlantic drift dive in four-to-five knot current, as one of its best dives, for experienced divers only! This is an exposed site, best dived between December and June, in the first part of the year. Another favourite site, Mt Irvine Wall is very sheltered, takes divers to around 20m, and is rich in sponges and nudibranchs. Despite the protected location, however, visibility and general diving conditions greatly deteriorate when there is a groundswell.

Special Interest: This is hummingbird land. A visit to Flying Fish Island is highly recommended.

Other Wildlife: The Caribbean manatee is sometimes found along the east coast of Trinidad. Hawksbill, leatherback, olive ridley and green turtles occur here.

Legal Aspects: Buccoo Reef/Bon Accord Lagoon is a legally established protected area.

Medical Facilities: The most conveniently located recompression chamber facilities are on Trinidad, in Venezuela, and on Barbados. For emergency information contact James Young of Dive Tobago Ltd.

3.31 : TURKS AND CAICOS

Location: Consisting of a group of eight relatively large and about forty smaller islands scattered across 160km of ocean, the Turks and Caicos Islands form a southerly extension of the Bahama chain of islands. They lie due north of Haiti and the westerly portion of the Dominican Republic, outside the chain of Antilles which encircle the true Caribbean Sea.

Physical Description: Low, flat, arid, coral limestone and sand islands, fringed by mangroves and surrounded by well-developed coral reefs in clear, oceanic tropical waters, the 40-island chain more than compensates underwater for any lack of luxuriance on land. The group contains over 200 miles of pristine white sand beaches.

Climate: The first half of the year is relatively dry with an average monthly rainfall of 31.5mm, while the second half is somewhat wetter (62.8mm average). Temperatures are similar to the Bahamas, ranging between 16°C and 35°C but averaging a comfortable 25°C in winter or 29°C in summer. Winds are predominantly easterly trades. The best diving periods are probably April to November although the latter part of this period can be spoilt by strong winds or even the rare hurricane. The seas tend to be quite rough in February and March.

Electricity Supply: 110 volts at 60 cycles.

Visitor Accommodation: The main tourism centres are on Providenciales and Grand Turk. The following is a list of what is currently available: Kittina Hotel, Grand Turk (946-2232); Salt Raker Inn, Grand Turk (946-2260); Turks Head Inn, Grand Turk (946-2466); Balfour Beach Cottages, Salt Cay; Mount Pleasant Guesthouse, Salt Cay; Admiral's Arms, South Caicos (946-3223); Corean's Cottages, South Caicos; Caicos Reef Lodge, South Caicos; Prospect of Whitby, North Caicos (946-4250); Meridian Club, Pine Cay (US contact: (813)

263 2327); Leeward Marina and Villas, Providenciales (946-4216); Third Turtle Inn, Providenciales (US contact: (305) 276 7372); Treasure Beach Apartments, Providenciales (946-4211/4214).

Diving Centres: Eight dive-operators, two live-aboard dive boats and 15 hotels offering diving packages are now based in the islands. Six of the fully equipped diving centres are on Providenciales while two are on Grand Turk. All divers must present a valid certification card before they hire equipment, which is readily available at the diving centres. For the most part, diving is from dive-boats with accompanying dive-masters. Listed centres and live-aboards are indicated below:

• *Grand Turk*: Blue Water Divers (PO Box 124, Grand Turk, Turks and Caicos Islands; 946-2432), 12 divers, and Omega Diving of Grand Turk (946-2232), 70 divers.

• *Providenciales*: Provo Turtle Divers, Third Turtle Inn (328-5285), a PADI centre,32 divers; Provo Aquatic Centre (946-4455; fax: 946-4605), 55 divers; Provo Undersea Adventures (946-4203), 16 divers; Seatopia (946-4553), 6 divers; Third Turtle Divers (946-4230), 24 divers.

•*Live-aboards*: *Aquanaut* (PO Box 101, Grand Turk), 6 berths; *Sea Dancer* (USA booking number is 800-367-3484), 12 berths.

Marine Environment, General: The islands are formed on two submarine (oolitic) sandbanks of the West Atlantic. The Caicos Bank (7,680sq. km) is fringed on its northern side by four quite large Caicos islands and many smaller islets with a string of reefs interpersed by sea-grass beds and a few small cays around its remaining, loosely defined triangle.

Separating this large bank from the smaller Turks bank is the 2km deep Turks Island Passage. The drop-off lies only a 400m from the beach at Cockburn Town, capital of Turks and Caicos. Underwater visibility is gin-clear, creating some superb diving conditions in comfortably warm seawater (sea surface temperatures 22°C to 28°C). Easterly trade winds result in generally calm conditions on westerly shores. Currents can be strong at times, particularly around the northern and southern tips of Grand Turk.

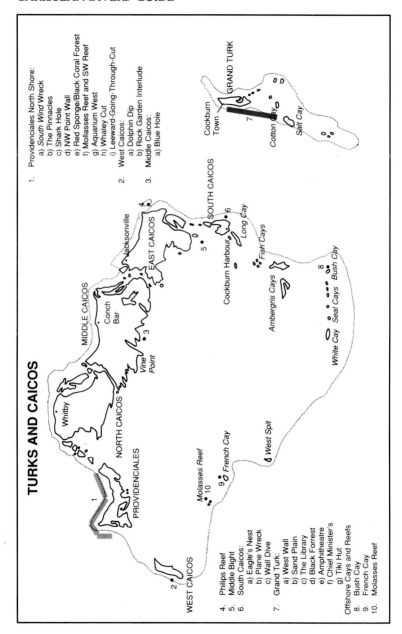

TURKS AND CAICOS

1. Providenciales North Shore:
   a) *South Wind* Wreck
   b) The Pinnacles
   c) Shark Hole
   d) NW Point Wall
   e) Red Sponge/Black Coral Forest
   f) Mollasses Reef and SW Reef
   g) Aquarium West
   h) Whaley Cut
   i) Leeward-Going-Through-Cut

2. West Caicos:
   a) Dolphin Dip
   b) Rock Garden Interlude

3. Middle Caicos:
   a) Blue Hole

4. Philips Reef
5. Middle Bight
6. South Caicos:
   a) Eagle's Nest
   b) Plane Wreck
   c) Wall Dive
7. Grand Turk:
   a) West Wall
   b) Sand Plain
   c) The Library
   d) Black Forrest
   e) Amphitheatre
   f) Chief Minister's
   g) Tiki Hut

Offshore Cays and Reefs
8. Bush Cay
9. French Cay
10. Molasses Reef

Recommended Dive Sites: Diving around Turks and Caicos is so good that a list of selected dive sites is almost superfluous. Spectacular caves, blue holes, massive and rich sea-grass beds, prolific coral reefs, walls, pinnacles, drift dives through pelagic populated channels, nurse shark aggregating sites, archaeological wrecks, turtle nesting islands, inquisitive bottle-nose dolphins, manta rays – just name your requirements and the dive-master will take you there! A few tips might however help you to locate the very best sites.

• *Dive sites easy to access from a base on Providenciales*:

The most dramatic diving is along the wall, half an hour or so from the Provo. A series of sites along the north shore are especially suitable for novice divers since there is no current and underwater visibility remains good.

1. Wreck of the *South Wind*: consists of the hurricane-disturbed remains of a wreck lying in 15m, on a steep slope. Tame Nassau groupers are a feature of the wreck.

2. The Pinnacles: tall, narrow coral pinnacles, near the edge of a wall. Shallow corals at around 9m with a sloping sandy seabed at 30m.

3. Shark Hole: is a narrow tunnel through the reef, from 18 to 40m. Sharks congregate over sand outside the lower end of the tunnel.

4. NW Point Wall: drops almost vertically from 15-18m to 1,830m! It is scalloped by gullies and chimneys, forming a most dramatic section of seascape inhabited by some of the larger species including nurse-sharks and other sharks, turtles and rays – even mantas.

5. Red Sponge/Black Coral Forest: pretty much as the name descibes, in a cave along the wall.

6. Molasses Reef and SW Reef: renowned for their ship-wrecks: old galleons with evidence of their presence still visible in the form of a few canon and coral encrusted anchors.

7. Aquarium West: is an attractive area with plenty of corals and coral-reef fish.

8. Whaley Cut is a break in the barrier-reef bordering the northern coast of Providenciales. Many large fish gather here. Other breaks in the northern reef are equally rich in marinelife.

259

9. A chance to see tame bottlenose dolphins is provided by diving off the north-east end of Providenciales, in the passage known as Leeward Going Through Cut.

• *Dive sites around West Caicos*:

1. Dolphin Dip: comprises a gully in the wall which seems to attract schools of dolphins. The edges of the gully, along the wall are heavily encrusted by a variety of invertebrates including big sponges and corals.

2. Rock Garden Interlude: is the name given to another of the wall dives along the West Caicos drop-off.

• *Dives around North Caicos*:

There is still much to be explored here, with plenty of exciting diving. At this stage it would be premature to list favourite sites since they are still being reconnoitred. Young green turtles may be seen among the sheltered creeks on North and Middle Caicos.

• *Dives around Middle Caicos*:

Just east of Vine Point on Middle Caicos, on top of the Caicos Bank, is a spectacular blue hole over 400m in diameter.

• *Dives off East Caicos:*

1. Philips Reef, off East Caicos, is reported to be in excellent condition, offering some superb diving.

2. Good shallow reefs, topped with elk-horn coral, lie between East Caicos and South Caicos, in the Middle Bight.

• *Dives around South Caicos*:

This is a dramatic and rewarding place to dive, very near the Turks Island Passage, and a focal point for some big sharks including bull sharks, blacktips and the odd hammerhead. The presence of a good through-flow of current not surprisingly attracts plenty of schooling fish and their predators.

1. Eagle's Nest: has a large resident population of southern stingrays together with schools of jacks, roving bull sharks and other big fish including, at least until recently, a 100kg jew-fish.

2. Plane Wreck: is just that: the wreck of an aircraft (Convair 340) in 17m, forming an interesting wreck dive.

3. A magnificent 'wall' dive lies just 180m off Cockburn Harbour at the southern end of South Caicos. The drop-off starts at around 16m

and upwellings of nutrient rich water emanating from the Turks Island Passage make this one of the richest marine dive sites in the entire group.

• *Dives around Grand Turk*:

On the westerly side of Grand Turk, looking across to East Caicos, lies the 2,730m deep Turks Island Passage. The sharp descent from the shallows into ocean depths is within a ten-minute boat ride from the beach. It is a truly impressive place to dive with the effects of water-flow through the channel enhancing marine-life.

1. One of the best sites to see manta rays is off the west wall of Grand Turk, outshore from Cockburn.

2 Garden Eels are prolific along the west coast of Grand Turk, on the sand plain at 8-15m. The species is *Nystactichthys halis*.

3. One of the main diving areas is the west reef system off Grand Turk. Dive sites here include The Library, rich in sea anemones, nocturnal cerianthid anemones, and nudibranchs; the Black Forest predictably rich in black corals on steep, relatively shallow over-hangs; the Amphitheatre near which humpback whales have been seen; Chief Minister's and Tiki Hut.

• *Offshore Cays and Reefs*:

1. Try the shallows around Bush Cay for nurse sharks.

2. French Cay on the western side of Caicos Bank has many nesting terns and a fair number of roving sharks.

3. Molasses Reef, south east of West Caicos, is the site of the oldest New World wreck ever found. It has been excavated by the Texas Institute of Nautical Archaeology.

Special Interest: Migrating humpback whales pass through Turks Island Passage from December to March, en route to breeding and birthing grounds on the Mouchoir and Silver Banks to the south. There are caves on Middle Caicos with stalactites and stalagmites. There is a commercial conch farm at Leeward-Going-Through-Cut.

Other Wildlife: Loggerhead, green and hawksbill turtles nest on many of the cays.

Conservation Issues: Over-fishing, including intensive spearfishing and poaching on some offshore reefs, has been a problem in the past. Locals used to use bleach to extract lobsters from their holes. A locally based and Washington-connected foundation, PRIDE (Protection of Reefs and Islands from Degradation and Exploitation) is active in educating and informing local people about conservation issues. This has included a programme of encouraging diving centres to 'rotate' dive sites. Mooring buoys have been placed at popular dive-sites and all the diving operators make a special effort to avoid any damage to the marine environment.

Legal Aspects: Visitors to the Turks and Caicos are not allowed to use spearguns. Turtle eggs are completely protected whilst turtles themselves are partially protected. The Fisheries Export Duty Ordinance, 1952, regulates the harvesting of conches and spiny lobsters. The Fisheries Protection Regulations, 1976, places a ban on the use of scuba or explosives for collection of any marinelife; prohibits fishing in Bell Sound and places controls on the use of spearguns.

Medical Facilities: Providenciales has a multi-lock 60-inch recompression chamber, owned by Dick Rukowski, and located at Erebus Inn (946-4240). The chamber is available for the treatment of diving accidents and is run by hyperbaric experts resident on the island.

3.32 : US VIRGIN ISLANDS

Location: The US Virgin Islands comprise around 50 islands, cays and rocks. The principal islands are St Croix, St John and St Thomas. Lying approximately 2,630km SSE of New York City and 1,770km ESE of Miami, they are all at the northern end of the Leeward Islands of the Lesser Antilles, not far from the east coast of Puerto Rico. While St John and St Thomas are in a small archipelago shared by the British Virgin Islands, St Croix, lies by itself, south of the main group, and in the Caribbean proper.

Physical Description: It was Columbus who first named these islands the Virgins, a reference to their unspoilt beauty. There are 50 or so islands strung out in a line which separates the Caribbean proper from the Atlantic Ocean.

Climate: There is little variation in temperature throughout the year, with the climate offering an almost perfect range from 25°C to 28°C. Average monthly temperatures are shown below:

Jan	25°C	May	26°C	Sept	27°C
Feb	25°C	June	27°C	Oct	27°C
Mar	24°C	July	28°C	Nov	26°C
April	26°C	Aug	28°C	Dec	24°C

Hurricanes may occur in autumn and some strong winds in winter months. Annual rainfall varies between 750 and 1,250mm. Heavy rainstorms in the autumn and winter months can cause considerable run-off and mixing of shallow water, together with increased turbidity.

Electricity Supply: 110 to 120 volts at 60 cycles.

Visitor Accommodation: One and a half million people a year visit the US Virgin Islands, so expect to find a sophisticated, tourist oriented economy offering a wide range of accommodation and plenty of activity underwater, on the water and on land. A recent survey revealed that 52 per cent of the visitors to the US Virgin Islands snorkel and dive but despite this, dive-sites are not usually crowded. Whatever budget you are working to, it should be possible to find somewhere suitable to stay. For those in search of pampered luxury then Virgin Grand St John could be the place, whereas students seeking low cost accommodation may try the campsite at Cinnamon Bay which offers bare sites for less than $10 per day. Accommodation on St Croix (somewhat set back by hurricane damage in 1989) also covers the full range from complete resorts with 18 hole golf courses to seaside hotels, central accommodation or in restored 18th century greathouses. Secret Harbour Beach Hotel, St Thomas (US reservations: (800) 524-2250; or (809) 775-6550) is beautifully located in one of St Thomas's most attractive bays (see AquaAction under Diving Centres). Limetree Beach Hotel, Bolongo Bay, is geared to divers and associated with the St Thomas Diving Club. Frenchman's Reef Beach Hotel on St Thomas is served by Sea Adventurers.

• *St John*: The Virgin Grand St John Beach Hotel and Villas (US contact: (800) 323-7249) is served by the Pro Dive Centre and teams up with them to offer five-night diving vacation packages together with other holiday plans aimed at scuba divers. The hotel complex boasts a 51cfm compressor, so there is no waiting around for air! Gallows Point Hotel is served by Low Key Watersports.

• *St Croix*: There was major hurricane damage on St Croix during 1989 and visitors are advised to check on the present situation before committing themselves. The Caravelle Hotel, owned by Sid and Amy Kalman, is ideally equipped for visiting divers and is served by VI Divers which also links up with Pink Fancy and Hotel On The Cay. Club Comanche Hotel (US contact: (800) 542-2066) is an attractive blend of old and new with some four-poster beds, a reconstructed sugar mill, and all the modern comforts a fly-dive holidaymaker might require. It offers diving packages with Dive Experience. The Buccaneer (US contact: (800) 223-1108) has 144 luxury rooms on 100ha of ocean frontage and works with Caribbean Sea Adventures. The Cormorant Beach Club, a 38-room hotel, offers accommodation to divers and is linked up with Scuba Tech.

Diving Centres: Since the US Virgin Islands fall within the jurisdiction of the US Coastguard Service all the dive operators must comply with standard US requirements.

• *St Thomas*: Diving centres include the magnificently located AquaAction (P.O.Box 12138, St Thomas, US Virgin Islands; 775-6285, ext. 274), owned by Julie Archibald, and based at Secret Harbour Beach Resort. This PADI 5-star instructor development centre is associated with the lovely hotel at Secret Harbour, uses a 8.5m dive boat, *Nina*, and offers divers special courses in open water, rescue, dive-master and other specialities. For underwater photographers they offer film processing. AquaAction also works with Seahorse Cottages and Harbour House Villas. Other centres on St Thomas include the Chris Sawyer Dive Center (775-7320) at the Compass Point Marina which specialises in underwater video, creating programmes for its guests and offering training in video and still photography techniques. The Sawyer Center operates *Fools Gold*, a 13m, 12-passenger craft. The St Thomas Diving Club (PO Box 7337, St Thomas, US Virgin Islands; 775-1800; fax: 775-3208), located at Bolongo Bay Beach and Tennis Club is owned by Bill Letts and managed by Lecia Richmond. Appropriately enough, Bill Lett's latest 9m dive-boat is called *Letts Dive*! In addition they run the 7.5m Delta, *Diver II* and the 20m *Mohawk II*. Sea Adventurers operates diving boats out from the dock at Frenchman's Reef Beach Hotel. The Pelican Diving Center is located in the lobby of Windward Passage Hotel where operations of their 13m 12-passenger diving boat, *MV Pelican*, are co-ordinated. Underwater Safaris of St Thomas is run by Mel Luff and conveniently located at the Ramada Yacht Haven Hotel and Marina with which they organise diving holiday packages. 'The oldest certified scuba school in the VI' is how Joe Vogel's Diving School (PO Box 7322; St Thomas, US Virgin Islands; 809-775-7610) is described and it is quite true that Joe, a NAUI instructor, has been at the game for almost 30 years. Joe specialises in taking small groups diving and even after all this time, he remains an enthusiast for diving in VI waters. Another 'old-hand' at local diving is Dave Fredebaugh who runs Caribbean Divers, an SSI and PADI full service diving facility (775-6384) which uses a 6m diving vessel, the *Different Drummer*. Dive the Virgins offers daily scuba tours for beginners. Finally, mention should be made of the Virgin Island Diving School which works primarily with cruise ships, providing their passengers with a taste of the delights of scuba diving.

• *St John*: Most of the diving companies on St John are associated with particular hotels but offer services outside their immediate catchment area. The focus of diving activity is at Cruz Bay, the main landing site for ferries and seaplanes carrying passengers to St John. The Pro Dive Center, owned by Cruz Bay Watersports Co. (PO Box 252, St John, US Virgin Islands; 776-6234) is a PADI 5-star training facility with three custom diving boats, offering a wide range of training courses and certification. Associated with the Virgin Grand St John Hotel and Villas, the centre is an ideal base for visiting divers. Pro Dive's main base is at their well equipped dive shop in Cruz Bay and their 8.5m diving boat Splash, is at the nearby marina. Their other base is at the hotel where they keep two other diving boats, the 12m, 2- passenger *Blast* and *Hi Dive*, a 9m, 16 passenger boat. All the boats are laid out for the convenience of divers, especially underwater photographers.

Another centre which offers a good range of facilities is Low Key Watersports, established by Bob Shinners, and located in the Wharfside Village. The centre operates a diving vessel, also named *Low Key* and arranges accommodation with the Gallows Point Hotel. Cinnamon Bay Watersports, owned by Captain Bob Conn operates the 13m, 12-passenger dive boat, *MV Cinnamon*, and has been taking divers around the area for almost ten years. This centre appeals especially to budget-conscious divers and Bob collects many of his divers from the Cinnamon Bay camp-site, mentioned above. Paradise Watersports, owned by Bob Carney, operate from Caneel Bay Hotel. This all round centre runs three dive boats, the *Privateer* (7.5m), *Caribe* (8m), and *Jumbi Jay* (11m). Stu Brown's diving operation in Cruz Bay, St John's Waterports, specialises in smaller diving groups and uses the 8.5m diving boat, *Spencer*.

• *St. Croix*: The following information is based on the situation before the 1989 hurricane, and visitors are advised to check with local sources before committing themselves. The diving centres on St Croix are all of a high standard and offer comprehensive facilities to divers. Dive shops are well equipped and diving instructors both well informed and enthusiastic. The island itself has a special ambience and it would be hard not to enjoy a diving holiday here.

VI Divers, run by Jimmy and Kathleen Antoine, has a dive store downtown, and an 11m dive boat, *Brain Storm 1*. Their principal hotel link-up is with Caravelle Hotel which is fully geared to the needs of divers. While all the diving centres seek to educate divers about marinelife, Michelle Pugh's Dive Experience (PO Box 4254, St Croix, US Virgin Islands; 773-3307) is a PADI 5-star training facility which places a special emphasis on conservation and care for the marine environment. Claiming to have the fastest boat on St Croix, the centre offers personalised underwater video and uses dive computers to maximise dive time. It teams up with Club Comanche Hotel (US contact: (800) 524-2066) to offer hotel and dive packages. Sea Shadows is a diving company associated with the Carmbola Beach Resort and Golf Club, qualifying as a NAUI Dream Resort. Scuba Tech (PO Box 5339, St Croix, US Virgin Islands; 778-9718 and 778-9650), based at the Salt River Marina, runs a 16-passenger catamaran, *Reefraker*, and offers PADI and NAUI certification courses. The centre works primarily with Cormorant Beach Club.

Caribbean Sea Adventures is an impressive diving outfit with more than a dozen vessels in their fleet, including the 7m *Seaspray* and 8m *Scorpio* designed to carry small groups, or the 12m *Phoenix* and the 11m *Deliverance* for larger teams. Cruzan Divers operates the 13m *Afternoon Delight* and the 6m *Drala* and runs its diving holidays in conjunction with the Frederiksted Hotel and the Royal Dane Hotel. Sea Sports Inc, is a PADI facility managed by Susan Rhoades and Dave Clark, who run a six-passenger Mako dive-boat and even offer divers use of water scooters. This centre links up with Sprat Hall Plantation and Cathy's Fancy. Underwater St Croix, based at Green Cay Marina, runs the 11.5m, 12-passenger boat, *Reliance*, and has a full range of NAUI courses.

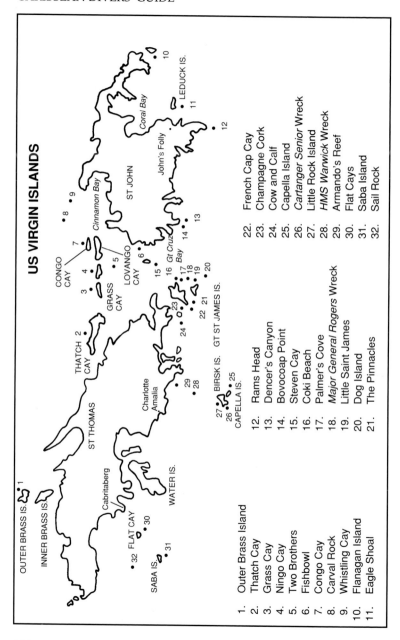

US VIRGIN ISLANDS

1. Outer Brass Island
2. Thatch Cay
3. Grass Cay
4. Ningo Cay
5. Two Brothers
6. Fishbowl
7. Congo Cay
8. Carval Rock
9. Whistling Cay
10. Flanagan Island
11. Eagle Shoal
12. Rams Head
13. Dencer's Canyon
14. Bovocoap Point
15. Steven Cay
16. Coki Beach
17. Palmer's Cove
18. Major General Rogers Wreck
19. Little Saint James
20. Dog Island
21. The Pinnacles
22. French Cap Cay
23. Champagne Cork
24. Cow and Calf
25. Capella Island
26. Cartanger Senior Wreck
27. Little Rock Island
28. HMS Warwick Wreck
29. Armando's Reef
30. Flat Cays
31. Saba Island
32. Sail Rock

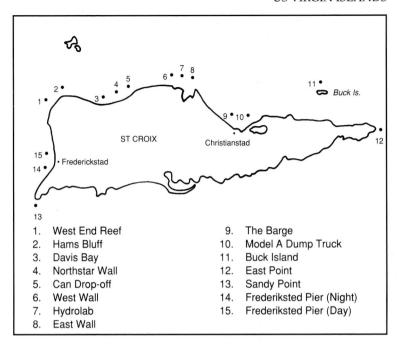

1. West End Reef
2. Hams Bluff
3. Davis Bay
4. Northstar Wall
5. Can Drop-off
6. West Wall
7. Hydrolab
8. East Wall
9. The Barge
10. Model A Dump Truck
11. Buck Island
12. East Point
13. Sandy Point
14. Frederiksted Pier (Night)
15. Frederiksted Pier (Day)

Marine Environment, General: Considerable scientific investigation has taken place around the US Virgin Islands and some first-class research facilities are available there, including the Ecological Research Station on St John, associated with the College of the Virgin Islands. The West Indies Laboratory, part of Farleigh Dickinson University, is located at Teague Bay, on the north-east coast of St Croix. A research laboratory at Benner Bay on St Thomas is run by the Department of Conservation and Cultural Affairs while NOAA's hydrolab is an in-situ underwater facility located at the apex of Salt River Canyon on St Croix.

St Croix has well developed bank barrier reefs, together with fringing and patch reefs. Key commercial marine resources include spiny lobsters, black coral and the queen conch. Local fish tend to have a relatively high level of contamination with ciguatera fish poisoning, and almost half of the 84 fish species caught around St Thomas being potential carriers of ciguatoxin!

Recommended Dive Sites: Buck Island on St Croix has a marked out underwater nature trail in its Underwater National Monument Park. The Cow and Calf consists of canyons and tunnels at around 12m. While offering some dramatic underwater scenery it is a safe dive for accompanied beginners. For wreck diving, try the Cartanzer, Senior which is a 58m long steel freighter lying in 12m of water and surrounded by large schools of snappers and yellow-tail. This is a good site for underwater photographers.

• *St Thomas*: Popular diving sites on St Thomas were recently reviewed in Skin Diver magazine (January 1989) which listed Sail Rock off the SW coast; Saba Island; Flat Cays; Little Buck Island; the wreck of the *Cartanzer Senior*; Submarine Alley; the wreck of *HMS Warrick*; the Cow and Calf and the associated Champagne Cork tunnel; Frenchcap Cay with the Pinnacles and Cathedrals; Little St James; Palmers Cove; the wreck of the *Major General Rogers* (off the Stouffer Virgin Grand Beach Resort at Smith Bay, in 21m); Coki Beach; Little Carval Rock; Thatch Cay with the Tunnels; Grass Cay with the Greenheads; and Congo Cay and Carval Rock with the Slice, which is an impressive steep-sided canyon between Congo Cay and the free-standing Carval Rock. The latter is for experienced divers only since current, surge and surf are all factors which must be taken into account while exploring the caves and channels around the famous rock.

• *St John*: The channel running between the east coast of St Thomas and the west coast of St John, known as Pillsbury Sound, is only about 3km wide so diving sites on either of these coasts are equally accessible to dive operators from both islands. Along the north coast of St John, Mary Point juts out with Whistling Cay lying just offshore, forming a popular dive-site with at least one tame moray eel and some nice coral formations. Due west of Cruz Bay lies Steven's Cay where an arc-shaped reef has been christened The Fishbowl. Most of the reefs around St John are part of the Virgin Islands National Park and Biosphere Reserve, and many of the diving sites provide more than adequate justification for this special status. The Sea Gardens, off Bovocoap Point on the south-west corner of the island, are a good example. Coral structures resplendent with delicate, brilliantly hued sea-fans, sea-whips and sponges, rise from the sea-floor at around 30m to within about 14m of the surface, making for a flexible dive plan, depending on experience, deco-profile and personal preference. Denver's Canyon is a nearby dive site where narrow ravines harbour resting nurse sharks, spiny lobsters and a diver-friendly 2m moray eel. Other popular sites include the Pinnacles; the Leaf in Reef Bay; the Ram's Head forming the south-easterly headland of the island and Eagle Shoal off the south-east coast.

• *St. Croix*: Some damage is bound to have taken place to dive sites as a result of the 1989 hurricanes. The following account is based upon pre-hurricane data and should be checked against local information.

There is no shortage of good diving sites around St Croix. The Model A Dump Truck dive is located at 40m on Scotch Bank Reef which is a well-formed reef stretching from Christiansted Harbour out towards Buck Island. A second reef system extends north-west from Christiansted Harbour; known as Long Reef, this has a steep wall cresting at 16-21m. The Barge, is just what it says, an upside down barge sunk in 21-29m, a short distance west of the harbour entrance. You could also pay a visit to the NOAA Hydrolab. It is located on sand flats close to the inner limits of the Salt River Marine Canyon. Two major reef walls occur in the same area; known simply as the East Wall and the West Wall, both dive sites are dramatic and full of marinelife, particularly sponges and gorgonians. Other favourite dive sites include Rustop Twist; Cane Bay Wall where, in addition to the thrill of a great wall dive you may be fortunate enough to meet a bottle-nosed dolphin or two; Northstar Wall; North Wall at Davis Bay; Hams Bluff; Butler Bay Wrecks including *Rosaomaira, Suffolk Maid* and *Northwind*; Sugar Slope; Rainbow Reef including the Spanish anchor; and finally one should not neglect the possibility of night dives at almost any convenient spot, particularly Frederiksted Pier.

Special Interest: The US Virgin Islands have a rich and fascinating history and formed a base for several renowned pirates.

Other Wildlife: Mongoose; deer; numerous wild parrots and other tropical birds.

Conservation Issues: It would be desirable to have a blanket ban on spearfishing. Hurricane damage has been significant on some reefs. Sadly, land management on certain islands, particularly St Croix, has led to increased run-off and consequent heavy sedimentation and coral mortality. Sand-dredging for on-land construction and reclamation has caused high turbidity at some sites, leading to large scale coral-kills. Those species which are commercially fished have all suffered serious population declines.

Legal Aspects: The Virgin Islands Coastal Zone Management Act of 1978 established a conservation programme under the title The Virgin Islands Coastal Zone Management Program. Law No 4848 prohibits harvesting of all corals from local waters. At the time of writing spearfishing is prohibited in marine parks but permitted elsewhere. Turtles are legally protected. Special protected marine zones include The Virgin Islands National Park and Biosphere Reserve and Buck Island National Monument. At the time of writing other areas are under consideration for protection.

Medical Facilities: The islands offer sophisticated medical facilities and plenty of highly qualified doctors. There is the De Castro Clinic in Cruz Bay and the St John Hospital and Community Centre at Centreline. St Thomas has a Medical Arts Complex and the St Thomas Hospital and Community Centre. St Croix has the St Croix Hospital and Community Health Centre, the Sunny Isle and Beeston Hill Medical Centre, and the Ingerborg Nesbitt Clinic in Frederiksted. A recompression chamber is situated at St Thomas Hospital and at the time of writing is operated by Dr Dave Boaz who is very experienced in hyperbaric medicine.